Over the Alps

Over the Alps

Reflections on Travel and Travel Writing,
with special reference to the Grand Tours
of Boswell, Beckford and Byron

by Patrick Anderson

Rupert Hart-Davis LONDON 1969

© Patrick Anderson 1969
First published 1969

Rupert Hart-Davis Ltd
3 Upper James Street
Golden Square, London W1

Printed in Great Britain by
Ebenezer Baylis and Son Ltd
The Trinity Press
Worcester and London

SBN 246 98591 7

For

Clifford, Patrick, Robert, Ursula, Kate, Geoffrey,
Frances and Derek: Colleagues and Friends

Acknowledgments

MY CHAPTER ON Boswell's travel writing is based on Professor F. A. Pottle's editions of the Journals, *Boswell's London Journal*, *Boswell in Holland*, the two volumes of *Boswell on the Grand Tour* (all published by Heinemann) and on *James Boswell: The Early Years*, F. A. Pottle (Heinemann) together with the essay on Boswell in *The Search For Good Sense*, F. L. Lucas (Cassell). For William Beckford's journeys I have relied on *The Travel-Diaries of William Beckford*, ed. Guy Chapman (Constable, 1928) which contains the early *Dreams, Waking Thoughts and Incidents* and its expansion, with omissions, into *Italy, with Sketches of Spain and Portugal*—both diaries in the form of letters—together with *Recollections of an Excursion to the Monasteries of Alcobaça and Batalha*. I have also used the franker *Journal of William Beckford in Portugal and Spain* 1987–1788, ed. Boyd Alexander, (Hart-Davis, 1954). For the life I have depended upon *Beckford: A Biography*, Guy Chapman (Hart-Davis, 1952) and *England's Wealthiest Son*, Boyd Alexander (The Centaur Press, 1962). The letters collected in *Life at Fonthill*, ed. Boyd Alexander (Hart-Davis 1957) give a picture of Beckford in middle age. For material on Ludwig of Bavaria I have used chiefly *Bavarian Fantasy*, Desmond Chapman-Huston (Murray 1955). For Byron's journeys I have used *The Poems of Byron* (Oxford Standard Authors), *Byron, Selections from Poetry, Letters and Journals*, ed. Peter Quennell (Nonesuch Press), *Lord Byron's Correspondence*, ed John Murray (Murray, 1922) and the very useful amalgamation of material in *Byron and Greece*, Harold Spender, (Murray 1924). I am also indebted to Professor L. A. Marchand's monumental life of Byron (Murray) and to Mr Peter Quennell's *Byron in Italy*. The following books have thrown light on various other aspects of my subject: *The Englishman Abroad*, H. & P. Massingham (Baker), *The Grand Tour*, Geoffrey Trease (Heinemann), *Italian Journey*, W. Goethe (Collins), *Earls of Creation*, J. Lees-Milne (Hamish Hamilton) *Lord Elgin and the Marbles*, W. St Clair (O.U.P.), *Spain*, Sacheverell Sitwell (Batsford), *Portugal and Madeira*, Sacheverell Sitwell (Batsford), *Baroque in Spain and Portugal*, J. Lees-Milne (Batsford). Other quotations are from standard editions—Evelyn, Gray, Walpole etc— or are acknowledged in the text. May I express my grateful acknowledgements to all these authors, editors and publishers.

The Department of English,   P.A.
Trent Park College

Contents

List of Illustrations

Acknowledgments and thanks are due to all the above sources, and to William Heinemann Ltd for their permission to reproduce Boswell's Corsican passport, from the Yale edition of *The Private Papers of James Boswell*, published by them in London.

1*

Every Man's Grand Tour

An Introduction

THEIR FORMAL EDUCATION completed – Eton and Cambridge, to be sure – the two young men set out on their travels. It was an Easter Sunday in late March, the wind was brisk, they crossed from Dover to Calais in five hours, and one of them was sea-sick. As soon as they landed it began to snow. They spent the night in Calais; 'an exceedingly old, but very pretty town' the one who had been ill wrote to his mother, 'and we hardly saw anything that was not new and so different from England, that it surprised me greatly.' The next morning they went to church and then took a post-chaise to Boulogne, travelling at the slow pace of six miles an hour, because the other young man, who was rich and rather distinguished, favoured an easy journey; the roads struck them as surprisingly good but the inns were 'terrible'. So to Abbeville by way of Montreuil, where they dined 'on stinking mutton cutlets, addled eggs, and ditch water.' Thence to Amiens and Paris, 'images quite unusual presenting themselves on all hands' and the whole journey taking six days instead of the more usual two. At Paris they stopped.

Images quite unusual, you notice, but little by way of specific description and nothing naively excited. 'The country we have passed through hitherto has been flat, open, but agreeably diversified with villages, fields well-cultivated, and little rivers.' This is all that the lazy amplitude of France evokes, even when they are travelling towards Montreuil and Abbeville and seeing on every side that extraordinary half-abstract landscape of fluidly tilting and lifting downs, almost featureless in their immensity but nevertheless giving the impression of expanded lungs, for there is more movement here than in the plain about Chartres. A distant line of trees looks as though it might slip off the curve of the earth altogether and dissolve away in the circum-ambient light. Boulogne, we are told, is more English than French and Abbeville has seventeen convents. As for Amiens, its cathedral is 'a huge Gothic building' – yes, of course – but scarcely 'just what that of Canterbury must have been before the Reformation'.

We could have done in fact with some evocation of atmosphere, perhaps in relation to a village of charm and character like Samer, one of the first nowadays to acquaint the traveller's eye with those shabby harmonies of grey, white, silver and pink which are so characteristic of France. (At Samer one buys one's first bottle of *vin ordinaire*.) With their formal arrangement of shutters, balconies and balustrades French houses can look very imperious or very pert. And yet a certain shabbiness, like the complacent acceptance of middle-age, or even a certain indifference, the product of a deeply conservative way of life, links the small château outside a French village and the embattled *hôtel de ville* in its centre with the huge faded advertisements and the slipshod pavé, the often blank and straggling streets, and thus with the tall trees and slow rivers of a countryside so assured that it yawns in one's face where, in England, everything smiles and primps for the camera.

We miss, too, the agitation of arrival in a foreign country; as when nowadays French officials offer one with cynical brusqueness (or so they did last summer) a handful of pamphlets, a bag of prunes, a cotton napkin stencilled with a map of their country in the shape of a vine-leaf and a folder of *Cheques Sourire*, 'which you are invited to hand to those of your French hosts who have been particularly nice and helpful to you' and which will, if they collect enough, reward them with a trip to Tahiti. Nor do we discover in these letters much sense that our young travellers were entering upon, or rather confirming, their inheritance, a fact of which they were too confidently aware to feel the necessity of comment, or that they might find material abroad to nourish a private fantasy, an Enchanted Garden, although in their different ways both were to cultivate an idiosyncrasy of the imagination in later life.

The rich and probably more sophisticated young man, who had only recently paid a nostalgic visit to his old school, and thought himself 'like Noah, just returned into his old world again, with all sorts of queer feels about me', now looked around him with a critical eye. What did the famous pleasures of Paris amount to? No more than cards, eating and the opera, he declared; the deficiencies of the latter were obvious enough, 'their music resembles a gooseberry tart as much as it does harmony'. His friend agreed: 'cracked voices, trilling diversions upon two notes and a half...Our astonishment at their absurdity, you can never conceive.' Fortunately the comedy was better, and then of course 'great part of our time is spent in seeing churches and palaces full of fine pictures' besides which (the poorer of the two travellers is still speaking) 'I could entertain myself this month merely with the common streets and the people in them.' His more fashionable colleague noted that 'the French love show; but there is a meanness throughout it all', a fine house having windows patched with paper and the food served there being also patched with 'sallads, butter, puff-paste, or some such miscarriage of a dish', an opinion seemingly not shared by the other: 'what tables we have seen have been so delicately served, and so profusely, that, after rising from one of them, one imagines it impossible ever to eat again.' The sophisticate had to admit that the French 'beat us vastly in buildings, both in number and magnificence'; on the other hand they had curious notions of honour, aristocrats and even princesses of the blood making money out of gaming-houses. And then there was the French exclusiveness, which many of us remark to this day; indeed General De Gaulle has suffused selfishness and self-complacency with the purple of his mystique. 'We have seen very little of the people themselves, who are not inclined to be propitious to strangers, especially if they do not play and speak the language readily.' The weather, too, continued bad.

They managed to get to Versailles, but rather hurriedly. Neither of them liked it: 'the great front is a lumber of littleness, composed of black brick, stuck full of bad old busts, and fringed with gold rails... There are avenues of water-pots, who disport themselves much in squirting up cascadelins. In short, 'tis a garden for a great child. Such was Louis Quatorze, who is here seen in his proper colours, where he commanded in person, unassisted by his armies and guards, and left to the pursuit of his own puerile ideas of glory.' Thus the sophisticate. And his friend found the principal façade equally boring: 'What a huge heap of littleness!...You cannot see a more disagreeable tout-ensemble', although he was inclined to relent about the garden-front and its prospect, the spacious terrace with its two basins, the sylvan semi-circle whose niches were filled 'with beautiful copies of all the famous antique statues in white marble' and in whose centre stood the basin of Latona, the great alley leading to the long, the almost interminable canal. All impressive indeed, but nevertheless deficient in something English, informal, spontaneous, and picturesque, for 'everything you behold savours too much of art; all is forced, all is constrained about you; statues and vases sowed everywhere without distinction; sugar loaves and minced pies of yew; scrawl work of box, and little squirting jets-d'eau, besides a great sameness in the walks.' How pleasant, we may feel, to be young, to be fresh, and to condemn the artificiality of a great king and his culture. Gooseberry music and mince-pie topiary! We expect our university travellers to be poised and to scoff, provided they can also be patient and observe. Palladian England, with its graceful façades hidden behind trees and parkland, and its quasi-democratic sociability and common-sense, was no preparation for such overweening extravagance. Nevertheless ,'here then we walk by moon-light, and hear the ladies and the nightingales sing.'

The pair moved on to Rheims, which the poor scholar found disappointing: 'There is little in it worth a stranger's curiosity, besides the cathedral church, which is a vast Gothic building of a surprising beauty and lightness, all covered with a procession of little statues, and other ornaments' and of course besides the fact that 'you have nothing to drink but the best champagne in the world.' The people there were not averse to pleasure but simply unpractised in it, untouched by even the little that Parisian society had to offer, and hence monotonously committed to endless games of cards briefly punctuated by a ridiculous *goûter*, 'which supplies the place of our tea', dinners or suppers being rarely given. That they would have liked to be gay was proved on the occasion when a walk in some gardens suddenly suggested supper under the trees, by the fountain, and this al fresco grouping led in its turn to singing and then to the hiring of a company of violinists and dancing to their accompaniment. Minuets warmed to country-dances, midnight paled to early dawn, whereupon the gay lady who had had the original idea sent the weary into their coaches while the rest danced before them in procession through the town, 'and waked every body in it', which caused the sophisticated traveller to propose making a custom of the thing, only the other ladies didn't seem too keen, 'so I believe it will drop, and they will return to their dull cards, and usual formalities.'

Dijon was pleasant, Lyons the reverse, and it was there that the fashionable young man's father, who was Prime Minister of England, sent word that they should abandon their plan to winter in the south of France and instead cross the Alps into Italy. For, of course, our young men were Horace Walpole and Thomas Gray. The year was 1739. That characteristic feature of eighteenth century education, the Grand Tour, was being embarked upon. And what was a Grand Tour without Alps, part 'horrid', part sublime (for the Chamonix glaciers were beginning to come into fashion), to be followed by the works of art and the historic cities of the classical south? It was Italy which had nourished the Elizabethans and Milton with the colour, passion and extravagance of its re-discovery of the cult of man, providing the subjects and atmosphere of plays, giving lessons in *real-politik* to some and the ideal of courtly honour and grace to others. And now, in quieter times, it was Italy which brought the classical authors learned at Eton and Westminster alive, as well as offering the richer young men the chance of buying statues and paintings to embellish the houses they would re-design and re-build in the light of the palaces they had admired and the ruins over which they had scrambled.

From Lyons, Walpole and Gray made an expedition to the Grande Chartreuse, a place to be visited later by Beckford, who padded his first travel-book with some cloudy pages devoted to its description, and also by the young Wordsworth and his friend Jones on their hike in 1790: more than thirty years later Wordsworth's sister Dorothy was to write, 'I do not think that any spot which he visited during his youth-ful travels with Robert Jones made so great an impression on his mind.' Walpole wrote to their mutual friend, Richard West, 'here we are, the lonely lords of glorious, desolate prospects' and Gray, enchanted by 'one of the most solemn, the most romantic, and the most astonishing scenes ever beheld', must have found material that went later into *The Progress of Poetry* and *The Bard*. Their later crossing of Mont Cenis was too like Evelyn's experience on the Simplon to be equally satisfying to Gray: 'The week we have since passed crossing the Alps, had not equalled the single day upon that mountain...Not a precipice, not a torrent, not a cliff, but is pregnant with religion and poetry.'

On the day before they arrived at Mont Cenis they had an un-pleasant experience. Walpole's spaniel was seized and eaten by a wolf and, as Gray remarks, if the dog Tory had not been there, 'and the creature had thought fit to lay hold of one of the horses; chaise, and we, and all must inevitably have tumbled above fifty fathoms perpendi-cular down the precipice.' The crossing itself, six miles up to a plateau of deep snow surrounding a frozen lake, and six much steeper miles down again, was fraught with danger. The chaise was dismantled, it and the baggage packed on mules, and 'we ourselves were wrapped up in our furs, and seated upon a sort of matted chair without legs, which is carried upon poles in the manner of a bier, and so began to ascend by the help of eight men.' It is Walpole who describes how 'on the very highest precipice of Mont Cenis, the devil of discord, in the similitude of sour wine, had got amongst the Alpine savages, and set them a-fighting with Gray and me in the chairs: they rushed him by me on a crag where there was scarce room for a cloven hoof. The least slip had tumbled us into such a fog, and such an eternity, as we should never have found our way out again.' No wonder that Gray, summing it all up from the safety of Turin, declared the crossing had been 'eight days journey through Greenland' and added 'Mont Cenis, I confess, carries the permission mountains have of being frightful rather too far.'

Walpole and Gray continued south, visiting Genoa, Bologna, Florence, Rome and Naples and, although they quarrelled in the end, they enjoyed much of what they saw. Walpole delighted in the carnival at Florence: 'I have done nothing but slip out of my domino into bed, and out of bed into my domino. The end of the carnival is frantic, bacchanalian'; but he was pleased to find that its freedom was untinged with malicious familiarity, the Italians being good-natured and fond of the English: 'Their little partiality for themselves, opposed to the violent vanity of the French, makes them very amiable in my eyes' while the city had 'so many other charms, that I shall not want excuses for my taste'. Later, too, he gives a splendid account of Herculaneum (Pompeii was not then discovered). The quieter Gray praises many a beautiful sight. There is Genoa, for instance: 'We find this place so very fine, that we are in fear of finding nothing finer. We are fallen in love with the Mediterranean Sea, and hold your lakes and rivers in vast contempt'; together with the landscape of Lombardy, 'one of the most beautiful imaginable...vast plantations of trees, chiefly mulberries and olives, and not a tree without a vine twining about it' (an Italian method of vine-planting often remarked by English visitors). There is art at Florence, 'the famous gallery, alone, is an amusement for months'; the Duomo at Siena, 'laboured with a Gothic niceness and delicacy in the old-fashioned way'; and of course Rome, although the city struck him as sadly neglected and decayed, besides which there was nothing to do in the evenings. All the same he didn't like Walpole's hurrying him back to the social life of Florence.

Both reveal reactions that will be familiar to most literary tourists, or indeed most tourists who write home. A fear of reproducing the guide-book: 'One hates writing descriptions that are to be found in every book of travels' (Walpole); the gradual dissipation of the sense of novelty: 'When I first came abroad every thing struck me, and I wrote its history but now I am grown so used to be surprised, that I don't perceive any flutter in myself when I meet with any novelties' (Gray); positive exhaustion: 'I have grown so lazy, and so tired of seeing sights ...I have contracted so great an aversion to inns and post-chaises, and have so absolutely lost all curiosity, that, except the towns in the straight road to Great Britain, I shall scarce see a jot more of foreign land' (Walpole); even a kind of boredom and nullity, but then they spent far too much time in Florence, as when Gray confesses that that city was 'an excellent place to employ all one's animal sensations in, but utterly contrary to one's rational powers. I have struck a medal upon myself; the device is thus, O, and the motto Nihilissimo...If you choose to be annihilated too, you cannot do better than undertake the journey.' What animal sensations, one wonders, did he in fact employ? Did he retreat to the Boboli Gardens like Beckford? A little low company might have been the answer. Others have found it so.

Earlier at Rome, before the return sojourn in Florence and the quarrel at Reggio, Gray describes a view of classical places and ruins, with the Tyrrhenian Sea in the distance, and then adds 'all this is charming' which he follows immediately with, 'Mr. Walpole says, our memory sees more than our eyes in this country. Which is extremely true; since, for realities, Windsor, or Richmond Hill, is infinitely preferable to Albano or Frascati.' One sees him reaching for what is really significant in his experience. The scene is charming but its charm becomes meaningful to him only through the play of the historic memory, the imaginative reconstruction of the classical past, while at the same time it confirms and refreshes (as I take it) the best in England. To Augustans the best was usually the Thames valley. Had he possessed more sensuousness he would have sunk deeper into the reality of the moment; or, in some trance-like state, the beauty of sunshine, landscape, sea, together with the expressive dilapidation, endearing untidiness and even apparent triviality of contemporary Rome, would have merged into a sense of a kind of continuous human present. He would have been in a heightened state of mind where imagination and an overmastering sense of life became inextricably mingled. He would have been pre-eminently the creator. But, in fact, he remained poised and cool, to the extent of preferring Windsor to Albano! Nevertheless, a line or two later in this letter of May, 1740 to West, he remarks that 'it is the most beautiful of Italian nights, full of the scent of orange trees and the murmur of a fountain', and that various important buildings are within sight of his window. 'This is all true', he exclaims, and the note of momentarily joyous discovery reminds one of Byron at the Capuchin convent in Athens in 1811: 'Hymettus before me, the Acropolis behind, the Temple of Jove to my right, the Stadium in front, the town to the left; eh, Sir, there's a situation, there's your picturesque!' But Byron expressly denied that all this was anything like London.

Their usual tone of cool urbanity was maintained when both young men summed up the effect the journey had had upon them. 'You won't find me much altered, I believe', wrote Walpole, 'at least outwardly. I am not grown a bit shorter, or a bit fatter, but am just the same long lean creature as usual. Then I talk no French, but to my footman; nor Italian, but to myself...' Gray, however, admitted some change: 'You must add, then, to your former idea, two years of age, a reasonable quantity of dullness, a great deal of silence, and something that rather resembles, than is, thinking; a confused notion of many strange and fine things that have swum before my eyes for some time, a want of love for general society, indeed an inability to it. On the good side you may add a sensibility to what others feel, and indulgence to their faults and weaknesses, a love of truth, a detestation of everything else. Then you are to deduct a little impatience, a little laughter, a great deal of pride, and some spirits.' This is admirably modest and wise; it is also, for a man of twenty-five, rather sad. Quite obviously this Grand Tour has little to do with romantic self-revelation, with the search for a 'country of the heart' or with the shattering experiences so beloved of youth. It has no relation to Tennyson's *Ulysses*:

> I am a part of all that I have met;
> Yet all experience is an arch wherethru'
> Gleams that untravell'd world, whose margin fades
> For ever and for ever when I move.

any more than it has to the more melodramatic accumulation of experience in A. E. Housman:

> Cities entered, oceans crossed,
> Knowledge gained and virtue lost,
> Cureless folly done and said,
> And the lovely way that led
> To the slimepit and the mire
> And the everlasting fire.

It is not C. P. Cavafy's *Ithaca*, and those returning from it do not carry the silken sun-born confidence of the youth described by Stefan George:

> Sein Blick ist schwer
> Schon vom Geheimnis das ich niemals weiss
> Und leicht umflort
> Dar er vom Lenz in unsern Winter traf.

Levelheaded Augustans such as Walpole and Gray introduce a book
which will be largely concerned with people so different from them as
to be almost their opposites: high-spirited Grand Tourists who went to
southern lands in order to discover themselves or at least to explore
their sensibilities in relation to some 'country of the heart'. Their
classicism was just as real but it was suffused with an existential urge;
in their differing ways they wanted to learn how to live. Discovering
Italy and, in particular, Corsica, James Boswell felt himself a better
man. William Beckford, too, although already a formed personality in
his youth, found freer modes of expression and a wider field for the
play of his aesthetic impulses in Italy and later in Portugal. And Byron,
fascinated by Albania and Turkey, declared that all young men should
be sent abroad to learn about life and manners, in which he clearly
included both the excitingly barbarous and the intriguingly exotic.
My choice of these three is based, firstly, on my belief that almost all
the best travel-writing is personal, as theirs was: an experience lived
rather than sights seen. The lived experience normally requires that
some time be spent abroad, a condition prescribed by the Grand Tour,
while its expression in terms of personality may suggest some depen-
dence on notes, journals and letters, and here, too, my chosen three
often reveal themselves in pre-publication spontaneity.

If the reader should question why I go back so comparatively far in
time — who could be more personal, he might instance, than Ruskin or
John Addington Symonds or D. H. Lawrence? — I must adduce the
second reason for my choice. This is the particular charm generated by
the period before the Industrial Revolution, a period whose general
tranquillity and gracefulness is always worth contemplation even if it
didn't distance and compose my figures while also providing a tension
between the classical and the romantic. The modernity of Boswell,
Beckford, and Byron is, I think, intense. Many of those who make some
sort of Grand Tour today, undergraduates with Land Rovers, hitch-
hikers to Greece and Israel, middle-aged escapists 'doing a Gauguin'
as far as possible from the package-tours, will recognise amongst their
companions, or in themselves, traces of the engaging Boswellian
careerist, the Beckfordian aesthete, the Byronic man of action and of
the world. Fascinating characters all three, their essential modernity
speaks to us more clearly just because they died more than a hundred
years ago and are neither entangled with an age we have largely
rejected nor so close to us as to lack solidity and shape. In other words,
their modernity is not part of our muddle. It exists in a period which in

many ways criticises our own. This is a period we may imagine turning toward us the searchlight faces of its Palladian porticos, the immense perspectives of its Baroque avenues, the tall silences of those gilded and stuccoed and be-mirrored saloons where the ceilings are perhaps by Tiepolo, the paintings by Poussin and Fragonard and Salvator Rosa, while a harpsichord waits for the ice and fire music of Telemann and Mozart and on the tables lie copies of Voltaire, Gibbon and the *Quattro Libri*, together with a portfolio of sturdy, earthy Hogarth prints.

This period is remote from us not so much in time as in the composure which informs it and the fact that it seems to conclude a long process of development rather than to reach out into the following century. In this sense it is the final sunny product of the civilising mission of Greece and Rome. The Age of 'Enlightenment' or 'Reason' or 'Taste', it is an important element in our travelling if we go no farther than Kenwood, Syon and Osterley, and it is the only great age from which many of us can afford to garner mementoes for use in our own houses, which may themselves date from the same period. We can, of course, exaggerate its stability, sentimentalise its charm. Courts were often stuffy, rulers almost invariably despotic. But we can hardly deny the visual delight of a time which added to the continuing classicism of the Renaissance the splendours of Baroque and Rococo. The first style had been born long before under the influence of the Jesuits in Italy but it was now for the most part that it moved into central and northern Europe, establishing its headquarters at Vienna where it became the expressive instrument of Habsburg power, but also influencing the Court and Palace of Versailles; furthermore, most of the great Baroque buildings of Spain, such as the west façade of the cathedral of Santiago de Compostela, and of Portugal, notably the royal palace of Mafra, also date from the eighteenth century. Although the style differed from country to country, with Austrian and Bavarian Baroque preserving the fluidity and humanism of the Roman originals far more than did the stiff, dogmatic edifices of Spain, one can usually find in a Baroque building an element of theatrical extravagance and impressiveness, a marked and often restless rhythm, a sense of things being portrayed at their peak intensity. In the colder light north of the Alps this magnificence tends to become intellectualised, rather hauntingly pure and nostalgic, as though it were a refrigerated dream of the emotionalism of the south. (You can see this in the Danubian monasteries of Melk and St Florian, half farm, half fairyland; in the Mirabell Palace at Salzburg or the Würzburg Residenz). Meanwhile Rococo, which is less a matter of structure than of decoration, transformed the rolling waves of Bernini, Borromini and Fischer von Erlach into a dazzling display of opalescent foam.

When I say that the pre-industrial age criticises our own, and that a kind of mainstream of classical humanism seems to falter and stop about the year 1830, I do seriously mean that those who search for values today—those who want to dredge the channels of our western tradition, those who want to brace our culture against the multiple shocks it is sustaining—should turn to the lessons embodied in Rococo Nymphenburg and Queluz, in Baroque Santa Maria della Salute or the Belvedere in Vienna, as well as in the more familiar Palladian buildings and gardens we are so lucky to have in England. I do not of course mean the contemplation of architecture alone, although the thorough experience of a building, its artefacts and its setting can have the widest implications and need not in the least imply that one is 'precious', 're-actionary', the inhabitant of an aesthetic ivory tower, although such criticism is fairly common; I mean the essential quality of that period which, first settled in the quiet lives of Walpole and Gray, quickens to a curious and even a disruptive modernity in Boswell, Beckford and Byron.

Certainly Walpole and Gray look settled from the stand-point of today. Both were men of great sensibility. A vivacious observer of the life of society, Walpole loved best of all the semi-rural retreat which he fashioned in a variant of the Rococo manner. How often he refers with infectious enthusiasm to his 'little Gothic castle at Strawberry Hill', 'that sweet little spot, little enough, but very sweet', with its 'enamelled meadows, with filigree hedges' and its cows and Turkish sheep 'all studied in their colours to becoming the view'. It was indeed 'a gay and tranquil scene', for the 'gloomth' was certainly not over-done, much of the furniture was modern and the garden itself had to be 'riant'...'I am all plantations and sprout away like any chaste nymph in the *Metamorphoses.*' Meanwhile the sadder and lonelier Gray concerned himself with his Pindaric versions of Celtic and Norse, his inter-leaved Linnaeus, and that 'plano-convex mirror', bound up like a pocket-book and worn as a fob, with which he composed views of mountains and landskips, of the sublime and the picturesque, during his tours in the country. The verse he distilled was rare and precious, each drop his own and yet faceted with glints and reflections of past authors, Homer or Virgil, Dante or Petrarch or Shakespeare. It was his century, after all, which caught the antiquities of Rome in the engravings of Piranesi and the shimmering water-world of Venice in the brush of Canaletto; Claude Lorrain was scarcely earlier. It was the same century which first went seriously to Dalmatia and Greece. Even the Enlightened can enjoy the idea of a Golden Age, while Good Sense clearly demands that one grow thoroughly familiar with what it is that one inherits.

Thus it is that the comments of Walpole and Gray as they cross the Alps will seem to us closer to the preceding century than to an Arnold or Ruskin, whose professorial earnestness is that of the dispossessed. John Evelyn is a case in point. Visiting Italy in 1643, he went by sea from the south of France, narrowly escaped shipwreck and then found himself skirting the shore, 'from whence, the wind blowing as it did, might perfectly be smelt the joys of Italy in the perfumes of orange, citron, and jessamine flowers for divers leagues seaward.' Later, amongst the Apennines, he revealed an imaginative respect for mountains however 'inhospitable' and 'horrid' they might be. 'As we ascended we encountered a very thick, solid, and dark body of clouds, which look'd like rocks at a little distance, which lasted neere a mile in going up; they were dry misty vapours, hanging undissolved for a vast thicknesse, and obscuring both the sun and earth, so that we seemed to be in the sea rather than in the cloudes, till, having pierced through it we came into a most serene heaven, as if we had been above all human conversation, the mountain appearing more like a great island than joyn'd to any other hills, for we could perceive nothing but a sea of thick cloudes rowling under our feete like huge waves, every now and then suffering the top of some other mountain to peepe through, which we could discover many miles off: and between some breeches of the cloudes we could see landskips and villages of the subjacent country. This was one of the most pleasant, newe, and altogether surprising objects I had ever beheld.' Reflected in its syntax, the patient almost dogged observation, the tone of perplexity and effort, earn the right to both 'a most serene heaven' and to the very Augustan pleasure in 'landskips and villages'.

On his way home Evelyn crossed the Alps by the Simplon and much that he wrote is little different from the descriptions of Walpole and Gray, with the exception of their humour and Gray's religious awe. He noticed 'strange, horrid and fearful crags and tracts, abounding in pine trees, and only inhabited by beares, wolves, and wild goates'. He grew depressed at the peasants' goitres, 'some of which I have seene as big as an hundred pounds bag of silver hanging over their chinns.' These were a perennial object of tourist curiosity. Although he enjoyed the prospect of the mountains from Lake Maggiore, and again from Lake Geneva, 'shewing their aspiring tops', and was to enjoy 'that goodly river the Rhone', he decided that their abrupt rising from the Lombard plain was 'as if Nature had here swept up the rubbish of the Earth in the Alps'. (For my part, I must agree that most mountains are best at a distance when there is no chance of one's having to climb them and so enter a world of almost invariably bad weather, monotonous pine forest, misanthropic crags and screes, dingy snow and the paranoiac mutterings and ravings of water-falls. In fact Addison's 'sort of agreeable shuddering at this most misshapen scenery' is quite as far as I will go. I am all for Ronald Firbank's wanting to 'shake' Switzerland. I suppose that, as a tribute to the puritanism of one's schooldays, when 'effort' was everything and *per ardua ad astra* a favourite motto, to have encountered and survived the attentions of these bullies can be regarded as a justification for sensuality farther south. Like breaking training after the big match.) Behind Evelyn we may perhaps catch the figure of Milton, writing in Latin on the death of his friend, 'Alas! what vagrant wandering drove me to go to strange shores, across the skyey ridges, and the snowlined Alps?' although he too, like Evelyn, had enjoyed himself in the south, basking in a literary celebrity he recalled in the manner of Theocritus: 'Oh, how wondrous happy was I when, stretched at ease by the prattlings of cool Arno, in its poplar grove, where the grass was softest, I could pluck now violets, now the tips of myrtles, and could hear Menalcas vying with Lycidas!' A classical education binds such men together whatever their century. One may even think of that new Catullus, not otherwise notably classical, John Donne:

> Nurse, oh my love is slain, I saw him go
> O'er the white Alps alone.

Leaving aside romantic attributes as yet faintly envisaged, Grand Tours could be much grander, and far more influential on the participants and their times, than Walpole and Gray's. Such was the quick year spent abroad by Richard Boyle, third Earl of Burlington, in 1714-15, when the twenty-year-old youth travelled with five or six companions, including a bear-leader and no less than two painters to provide him with views, in addition to several servants, and during which he bought a substantial collection of Old Masters as well as marbles, vases, musical instruments and books, his account book giving the enormous total of 868 trunks and crates for his baggage home. In Italy he had met and been advised by William Kent; on his return two books, Colin Campbell's *Vitruvius Britannicus* and a translation of *The Architecture of A. Palladio*, gave his hurried tour a new perspective and in 1719 he was back in Italy, and particularly at Vicenza, his love of music and painting now incorporated in that passion for architecture which gave us Burlington House and the villa at Chiswick, allied Palladianism with the Whigs and protected English taste (as when Gray and Walpole condemned Versailles) from the full European extravagance. Equally magnificent in purchases, and also under the influence of Kent, was the six years' residence abroad of Thomas Coke, the creator of Holkham Hall, who left England at the age of fifteen in 1712, studied for a time at the Academy of Turin and journeyed as far as Sicily and Malta. It was clever of a young boy to get abroad so early, and to respond to an excellent tutor like Dr Hobart, and to plan, even in adolescence, the architectural transformation of his ancestral home. For Coke, who bought whole priceless libraries of books and manuscripts, and acquired here a colossal bust of the Emperor Lucius Verus and there a gigantic statue of Jupiter, also studied architecture, visiting palace after palace, taking measurements and making drawings, dreaming the while of the splendid life he would lead amongst his treasures, half brutal foul-mouthed squire, half Latinist and aesthete.

Boyle and Coke went abroad some years before the Grand Tour reached its period of maximum popularity, a popularity only ended by the Napoleonic wars and then by the spread of railways and the rise of Thomas Cook, which made the 'once-for-all' aspect of much Grand Touring no longer necessary. But the idea of completing one's education, polishing one's manners and perhaps acquiring some additional status through continental travel had persisted through three centuries. Sir Philip Sidney, for instance, sailed from England in 1572 at the age of seventeen. The comments he made on his tour suggest that it was far from unusual even then: 'A great number of us never thought why we went, but a certain tickling humour to do as other men had done.' By no means all Grand Tourists were schoolboys or youths with bear-leaders to protect them from 'popery and filthy living' on the one hand, or the republicanism of Geneva on the other, and to see that they did not fall into the hands of banditti, Barbary pirates, match-making mothers, or the Inquisition. In fact some, like Addison, became for a short time bear-leaders themselves.

As they all trooped down to Italy, 'Nature's darling', by way of France or Germany, a multitude of local passports, bills of exchange and *bolletini di sanità* in their wallets, and their hands fumbling amongst the soldi and pistoles and ducatoons in order to bargain for a *vetturino* (with its packet-deal advantages) or to pay yet another *octroi*, it is naturally the career-men and writers whom we know best. Henry Wotton went abroad alone at the age of twenty-one in 1589 and supplemented his studies in Germany and Italy with intelligence work, visiting Rome in disguise and having to make an abrupt escape from his *pensione* when he thought he was recognised. Thomas Coryat was already a man of about thirty (the same age as Milton) and combined a reputation as a Court buffoon with that of a Mermaid Tavern wit; his tour, which began in 1608, was entirely for his own pleasure and the fun of writing a book. A rough crossing revealed him as already 'a carpenter of words' for he 'varnished the exterior parts of the ship with the excremental ebullitions of my tumultuous stomach', and thereafter he showed the greatest gusto for all kinds of life, enjoying most things from the dried frogs of Cremona ('they did exceedingly delight my palate') to the statistic of Venice, in whose summer heat he lay 'stark naked most commonly every night', brooding upon the fact that there were no less than 20,000 prostitutes in the city, and that he had himself paid a call upon a 'noble courtesan' without being contaminated or corrupted. Joseph Addison was an Oxford don of twenty-seven, with a government grant to help him prepare for a career in diplomacy, as, after prolonged study of continental matters at home, a re-reading of the classical authors and some intensive study of French at Blois, he at last traversed 'classic ground'. 'One can scarce hear the name of a Hill or a river near it that does not bring to mind a piece of a Classic Author, nor cast one's Eyes upon a single Spot that has not been the Scene of some extraordinary action,' he wrote from Rome in 1701. Edward Gibbon was twenty-five, had been abroad before and was already an author, when he started the scholarly trip that would bring him even more memorably to Rome in 1765 : 'It was on the fifteenth of October, in the gloom of evening, as I sat musing in the Capitol, while the barefoot friars were chanting their litanies in the temple of Jupiter, that I conceived the first thought of my history.' As for Smollett, Sterne and Garrick, they were middle-aged men, and the first two were travelling largely for their health.

Yet Grand Tours such as Gray and Walpole's were often the subject of criticism during the eighteenth century. Lord Chesterfield impressed upon his illegitimate son the absurdity of young men travelling to the Continent only to herd together because they did not know the language and had no curiosity about the history and manners of the countries they visited: 'they go abroad, as they call it; but, in truth, they stay at home all that while; for being very awkward, confoundedly ashamed, and not speaking the languages, they go into no foreign company, at least none good; but dine and sup with one another only, at the tavern.' Adam Smith agreed with him. 'Our young people, it is said, generally return home much improved by their travels', an opinion to which he strongly dissented since most of the privileged youth returned more conceited, unprincipled and dissipated than before. 'Nothing but the discredit into which the universities are allowing themselves to fall, could ever have brought into repute so very absurd a practice as that of travelling at this early period of life.' The wiser tourist, wrote John Moore in 1795, would 'perceive how odious those travellers make themselves, who laugh at the religion, ridicule the customs and insult the police of the countries through which they pass, and who never fail to insinuate to the inhabitants that they are slaves and bigots.'

This is not to say that a bit of prejudice or hyper-sensitivity doesn't add spice to a traveller's account. Minds can be too fair and high. One feels at home when one reads Tobias Smollett's opinion of 1763: 'of all the people I have ever known, I think the French are the least capable of feeling for the distress of their fellow creatures.' One is at least amused by Lady Wortley Montagu's contention that 'the French grin is equally remote from the cheerful sincerity of a smile, and the cordial mirth of an honest English horse-laugh.' But one feels that criticism demands an interesting personality in the critic, if not also a parallel display of understanding and love. We all have our pet hates. 'I dislike Belgium,' Matthew Arnold was to declare, 'and think the Belgians, on the whole, the most contemptible people in Europe.' The condemnation of one foreign country often leads to the praise of another.

Lord Chesterfield—if we may digress for a few moments to glance at the whole question of travel and travel-writing—maintained that a tourist should become amiably involved. 'It is certain that no man can be much pleased himself, or please others much, in any place where he is only a bird of passage for eight to ten days...This is the real utility of travelling, when, by constructing a familiarity at any place, you get into the inside of it, and see it in its undress...you must show a willingness, a desire, an impatience, of forming connections, *il faut s'y prêter, et y mettre du liant, du désir de plaire.*'

To get inside a place, to form connections and please, was not this the way of George Borrow in Spain, captured in a book full of incident, dialogue and humour; or of the young Lord Byron to whom his landlady in Seville offered a lock of her hair, 'about three feet in length', a share of her private apartment and a provocative farewell, *Adios, tu hermoso! me gusto mucho;* of Kingslake amongst the girls of Smyrna, transcendent in beauty: 'their features are touched with a savage pencil, hardening the outline of the eyes and eyebrows, and lending an unnatural fire to the stern, grave looks with which they pierce your brain'; of Lawrence on the shores of Lake Garda, talking with his Il Duro: 'I knew he liked me very much, almost loved me... He was as clear and fine as semi-transparent rock, as a substance in moonlight'; or of Norman Douglas in Calabria, strolling beside an orphan guide: 'I made every effort to be pleasant to him...This radiantly-vicious child was the embodiment of the joy of life, the perfect immoralist!' One thinks of few of the better travel-books which are not much concerned with people; far more so than giving a careful and consistent guide to the sights, let alone the historical and political background.

And of course for people, for pleasing connections, one can go very much farther afield. One can go to Singapore and Borneo with Conrad who, despite the brevity of his experiences in Malaysia, evoked many a brown-skinned, sarong-clad figure against a background of river and swamp, defending the culture of his Malays and Bugis and Dyaks with an emphatic 'there is a bond between us and that humanity so far away.' Turn to Henri Fauconnier's *Malaisie*, that masterpiece of the jungle orient, and you will step even more surely across the soft red earth of some *kampong* amongst the coconut-palms, threading your way between the houses of bamboo and attap, the patches of spider lily and bowers of passion-fruit, with the hillsides misted with the silver-green of rubber trees and in your nostrils the fierce scent of pigshit and dried fish, of oil burning acridly in the frying-pans and of joss-sticks and perhaps of durian, that fruit which reminds the white man, the *orang puteh*, of 'eating custard in a lavatory'. But my own experience is turning a generally Malay community into a predominantly Chinese one. In either case the newcomer to the Tropics is likely to find himself an actor under a warm amber flood, trailing a giggling picnic of children, greeted with huge gold-toothed smiles from many quarters, although it is a Tamil youth glossy and indolent behind a freckling lattice or a

Malay girl in a sultry combination of electric-blue chenille scarf, lace kebaya and marmalade-coloured sarong who rivets his attention. Conrad's bond of common humanity is enlivened by this sense of privileged strangeness. The stage upon which you move is a bright but enigmatic enchantment; the flowers and fruits — the frangi-pani and bougainvillea, the purple mangosteens and hairy pink rambutans — have the look of stage properties; and, soon exhausted, ludicrously wilting in the heat, with the greasepaint, so to speak, running down your face, you long to pierce through to the reality behind. You have heard of the Malay girl who placed a moon-flower on the pillow of her young master. In *Malaisie* you read of a Tamil being unwound by her French lover from voluminous garments. You buy a nugget of sandal-wood, perhaps, to imagine, or to remind yourself, of the scent of skin whose dark colour is full of strange lights. Such was the skin of the courtesan Kuchiuk Hanem, with whom Flaubert slept at Isna on the Nile. She was accompanied by a tame lamb, spotted with henna and muzzled in black velvet...

For pleasing connections you can go to India, to the two Maharajahs, say, of Mr J. R. Ackerley and Mr E. M. Forster,[1] the former musing: 'Goodness, wisdom, and beauty — that is what the Greeks worshipped, and that is what I want...a good, wise, and beautiful friend', while the latter could be as childlike and charming: 'He was so sweet when I arrived — darted up from behind and put his hand over my eyes.' There is the Nepal of Mr John Morris and his friend, Umar Sing, and the Arabia of Mr Wilfred Thesiger, so strong in admiration for his follower, Salim bin Ghabaisha, a youth with a mane of blue-black hair and a simple length of indigo cloth wound about him, the best shot, the most fiery temperament, of all the Rashid: 'Antinous must have looked like this, I thought, when Hadrian first saw him in the Phrygian woods.' (And the mind darts from the sands of the Open Quarter to the museum at Delphi, where that now opulent and un-Arabian youth sulks nobly in a room set apart from the other sculptures, his creamy flesh contrasting with the porous and gritty figures of the Archaic period, flushed as they are with mauve and rose.)

It is this imaginative and spiritual involvement which both prompts and justifies the criticism that travel writers often level at the countries of their choice. Travel can be a kind of second life. Freed from routine and the compromises it necessitates, having shed a good deal of respon-sibility and perhaps acquired rather grander spending-habits than are

[1] In *Hindoo Holiday* and *The Hill of Devi*.

normal at home, the traveller assumes a less inhibited and even a hazardously free personality. He is, after all, out for experience, which can scarcely be said of his daily trips to an office; and the experience he lays himself open to may contain elements rarely present in his ordinary life. Indeed these periods of leisure acquire their own cohesion; the traveller is aware of cross-references from holiday to holiday which have little or no relation to his workaday life. He brings new sides of his personality into play. The adjustment is complicated and so, when the moment of intensity comes, when he is caught by a new landscape or city or country, his sense of appropriation contains all sorts of half-realised vulnerabilities and re-patternings of attitude. 'My Greece,' he says, or 'my Toledo', and he may begin at once a lover's quarrel with a mistress whose objective existence is even more precarious than that of the human variety.

Certainly the best travel writers never gush. They may indulge in fine writing — and what's wrong with that if the experience justifies it? — but they also probe and recoil, making use of the comic and the satiric sense. I can't recall a good book of travel which is all romance and praise. Doughty is miserable through much of *Arabia Deserta*, Kinglake's chief event is a horrible epidemic of the Plague, Lawrence loathes almost as much as he loves in Italy and Mexico, Norman Douglas sprinkles his huge erudition with irritations and prejudices as well as roguish queries, bland refusals to expatiate, convtionalersa fits and starts. The experience of the chosen land brings out different assertions of the personality from writer to writer. Thus in Southern Italy Gissing is haunted and tearful, Douglas blithely at ease, while Edward Lear ambles from sketchable view to sketchable view, responding with his dry gentlemanly wit to various misfortunes from elderly bores to rooms made malodorous with silkworms, from an infant who falls into a dish of macaroni to a family which takes umbrage when he gently insists that England too can produce fruit. Sardinia can make D. H. Lawrence very angry indeed, as when he encounters a shamelessly food-spotted waiter: ' "Dirty, disgusting swine!" said I, and I was in a rage.' This sort of rage, by the way, is a lover's protest when his mistress puts on ugly clothes or too much make-up, or when she takes him to be just another lecherous male: I know it well from Greece. Other writers, especially young ones, present personalities which are less decided, more susceptible in their lack of definition; this enables them to hint at a mysterious inner core, a subtle flowering towards life, which they may or may not fully understand. What lay behind the bright glance of Isherwood in Berlin? Certainly not a camera. An example would be Mr Kevin Andrews' beautiful book on Greece, *The Flight of Ikaros*, which, incidentally, is far from uncritical, especially where Greek cruelty is concerned. Still other writers keep their ends up by being smart or flip.

You can be both these things and still cherish a country of the heart, as Robert Byron did on Athos and in Persia; or you can play wittily with a Grand Tour from which you expect sporadic intensities rather than a major commitment, as Aldous Huxley did in Central America; or you can live for high spirits, curiosities and squalors, which was the way of Evelyn Waugh in Aden, Abyssinia and Brazil, countries with which he felt no particular imaginative identification. What matters is (I) your personality and personal stance, with all the possible variations in the degree to which you are inward or outward, sensible or foolish, knowledgeable or naive, providing you can persuade the reader that you are sufficiently interesting for what happens to you to be of some importance. You can be interesting because you are young and unformed, or because you have the huge erudition of a Norman Douglas (subverted as it is by Greek naughtiness) or of a Patrick Leigh-Fermor (a personally unobtrusive writer who nevertheless exposes himself in the exuberance of his style); you can even be a sermonising sage like Lawrence (who makes himself bearable by the keenness of his eye and his nerves) or Henry Miller (whose prejudice and intellectual shallowness are relieved by an earthy gusto). Of course (II) something *must* happen to you, something *must* be seen, and it is likely that this exterior world will have much to do with individuals you meet, including people the Foreign Office would never dream of giving you an introduction to, together with the general atmosphere of places and a fair proportion of discords and discrepancies, not omitting your own humiliations and hardships. The result (III) is that balance between inner and outer which suggests experience appropriated, a vision achieved.

As a book-reviewer who is often asked to comment upon travel-books, I can give a couple of examples. Some years ago the poet James Kirkup described a period he spent as lecturer at the University of Malaya in the city of Kuala Lumpur, or, as Cocteau called it, Kuala l'impure. His book was characterised by a mixture of sensuously poetic evocation and a fairly extreme use of the flip manner, which in fact he extended to the Firbankian camp. Puns, notebook jottings without verbs, startlingly interpolated aphorisms led to such things as 'discuss-

Boswell by Sir Joshua Reynolds

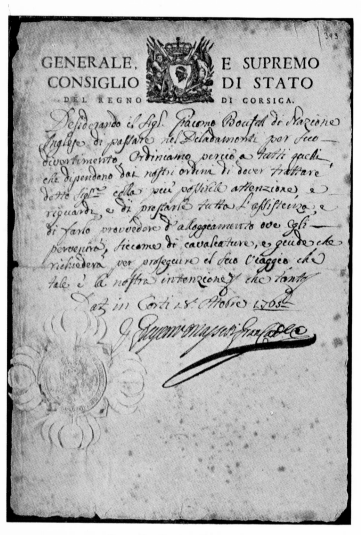

Boswell's Corsican Passport

ing erogenous zones with a Buddhist priest' and 'when you kiss a
person with gold teeth the kiss is warm'. He declared that he was
consoled during atrocious thunderstorms by his servant's appearing
with a kaleidoscope and a bottle of hock decorated with a big ribbon.
Bored with examination papers, he sprinkled them with scents of his
own creation, 'Naughty Time' and 'Perfect Disgrace'. All this was great
fun but suggested an imbalance between personality and exterior
subject; an addict of Japan, he disliked Malaya. His disgruntled concentration on himself was doubtless a result of this dislike but it con-
veyed the sense of a persona melodramatically conceived, whose out-
rageousness did not lead back to a central core of experience. On the
other hand, I could instance a recent account of an African trip by a
distinguished journalist which followed the aspects outlined above but
nevertheless failed because the personalities (a wife was drawn in) were
too suburban and shallow to deserve the emphasis they got, while the
mysterious continent was eaten away by an alternation of staccato
snapshots and cosy family giggles about the mechanics of the tour.
'Aren't we nice?...Isn't the wife sensible?...And those animals —
aren't they jolly, aren't they cute?' The good 'smart' writers always
know when to stop flexing their muscles and exchanging their in-jokes,
and to stand in awe before the Mayan ruin or the lions coming down
to the water-hole.

The travel book extends from the journal, which can be a novelist's
technique, to the novel itself. *Kangaroo* is probably a better description
of a part of Australia than Lawrence's touristic writings are of Italy.
Mr Lawrence Durrell conveys more of the Levant in the *Alexandria
Quartet* than he does in those factitiously assembled groups of intellectuals who discourse so learnedly on Corfu and Rhodes in his
books about the Greek islands. And the essence of Norman Douglas's
philosophy is found, of course, in *South Wind*. To return to the period of
Lord Chesterfield, we have Sterne's *Sentimental Journey*, a journal
become a novel, but with the author's personality entirely and pro-
vocatively pervasive. The same is true of William Beckford's *Visit To
The Monasteries* and, if to a lesser extent, of Boswell's *Corsican Journal*.
What, for that matter, are Byron's *Childe Harold* and *Don Juan* but
novels in verse? All these works are based on my proposed balance
between an interesting personality and an exterior world imaginatively
and critically seen.

If we now return to the Grand Tour it is to find romanticism taking
the place of Augustan men of the world exploring their inheritance of

2

Western culture (the aristocratic illiterates need not detain us). Crossing the Alps becomes sometimes a return to the schoolroom, more often an ecstasy of escape. Reactionary governments, the spread of industrialism, the dominance of a philistine middle-class drive the lonely, the spirited, the maladjusted, the sentimental, the sexually peculiar to the sunshine of Italy. Thus Shelley writes in April, 1818: '...no sooner had we arrived at Italy, than the loveliness of the earth and the serenity of the sky made the greatest difference to my sensations. I depend on these things for life; for in the smoke of cities, and the tumult of human kind, and the chilling fogs and rain of our own country, I can hardly be said to live.' At the other extreme is Dr Arnold, standing on the shore of Lake Como in 1829 and being firm with himself: 'I fancy how delightful it would be to bring one's family and live here; but then, happily, I think and feel how little such voluptuous enjoyment would repay for abandoning the line of usefulness and activity which I have in England...' This moralism reminds one of Ruskin, so artistically gifted and finally so mad, who belonged to both Alps and olive groves (as did those rebels, Samuel Butler and John Addington Symonds) but whose extraordinary sensuousness was constantly distorted by the prejudice and arrogance appropriate to a Victorian sage.

Of the ecstatic travellers one of the first must have been Winckelmann who finally reached Italy in 1755: 'One gets spoiled here; but God owed me this: in my youth I suffered too much.' But the most splendid, not least because he had his feet firmly on the ground, professed a classical outlook and travelled to return, was Goethe, who crossed the Alps in the autumn of 1786. In wonderful but surprisingly 'unpoetic' letters Goethe describes how he slipped away from his irksome administrative duties at Weimar and sought the classical South. He is half a scientist: he has an acute eye for mineralogy, for cloud-effects and weather, for plants and crops; he describes the methods of making polenta and discusses the effects of a constipatory diet upon health; he notices that vines near the road are sprayed with lime and he analyses the democratic implications of an amphitheatre, which he describes as based on the natural shape a crowd forms when watching something on a flat plane. By way of Munich and Carlsbad he enters the Brenner and the Tyrol. Part of the mountains he passes in the night-time, as did Beckford. (Alpine travel by night seems to have been commonplace; Dickens has a splendid description of this.) But the change to a happier climate and a new way of life is all-important. 'I am longing for grapes and figs,' he exclaims and is soon eating the latter for the first time. 'At present I am pre-occupied with sense-impressions,' he remarks in his serious half-scientific German way. 'Can I learn to look at things with clear, fresh eyes? How much can I take in at a single glance?' The weather is at first changeable, so that he is constantly putting on or taking off clothes, then bright and hot, and 'one can believe again in a God'. The mountain people show a peculiar fondness for peacock feathers; indeed, 'a person who intends to travel in the mountains should carry some with him, for such a feather, given at the right moment, will serve as the most welcome gratuity.' With the Adige near, he proceeds to Bolzano and Trento. Maize, mulberries, apples, quinces and nuts delight him. 'The days are long, nothing distracting my thoughts, and the glories of the mountain scenery do not stifle my poetic imagination: on the contrary, favoured by motion and the open air, they excite it.' When he hears the crickets at twilight he feels 'at home in the world, neither a stranger nor an exile. I enjoy everything as if I had been born and bred here and had just returned from a whaling expedition to Greenland.'

Near Lake Garda, which he insists on exploring, he sees his first olives and they are laden with fruit. (I do not know how far north olives can be found but recall how, at the tip of the Sirmione peninsula, in the environs of the so-called Villa of Catullus, whose broken arches frame the burning blue lake and the Alps around its upper extremity, there writhe olive trees which seem like heralds of the south, danger-ously exposed...but then Lawrence speaks of the shores of Garda 'fuming' with these vapour-like trees.) The rippling of the lake water is Goethe's first experience of seeing the subject of a Latin poem, Virgil's 'Fluctibus et fremitu assurgens Benace marino'. He gets to Verona, (where I once used him as a guide to find a very different city from his), and there, visiting his first classical ruins, he produces this beautiful sentence: 'The wind that blows from the tombs of the ancients is charged with a fragrance as if it had passed over a hill of roses.' But to my mind it is almost equally important that, in a smaller town on the way there, he had demanded the lavatory at an inn, whereupon the courtyard was shown him. '*Dove?*' he inquired, using 'a language I have always loved...I must put my linguistic talents to the test', as he says elsewhere, and the cheery answer came back, '*Da per tutto, dove vuol!*'

Goethe travelled widely in Italy, to Pompeii, Paestum and Sicily as well as to Rome; only the projected visit to Greece fell through. His enthusiasm was unbounded. 'I count it as a second birthday, a true rebirth, from the day I entered Rome.' It was 'a new youth, a second

youth, a new man, a new life...I think I have been changed to the
very marrow of my bones...I feel the sum of my forces compacting.'
The combination of antiquity and nature gave him that feeling of sane
earthiness which he called the vital principle of substantiality. For two
years he wrote, sketched, made plaster casts and conducted love affairs.
It was all so easy. *Desire followed the look, enjoyment followed desire.* And
later his compatriot, Heinrich Heine, making approximately the same
journey, was full of praise for the self-liberator (who, incidentally, on
his return to Weimar was nicknamed 'Priapus'): 'Goethe holds up a
mirror to nature, or, to state it more correctly, he is himself the
mirror. Nature longed to know herself, and she created Goethe.' With
Heine we have again those exclamations of delight which became more
or less *de rigueur* for Nordics crossing the Alps. 'Here in Italy everything
is so beautiful...it is more luxurious to weep under laurel groves than
under sullen, jagged firs; day-dreams are far sweeter beneath the ideal
cloud-pictures of the deep blue Italian skies, than under the ashy grey
German work-a-day heavens...' We murmur our assent, and add if we
are wise that there are plenty of cold days, draughty rooms, and
melancholy rain-sodden streets in Italy, Greece, Spain and Portugal —
and even in North Africa.

But for my part I find myself returning to that answer Goethe was
given when he asked for the lavatory shortly after his arrival. '*Da per
tutto, dove vuol!*' Isn't that, if very mildly, *it* — the change, the south, the
moment of adjustment, the squid soup, the pinched bottom, the boys
changing into their swimming-trunks in the Greek chapel, the drone
of bees round one's glass of mint tea on the cliffs of Rabat? 'Everywhere, everywhere. Go where you like!' It's the moment when Lucy
Honeychurch opens the window on her first morning in Florence, sees
the endearing muddle and vivacity of the street below, sees the tram
conductor spit in the faces of the urchins clinging to his vehicle (how
un-English, how disgusting!) and, taking it in her stride, does not
flinch. Accept that, and you're south. More poetically, but also from
a work by E. M. Forster, it is the moment when the student's notebook
on the Deist Controversy, emblem of laborious and probably pedantic
work, falls by accident into the translucent depths of the Mediterranean
where, as its owner realises, it becomes transformed into a thing of
beauty, nacreous, glimmering, like those enamelled tin plates for which
we dived as schoolboys. Not every revelation of foreignness can have
the absolute shock of these Nilotic negroes seen by Wilfred Thesiger,
'a pastoral people who own great herds of cattle, they are a virile race

of tall, stark-naked savages with handsome arrogant faces and long hair dyed golden with cow's urine'; not every foreign custom can seem as distant from suburbia as an Arabian circumcision ceremony described by the same author, with the young men 'looking like girls with their flowing hair and delicate features', the flayed members, and then the final triumph, each youth 'leaping and capering while the blood ran down his legs.'[1]

Yet this sense of difference always bears with it a sense of familiarity. Crossing the Alps (which to me at least is a more significant concept than merely crossing the Channel) means one of two things: in European places we bathe in the mainstream of Western, and largely classical, culture, growing buoyant with history embodied in atmosphere and art — we measure ourselves against the age-old potentialities of man; in places usually but not always beyond Europe, in North Africa, in Mexico, in the East, where there may be little history that we know or that seems to have any close relation to us, it is our dreams and unconscious desires which have greater play — we discover new and perhaps astonishing things about ourselves in an exotic setting. A Greek temple appears immediately familiar; a Buddhist pagoda can be equally appealing on a less conscious level. Both experiences, a walk through, say, Siena, a city instinct with history and art, and the exploration of a Berber village oasis in Morocco, can enlist some deep sort of personal engagement, can reveal some glimpse of inner reality, perhaps a reality beyond time; and it is such engagements and revelations which suggest, although the phrase is romantically loose, a form of the 'Enchanted Garden' where history grows so rich that it ceases to move forwards or backwards along a single plane, or where the atmosphere is so strangely or so beautifully beguiling that, a child again, one hears voices from Eden, catches shapes and gestures of an archetypal humanity.

These kinds of travelling are inter-related but it is the second, involving an Enchanted Garden of the Unconscious and the Repressed Wish, which we seem to hear from that strange, unsatisfied man, Richard Rumbold, in his first morning in Ceylon: 'A flawless, milky radiance was streaming through the open window, and I rang the bell. (The servant entered.) The unhurried gentleness of his movements in the warm, sleepy air and diaphanous morning light seemed to evoke some *alter ego* in myself, some dormant being repressed in early years by English standards of heartiness.'[2]

[1] *Arabian Sands*, (Longmans). [2] *A Message in Code, the Diary of Richard Rumbold, 1932–1960*, edited by William Plomer. (Weidenfeld and Nicolson).

Some seek to stray for ever in such paradises and, if they are really happy, one cannot blame them. 'I found in Spain a kind of freedom and spontaneity that I missed at home,' writes Gerald Brenan. 'And then have not northerners always had to go to the Mediterranean to learn the art of life? In these matters the English are still philistines.'

Such sentiments are close to those of Norman Douglas. But Douglas, who claimed that we should 'Mediterraneanise ourselves for a season' and that the true traveller has 'a prerogative to which the biliously moral middle-classes can never aspire; to be an Arab when it suits him', nevertheless confessed in *Alone* (1921) that he went to Italy not only to be in contact with beauty and antiquity but, and indeed above all, for '*the pleasure of memory and reconstruction at a distance.*' To do this 'in some November fog' made the manifold discomforts, the whole 'weltering ocean of unpleasantness', worthwhile.

If I may conclude this chapter with some personal comments, I would add that I am much less in favour of total expatriation than I used to be. I would rather consider myself a European than a potential expatriate. To my mind the romantic quest should be tempered with a little eighteenth century good-sense and sociability. I feel that one is not finally overwhelmed by the places one visits, or lost in the aesthetic and sensuous pleasures they promote, although Wordsworth's assertion of his spiritual independence when confronted by the Italian Lakes does, I confess, make me smile, especially in view of his fear that he might be seduced beyond all 'reasonable bounds':

> Not rich one moment to be poor for ever,
> Not prostrate, overborn, as if the mind
> Itself were nothing, a mean pensioner
> On outward forms, did we in presence stand
> Of that magnificent region.[1]

Travel has, I think, influenced most of the stages of my life, for I have spent something like sixteen years away from England; in Russia as a baby, in the United States and Canada at the beginning of manhood, in the Far East in my early thirties, and exploring Southern Europe, especially Greece, with approaching middle age. Like hundreds of other people I go towards and across the Alps in search of the beautiful, curious and diverting rather than for a rest or a conventional good time. I enjoy looking at buildings and their embellishments of sculpture and painting, although I prefer my works of art in an organic setting

[1] *The Prelude*, Book VI.

(church or palace, courtyards, gardens, townscape) rather than in a museum or art gallery. I like just as much to be encompassed by a beautiful countryside, to be penetrated by an atmosphere whether of town or country and, I suppose above all, to be hammered and dazed and intoxicated into sensuous animal life by a really strong sun. I cannot think I am in the least out of the ordinary in all of this. A vast tourist industry has been founded on the love of sun and sea; and if sightseeing is often as superficial as it is exhausting, I imagine that few would deny the life-enhancing effect of works of art, particularly when their individual beauties accumulate into the transmission of a quality or way of life which challenges our own. (Such accumulation is probably made easier by a warm climate; it certainly demands the sound attitudes, and even alas the poverty, which prevent the destruction of old buildings.) The same can also be true of local manners and customs in their circumambient atmospheres; sometimes it is another period in history, sometimes a geographically distinct set of values, often a combination of both, which sets us thinking about the quality of our own living. And what other subject is more important? I rest my case on what may strike others as didacticism and naivete: 'Look at Oxford Street, look at Harlow New Town...You would be better people if you reverenced the past and the picture it gives us of what man can be and do.' One must feel *at home in the world, neither a stranger nor an exile.*

I have to admit, though, that other aspects of my fondness for travel may be rather more suspect. I happen to be bad at languages, or possibly just lazy in acquiring them, and I realise that a result of this is that I nowadays meet too few people and almost certainly spend too much time in solitary contemplation of a vaguely aesthetic kind. Perhaps it is indicative that in choosing the subjects for this book, and one doesn't choose a hero without having a sympathy for him and finding in him some trace of the *alter ego*, I have selected in Boswell and Byron two travellers who were tremendously interested in people and who cared almost nothing for art and architecture. Indeed all three of my subjects *involved* themselves at one time or another in the life and politics of their foreign countries (as I think I can honestly say that I involved myself in English-speaking but relatively art-free Montreal and Singapore).

But whether or not I am ageing into a solitary aesthete and *voyeur*, I have to make the further admission that I regard travel with a strange fervency. Almost always inexpert and frequently incompetent over practical affairs, often in a bad temper because what I feel to be my sympathetic vision is at odds with my nervousness and shyness and my inability to get across, I have nonetheless to regard myself as the mystic of the midnight slum-bar and the noontide seascape. In the fresh and gay air of being once more on the move, in the quickened sense of belonging to a coherence far bigger than myself, I seem to find an inner reality. I exist. In some curious way I am positioned and focussed as a more religious man would be by his knowledge of the presence of God. I become a sensuous being, full of life and emotion. I am on the map: the map of history, yes, but the map of something less definable but more important too…a kind of eternal humanity which at times feels also like an eternal childhood. Do others share these feelings? *Are these ideas* (in Eliot's words) *right or wrong?*

As for this sense of inner reality, allied to the experience of time-lessness which I have already mentioned, I find that it can perhaps be best produced by the two extremes of great bareness and simplicity, such as the haunted simplicity of Greece, or of the fantastic richness (sometimes historical, more often decorative) of some of the buildings of Austria and Bavaria, of Italy, Portugal and Spain. In either case the imagination is fully at work. In Greece it works by a kind of expansion, reconstructing in a quite unhistorical way the lost worlds of Delos or Bassae with the aid of the sunny, cicada-shrill emptiness itself: a dilapidated cottage, a peasant's smile, a straying goat may be part of the process. Before the Transparente at Toledo, St Mark's basilica in Venice, the façades of San Pablo and San Gregorio in Valladolid, or under Tiepolo's great ceiling of the Four Continents surrounding Olympus at Würzburg, the method may be rather that of contraction, for here the richness is so great that the enchanted but bewildered mind must be adjusted to assimilate what it sees. 'So life can be like this after all' is finally the gist of its response, as it slowly takes in the overwhelmingly confident rhythms of a Baroque masterpiece such as the church of St Nikolaus in Prague, or moves, inevitably childlike, through the glittering perfection of the Amalienburg pavilion at Nymphenburg. My classicism is, in fact, more than half romantic. I like periods when man in his magnificence imposed a clarity so great that it emphasised the surrounding shadow, as does an archaic kouros, or when he expressed himself in designs so elaborate and even excessive (Batalha and Tomar in Portugal) that they cause a sort of clenching of the personality, which may become defensively frivolous or even pedantic, although here, rather more than in the virile and creative air of Greece, their full appreciation is likely to involve a kind of dreaming. This is one of my excuses for devoting so much of my book to William Beckford, that prince of reverie. But, in this matter of an 'inner reality', about which I still understand rather little, I can only say that I am as suspicious of its evident connection with dream as I am of its aestheticism. One can't simply let go. And, as a corrective to this temptation, and an inducement to be interested in other people, it is fortunate that of the travellers about whom I want to write, chronology offers first the energetic if slightly ludicrous figure of James Boswell.

'Cry like a parrot, chatter like an ape'

James Boswell in Europe

JAMES BOSWELL OF AUCHINLECK was in the habit of writing memoranda to himself. Such notes provided a moral stiffening for the day ahead. Their authorship was seemingly shared between the Ego and the Super-Ego, the latter reminding Boswell in Presbyterian accents to 'be like Father' and to 'chase libertine fancies', while the former, having chimed in with 'you are now happily free from sickly ideas of vice', was likely to continue on its own with a self-congratulatory boost, 'upon my word, you are a fine fellow', before perhaps divagating to the extent of 'think to have fine Saxon girls', a suggestion soon narrowed to 'swear solemn with drawn sword not to be with women *sine* condom *nisi* Swiss lass' and then further limited by 'swear, never to be with girl till you see Rousseau'.

It was quite characteristic, then, for Boswell to begin his two and a half years of foreign travel (from August 1763 to February 1766) with the following reminder: 'Set out for Harwich like Father, grave and comfortable. Be alert all along, yet composed. Speak little, make no intimates. Be in earnest to improve. It is not you alone concerned but your worthy father...See to attain a fixed and consistent character, to have dignity. Never despair.' And, although it is difficult to imagine Boswell ever being grave or silent for long, or wishing to dispense with intimates, whether complaisant females or father-substitutes, while his ebullient character was only 'fixed' in the consistency of immaturity, one must agree that his period abroad was a great success. He fought his very real 'despair' by sitting up all night journalising or by exercises to promote the circulation of the blood; travelling rough, and he travelled very rough indeed, was in itself a therapy. Furthermore, if his basic insecurity, whether social or ontological, was scarcely to 'improve', he provided himself with more adventures and experiences than fall to the lot of most young men in their middle twenties. Having discovered the primitive and noble simplicity of a little-known island people fighting for its freedom, he emerged, with some help from himself in the role of press-agent, as Corsica Boswell. 'I had got upon a rock in Corsica, and jumped into the middle of life.' But while his book prospered, the island capitulated to the French. There is much truth in the words he wrote in someone's *album amicorum* at Dessau in October, 1764: 'Never has a foreigner relished his travelling more than I. I travel as a philosopher. I am not so rude as Diogenes, but I am, like him, in search of men: beings worthy to uphold the dignity of human nature.' Himself so precariously dignified, as his Swiss servant Jacob would one day point out—at one moment the feudal baron, at the next fussing with the baggage or confessing that he has been *avec les filles* and has had his pocket picked—and also so intellectually limited, such a child, such a show-off, so incorrigibly vain, so frequently jejune, Boswell nevertheless did search for the good life and the true philosophy.

The first impression made upon us by the mixture of journals, memoranda and letters which comprise *Boswell in Holland* and the two volumes of *Boswell On The Grand Tour* is surely that of abundant life and variety. There is always something happening. There is never a dull moment. Our hero or anti-hero is constantly getting into a new scrape, admitting to a new self-dramatisation or embarking on another conversation about free will and predestination and the nature of the soul. A born reporter, he meets far more famous and genuinely important people than do Beckford and Byron. He is neither a balletic sprite nor a sardonic man of the world. A true adventurer, he is democratically involved in the mechanics and circumstantial details of travelling, about which he comments with lively good humour. He is young and in a way ordinary to the point of genius—or farce. The sheer scope of his experience commands our attention and, as we briefly survey his adventures, not only will the Grand Tour assume greater detail than is available in the pages of Walpole and Gray but the personality of the young traveller will also assert itself.

First we have the eight months spent at or, rather, near the University of Utrecht, for Boswell only got abroad as a student of his father's profession of the law. This was a ferocious regimen of study and high-thinking against a background of stuffiness and fog, prefaced by intense loneliness, dwindling into recurrent 'hypochondria' but relieved by a Christmas of 'brilliant dissipation' at the Hague, and by the affair with the capricious, free-thinking, insufficiently respectful and hence quite unsuitable probationary wife, Belle de Zuylen (or Zélide), a friendship that was not concluded until 1768 when, Boswell having told her of his fears about her 'levity and infidel notions', she replied with a letter he summed up in a single word, *termagant*. (More than

twenty years later, at the age of forty-six, this brilliant literary lady
would become the intimate of the nineteen-year-old Benjamin Constant.) This was the period of the Inviolable Plan: 'You have an
excellent heart and bright parts... For some years past you have been
idle, dissipated, absurd, and unhappy. Let those years be thought of
no more.' Each weekday Boswell devoted four hours to French, including the writing of an essay, and three to law; each morning an
octavo page was filled with a memorandum not only giving directions
for the day ahead but analysing yesterday's failures; each evening, including Sundays, exactly ten lines of heroic verse were composed.
Then there was the Greek, and the Latin literature, and Trotz's midday
lecture on Civil Law, and fencing lessons with a master who claimed
to be over ninety—no roistering or drabbing, no billiards, but card-
parties and concerts he did permit himself, together with his single
student club, a group of Hungarians who addressed each other in Latin.

Then, in June 1764, academic studies were over and he was gloriously released. He set out for Brunswick and Berlin, his main object
being to meet and lionise Frederick the Great. But the King was at
Potsdam, where presentations were not permitted, and all his efforts,
all his cajoling letters to officials, turned out to be in vain. He could
only observe at a distance. 'I then went to the Parade. I saw the King.
It was a glorious sight. He was dressed in a suit of plain blue, with a
star and a plain hat with a white feather. He had in his hand a cane.
The sun shone bright. He stood before his palace, with an air of iron
confidence that could not be opposed. As a loadstone moves needles,
or a storm bows the lofty oaks, did Frederick the Great make the Prussian officers bend submissive as he walked majestic in the midst of
them.' Boswell must return to Berlin, to his comfortable lodgings at the
house of the President of Police, and a walk *sous les marroniers* (presumably *Unter den Linden*) with the ladies—'Is this not living? It is. I
am quite a new man'—and then some pleasant hours over the hobbies
of the young Kircheisens, his host's children, ('I like young people who
have tastes of this kind. I never tire,') while he inspected the boy's
prints and pebbles and the girl's drawings and china. Much of his life
at Berlin seems bustling and bourgeois. He visited curiosities, heard
scientific talks, played 'seek the pin' and Ringelspiel, narrowly escaped
a duel, enjoyed his food, and at night grew 'hearty' with friends. But he
saw Frederick again at Charlottenburg where the ceremonies consequent upon the betrothal of the Prince of Prussia to the daughter of the
Duke of Brunswick were taking place: 'No strangers were invited to

the feasts, so I was only a single spectator. I had a full view of the King. I was very well amused.' Then, the next day, during a concert in the royal garden, 'I also saw the King a long time in the garden...I was quite enthusiastic and talked of the King with prodigious warmth' – so much so, indeed, that a companion had to restrain him, for he was even contemplating throwing himself at Frederick's feet in order to hear the man talk. Finally, after an interlude spent on a return visit to Bruns-wick, poor Boswell attempted to catch the royal notice by wearing a blue Scot's bonnet at a parade, a piece of exhibitionism which, although commented on elsewhere, never once drew the gaze of his hero. Characteristically, he became piqued and critical. He was not used to being thwarted in matters like this. An officer had told him that the King had neither religion nor humanity, another declared that his soldiers were unhappy, and so Boswell, who in his 'enthusiastic love of great men' had been reading Frederick's works every morning dur-ing July, was able to say by the end of September that 'the King is feared like a wild beast. I am quite out of conceit with monarchy!' Later, and here is a modern note indeed, he would deplore the results of the bombardment of the 'beautiful city of Dresden', an act done out of mere spite. 'I hated the barbarous hero.'

At Brunswick things had been very different. Boswell had been accepted by the court, even dancing a minuet with the Hereditary Princess, sister of George the Third. He had also met another hero, that Prince Ferdinand who commanded the British troops in the Seven Years War. 'He absolutely electrified me. Every time I looked at him, I felt a noble shock.' But even here some disillusionment set in. At an *operette* on the 9th of August, 'I sat in the Duke's *loge* and was fine with the ladies of the Court. My mind was clear and firm and fertile. It con-tained in itself both male and female powers: brilliant fancies were begotten, and brilliant fancies were brought forth.' Nevertheless, taking his leave on the 21st, 'I expected still more civilities than I received...I magnify all events in my own favour, and with the wind of vanity blow them up to size immense.'

It is now that the third stage of his European sojourn begins: the search, that is, for a Princely Friend. 'Since I have been in Germany it has been my wish to find a prince of merit who might take a real regard for me, and with whose ennobling friendship I might be honoured all my life.' Lord Auchinleck had been opposed to his travelling: 'In general I must tell you that travelling is a very useless thing...I could wish to see you 'gainst winter at home', and had so far conceded no more than a trip through Flanders to Paris or such a tour through the German courts as Boswell had already embarked upon. 'Manage father with affection' and a letter pleading for an extension to Italy had failed to alter the old man's mind. But now a firm promise to pursue the law on his return home together with the aid of letters written by influential friends, notably that old Jacobite the Earl Marischal of Scotland, who was a high official at the Prussian Court, might at last do the trick. There would be an answer at Geneva. In the meantime Boswell set off to visit Anhalt-Zerbst, Anhalt-Dessau, Saxony, Saxe-Gotha-Altenberg, Hesse-Kassel, Mainz, the Palatinate, Baden-Durlach and Baden-Baden. 'Campaigning' as he called it—travelling on the rough planks of *postwagens*, sleeping on tables or in the steaming straw of communal rooms at inns and sometimes not taking off his clothes for ten days— he explored the world of German *Kleinstaaterie*.

Changing into his scarlet and gold, or the 'flowered velvet of five colours' which prompted the princess at Gotha to exclaim, '*Mais, vous êtes beau!*', he was presented at seven courts. He also visited Wittenburg where he wrote a letter to Dr Johnson, so recently met and yet so captivated that he had accompanied Boswell to Harwich, from the tomb of the Protestant reformer, Melanchthon: the tomb proving to be a slab, he must lie flat on his stomach to make the gesture truly authentic (which of course gathered a crowd) and was then too afraid to send the effusion, it being 'too superstitious and too enthusiastic'. At Leipzig he admired the University; thirty-one years later his son would go there. In the Free City of Frankfurt he strolled 'with pleasant *étourderie* in the streets'. As for the princely friend, he could not find him at Dessau for Leopold Friedrich Franz happened to be away, but nevertheless he was well entertained. He was taken on a stag hunt, presented with one of the creature's feet as 'a mark of distinction' and encouraged (as Monsieur de Boswell, oak-garland in his hat) to entertain feudal speculations: 'A Scots baron cannot do better than travel in Germany. When he goes to Italy and France, he lives with artificial men cooped up in towns and formed in such a manner that Nature is quite destroyed' (27th September, 1764). He was, in fact, so pleased with his reception that he declared 'I am made for travelling'. At Gotha, too, he got on very well; 'The Duke and Duchess were plain old people.' At a court ball he wore a very genteel domino, white with red ribbons, and pleased himself 'with the idea of being in Spain' for he was always fond of a new persona. Mannheim, however, was a great disappointment; the Elector Palatine was haughty and did not invite him to dine; he revenged

himself in some of those heroic couplets, usually execrable, which he
often wrote as an exercise:

> Burnt be his palace to the very ground,
> And let no vestige where it stood be found.
> For hospitality ne'er enter'd there,
> But studied grandeur, to make blockheads stare.

And then at Karlsruhe, almost the last of his courts, he discovered
his friend. The Margrave of Baden-Durlach was reserved but amiable;
often host to Voltaire, he had progressive ideas, spoke English and
enjoyed the support of an artistic wife. Nevertheless, a fact noted by
Boswell with satisfaction, His Highness was reported to love the girls:
'Something big and fresh that he can get without pains, for he is
modest.' This philosophic amorist showed himself 'attentive to every
little anecdote' with the result that 'I found I was truly agreeable to
him'. In circumstances such as these Boswell, declaring his own mind
to be 'like an air-pump which receives and ejects ideas with wonderful
facility', was inclined to grow ebullient, confessional, anxious to be
assured he had 'force', 'genius', 'soul', and anxious, too, for the confirmation of a mutual bond which could be manifested in future correspondence. Floating happily amongst the shelves of books and cabinets
of medals, the concerts and the dancing, the new buildings and the
scientifically designed orchards, the pronouncements of the professors
and the cries from the pheasants in their 'beautiful and wild' preserve,
Boswell clung to his Margrave as often as he could. 'I told him how I
had formerly been an excellent mimic, but that I had given it up
absolutely, as it debased my character and procured me enemies', a
confession soon followed by some worldly anecdotes of Newmarket,
where Boswell had in fact been far from a success. Although the
Margrave seemed 'a moderate sceptic' Boswell was firm on religion: 'I
gave him freely my notions. I maintained the religion of Jesus as displayed in the four Gospels.' They discussed the soul. ' "When the act
of generation is performed," said he, "is there some power ready to
put in a soul at the critical moment, and to take it out again if the experiment fails?" We laughed very heartily at this speculative pleasantry...'
Laugh he might but in this mood Boswell was a force to reckon with.
'A young courtier passed the evening at my lodging. He owned himself
an infidel and a materialist, without any notion of futurity. I talked to
him with firm veracity; I showed him how inferior he was to me.'

A serio-comic aspect of this friendship of a week was Boswell's attempt to wheedle an honour out of the Margrave, namely the star and ribbon of the Order of Fidelity. He had been told that Karl Friedrich was 'a little nice' in giving it but the Margrave himself had explained that recipients had only to be good gentlemen. He *had* been offered the prince's correspondence ('I shall write to you sometimes; I shall be very glad to receive your letters') and this offer struck him as unsolicited and spontaneous, although he admitted to having prepared the way to it by asking: 'Is it possible, Sir, that after I am gone from you I may give you any mark of my gratitude?'—a pretty sure way of soliciting a gracious reply. Did not the promised correspondence include, so to speak, the mere gift of a German knighthood? At the last meeting he came out boldly with the request, looking at his friend 'steadily' the while. And the Margrave seemed favourable to the idea, no doubt especially so as Boswell had already explained that on both his father's and mother's sides he had royal connections. 'Let me have your genealogy attested, and when you return, we shall see.' Boswell's immediate reaction was 'oh, I shall have it' and that evening he told his servant Jacob, 'you shall have a master with a star'. But he never returned to Baden-Durlach and the correspondence languished. Karl Friedrich wrote him a single letter which he received at Geneva, misspelled, ungrammatical but evidently sincere. 'j beg you would be persuadet that j value the satisfaction of entering in correspondence with very much...you will oblige me Sir, by writing to me alwais openly and freely, and without Ceremonie.' Some of Boswell's letters seem to have been lost in the post, perhaps including the last sad one from Calais in February, 1766: 'your silence made me suppose that you had altered your opinion of me, either from bad information or from that fickleness to which the great are so unhappily subject.' Boswell was never to know that in the Grand-Ducal archives at Karlsruhe there reposes the copy of a letter written by the Margrave in May, 1768, a letter which positively bewails the fact that its author has received nothing from Boswell and can only hope that now he has returned to England he will be able to write. 'For to judge from the affectuous mind you once showed to me, I dare hope that it is no oblivion which stopped the courses of this literary commerce...In this sweet expectation, I am, with all my heart, Sir, your affectionate...' Perhaps the court bureaucracy interfered. But how Boswell would have relished that *sweet* and *affectionate* ending!

The next stage of Boswell's tour is the most famous. Within the course of a few weeks, in December 1764, he laid siege to the two greatest thinkers of the age. After the enlightened despotism of Frederick the Great, whose terrified soldiers he had described as being as numerous and dispensable as herrings, and the physiocratic liberalism of that other autocratic ruler, the Margrave, he moved to the very fountain-head of the ideas that were changing the world. Significantly both Rousseau and Voltaire were living in a kind of exile. Rousseau, at fifty-two only recently famous, for *La Nouvelle Héloïse*, *Emile* and *Du Contrat Social* had all been published in 1761–1762, had fled from Paris to Yverdon, a dependency of the state of Berne, and thence to the nearby mountain village of Môtiers, which was controlled by the King of Prussia and in fact governed by Boswell's friend, the Earl Marischal. This exile was therefore real enough. Meanwhile the septuagenarian Voltaire had retired to Ferney, only four miles from the democratic but Calvinist city of Geneva (Rousseau's birthplace although violently opposed to his views) but itself within the borders of France; in the event of danger he had prepared boltholes in both the adjacent Canton of Vaud and the Kingdom of Sardinia. The situation of the two sages was dramatically contrasted. Rousseau lived in chaste solitude with his former mistress in a simple house where dinner was served in the kitchen, Voltaire in an elegant château with its own theatre and manorial village, a flock of servants and a plenitude of guests. Yet both men were frail. An obstruction of the urethra forced Rousseau to wear an Armenian kaftan and to have frequent recourse to both chamber-pot and probe, while the toothless, skeletal Voltaire was likely to appear in slate-blue dressing-gown and night-cap, not sitting down with the company at dinner and frequently withdrawing to converse and play chess with a pet Jesuit abbé. Voltaire was a sophisticate and a wit, Rousseau an emotionalist with a passion for scenery and botanising. Voltaire was a tough-minded deist who could poke fun at all religious forms and pretensions, Rousseau a warmly vague believer. Voltaire had for long been famous as an epic and dramatic poet, the author of fifty plays: Rousseau, formerly a footman, teacher, musician and musical hack, was but recently arrived. To these contrasts must be added the fact, unknown to Boswell, that at the very moment of his encountering the two sages the quarrel existing between them was about to explode, with the result that Rousseau's brief period of happiness was to vanish for ever, he was to be driven from Môtiers and to find his paranoia developing into madness. For Rousseau's *Letters Written from the Mountain* attacking the Genevan oligarchy which had condemned *Emile* appeared in Geneva on December 18th, 1764, and

Voltaire's anonymous pamphlet, *How the Citizens Feel*, with its revelation that Rousseau had abandoned his children, followed on the 27th. This will give some idea of the dreadful relevance of Boswell's reporting. Nor is this all. Rousseau, who was of great assistance in getting Boswell recognised in Corsica, appears again at the end of the European tour. By then much of his magic had evaporated and Boswell, escorting his mistress, Thérèse Le Vasseur, to join him in England, seems to have conducted an affair with the middle-aged 'girl'. 'Yesterday morning had gone to bed very early, and had done it once: thirteen in all.' The ludicrousness of the situation lay in the fact that Boswell only wanted *dicta philosophi* to fill out his journal and that the amorous Thérèse disconcerted him by criticising him as a lover—always dangerous with Boswell, whose potency was precarious—and then insisting on administering a course in love. But such is the characteristic Boswellian richness: to sleep with the mother of those five abandoned children, reluctantly allowing your notebook to fall from your hand, and then to be humiliated for your pains. There is always a story. The teller is even more of a victim than the told. And what dominates both is the appalling, endearing mess reproduced by Human Nature and 'Life is just like that'.

Boswell succeeded in getting six interviews with the ill and touchy Rousseau on five different days. He allowed an interval of nine days to elapse between the third meeting on December 5th and his return on the 14th in order that the sage should have time to read and ponder the 'Sketch of My Own Life' he had written for him. During these meetings Boswell is at full stretch: all the resources of his personality from the need to confess and to be instructed to the calculating gall of a professional journalist are brought into play. He is at once insensitively persistent and, on a deeper level, sympathetic and imaginative. The result, despite the fact that the Journal was never worked up into a published account, is one of the great moments of the eighteenth century: a flourish of personalities on the rocky threshold of romanticism.

There is something heroic about the opening episode. Boswell heard that Rousseau often turned visitors away. He nevertheless decided not to use his letter of recommendation from the Earl Marischal and not to enlist the services of the local squire, who would have been ready to ensure his acceptance; he decided instead to rely entirely on his own heart and genius and on his ability as a pyschologist and a writer, preparing with extreme care, three drafts in fact, the letter which gained him admission. First there was a paragraph of extreme, dramatic and therefore potentially amusing concision: 'I am a Scots gentleman of ancient family. Now you know my rank. I am twenty-four years old. Now you know my age' and so on. Next came the frank admission of Rousseau's inaccessibility: 'I have heard, Sir, that you are very difficult, that you have rejected the visits of several people of the first distinction. For that, Sir, I respect you the more...' And then the note of individualism could be sounded loud and clear, manly in itself but suffused with tender tenor overtones of past suffering and present enthusiasm: 'I present myself, Sir, as a man of singular merit, as a man with a feeling heart, a lively but melancholy spirit.' To be soon followed, of course by 'your writings, Sir, have melted my heart, have elevated my soul, have fired my imagination.' After which it was only necessary to ensure that Rousseau did not plead the excuse of his sickness, 'You will find in me a simplicity that will put you to no trouble, a cordiality that may help you to forget your pains', and to beg, a little demandingly in the circumstances, that they should meet tête-à-tête.

Once inside the door Boswell decided to be hearty and informal, glad that they were both taking a turn about the room rather than sitting fixed in chairs; soon he was thumping Jean-Jacques on the shoulder. It must have been a remarkable sight: the uneasy kaftan-clad recluse and the boisterous youth in his scarlet and gold lace, his buckskin breeches and boots, together with an overcoat of green camlet trimmed with fox and, under his arm, 'a hat with a solid gold lace, at least with the air of being solid'. Young men visiting their mentors often bulk raw and bleak, hanging on the words of wisdom with a deadweight of tenacity, but a shy professor must have winced at the companionship of this brilliantly accoutred hearty. Throughout the meetings there runs, indeed, the theme of Rousseau's wanting to escape. The first meeting must be 'short': and when Boswell concluded by saying he would be back, Rousseau began to demur: 'Oh, as to that I can't tell,' for he was overwhelmed with visits from *idle* people, he was pestered with letters, and no, the fact that he left the room with Boswell didn't mean that he wished to accompany him further: 'I am going for a walk in the passage. Goodbye.' The second meeting, with Rousseau 'more gay' and at one point making an exceedingly weak pun (nonetheless described by Boswell as 'a precious pearl'), ended with nothing less than, 'you are irksome to me' followed by a forthright 'go away'. The third terminated with 'I don't promise to see you, I am in pain. I need a chamber-pot every minute.' The fourth visit was an extremely short morning one; it is possible that Rousseau had already inserted the probe before his guest arrived. Boswell was told he could come again in the afternoon but must expect no more than a quarter of an hour and should place his watch upon the table, a time-limit Boswell said he would extend to twenty minutes. But Boswell's persistence somehow turned his irksomeness into a joke. Rousseau evidently liked him. On the 15th of December he was actually invited to dinner.

In between these visits Boswell walked or rode in the mountains. 'To prepare myself for the great interview (the first), I walked out alone. I strolled pensive by the side of the river Reuse in a beautiful wild valley surrounded by immense mountains, some crowned with frowning rocks, others with clustering pines, and others with glittering snow. The fresh, healthful air and the romantic prospect around me gave me a vigorous and solemn tone.' But Boswell's was not a visual gift, let alone an aesthetic one; occasionally he comments upon a building or a work of art but he never really enters into such things and he is incapable of composing a picture, an atmospheric scene; yet the romantic note reaches us — the Wordsworthian combination of mountains, health and solemnity — although the phrase about the 'wild' valley and the 'immense mountains' was not to be adventurously expanded but repeated word for word in two letters sent from Môtiers. On December 5th, after the third visit, he did not leave the village till 6 p.m.; he was in fact busy writing first the sketch of his life and then a letter to a friend, Johnston, so great was his desire to set the seal of authority upon his experience, and it is in this letter that he explains, 'I am to be alone on horseback in a dark winter night, while the earth is covered with snow. My present sentiments give me a force and vigour like the lion in the desert.' The mountain setting was appealed to again on the last day with Rousseau. 'At seven in the morning I got on horseback and rode about a league to St Sulpice, where I saw the source of the Reuse...It is a prodigious romantic place.' Doubtless his mind was full of the *Nouvelle Héloïse*.

Apart from his riding and walking he had an eye for other people and much of the time he must have been writing the notes later worked up into the Journal, never with hindsight, always limited to the feelings and circumstances of that particular day, together with memoranda about the subjects to be discussed such as: hypochondria and suicide; his desire to have a Swiss girl (there was a splendid example at the inn at Colombier); Scots familiarity and sarcasm, did it justify duelling when offence had been taken?; how to follow Nature; and, a point prepared to be the climax of the final talk, would Rousseau consider himself bound to him by the finest, the most delicately intimate thread?

Of such things they talked. They talked of cats, admired by Rousseau, disliked by Boswell, and of the Prussian king; of ecclesiastics who made religion more and more incomprehensible and of sensualists who reduced the human spirit to the state of a corpse; of Dr Johnson and the Abbé de Saint-Pierre; of M.P.'s who must stick to their principles even if this makes them appear to be fools; of books, and Rousseau declared that even his own were rigmarole compared to meditation; of M. de Voltaire, who had injured Rousseau and therefore did not like him, but whose talk was most enjoyable; of how Rousseau would react to the democratic familiarity of the Scots (he would like it) which was often brutal and malicious (no, he would not like *that*). A key moment was when Boswell tried out his usual arguments in favour of lechery, a battery of baronial *droit-de-seigneur*, oriental concubinage and the fertility of the Biblical patriarchs, followed, when these guns had been successively silenced, by a brief fusillade about following the promiscuous manners of France and Italy when in those countries. Another was his query about Rousseau's religion: ' "But tell me sincerely, are you a Christian?" I looked at him with a searching eye...Each stood steady and watched each other's looks. He struck his breast, and replied, "Yes, I pique myself upon being one." ' A third related to his own sense of guilt and how he could expiate this: 'Say to yourself in the morning, "Come now, I am going to *pay off* so much evil"...there is no expiation of evil except good.' But Rousseau, being all for independence, refused to be Boswell's spiritual director. 'You are a fine fellow,' he said when the young man left, tears in his eyes.

The assault upon Voltaire was different. He was not regarded by Boswell as a potential guru and he was altogether too sophisticated a person to be thumped on the shoulder. Their several conversations, while revealing very well the dry irony to which Voltaire was addicted —one can hear his voice and sense his simpering manner—do not amount to a great deal, perhaps because the Frenchman took Boswell less seriously while he himself never made a coherent record. During the first exchange, of only half an hour's duration, what did Voltaire say? That Scots artists could not be successful because you cannot paint when your feet are cold...that of course Boswell and Johnson may undertake a tour of the Hebrides if they please, provided they do not insist that Voltaire accompany them...that he no longer speaks English because he is unable to lay his tongue against non-existent teeth...and that here is his friend the Abbé Pierre, a young man of sixty, 'a broken soldier of the Company of Jesus'. Later, when Boswell had got himself invited for a couple of nights so that he didn't have to rush back to Geneva in order to enter the walled city before its gates closed, he was able to hear Voltaire attacking Shakespeare, which had become almost an obsession with him – often two good lines, never six; you English are alone in admiring him because you have no taste – and nonchalantly summing-up Milton, Dryden and Pope. But religion was the great subject. In his long letter to his friend Temple, Boswell described what happened: 'I placed myself by him. I touched the keys in unison with his imagination. I wish you had heard the music. He was all brilliance. He gave me continual flashes of wit...At last we came to religion. Then did he rage. The company went to supper. Mr de Voltaire and I remained in the drawing-room with a great bible before us; and if ever two mortal men disputed with vehemence, we did. Yes, upon that occasion he was one individual and I another. For a certain portion of time there was a fair opposition between Voltaire and Boswell.' Indeed at one moment Voltaire fainted, or pretended to faint. 'He recovered, I resumed our conversation, but changed the tone. I talked to him serious and earnest.' Yet all that Boswell could extract was a veneration for the Supreme Being. 'I was sorry. I doubted his sincerity. I called to him with emotion, "Are you sincere? Are you really sincere?" He answered, "Before God, I am." ' Finally, on the afternoon of Boswell's departure, an ill and understandably reluctant Voltaire was persuaded to emerge from his privacy to hear his guest tell him 'I thought to see a very great, but a very bad, man', an opinion now abandoned except for some doubts about that article on the Soul in the *Dictionnaire philosophique*. Surely there is something more imaginative, more noble to the concept of the soul than Voltaire allows? 'Yes. You have a noble desire to be King of Europe. I wish it for you, and I ask your protection. But it is not probable.' What, then, about worship? 'Let us meet four times a year in a grand temple, with music, and thank God for all his gifts. There is one sun. There is one God. Let us have one religion. Then all mankind will be brethren.' BOSWELL. 'May I write in English, and you'll answer?' VOLTAIRE. 'Yes. Farewell.'

Boswell was not entirely happy at Ferney. The exuberance with which he had risen at Geneva on Sunday, December 23rd – 'I got up in fine spirits, and sung and was gay even at the seat of Presbyterianism on a Sunday'—together with the reference to the 'magician' and the 'enchanted castle' formed only one of his moods; he was also from time to time 'hipped' (hypochondriacal) and dull. Ferney was just another country house in which one could suffer a 'heavy ennui'. Scoffing urbanity was likely to please Boswell as little as it did Beckford during his Genevan days. Besides, one of the other guests, the artistic and poetic Chevalier de Boufflers, was clearly so much more brilliant than he. This counter-point of unease, however, only serves to accentuate Boswell's pertinacious technique as tourist and lion-hunter. There is the letter written to Voltaire's niece, Mme Denis, with the request that he may stay the night: an extraordinary exercise in adaptability of tone, when you compare it to that sent Rousseau, full of jokes that hover between frivolity and bawdiness—let them provide him with a garret or two chairs in the bedchamber of her maid—full of flattery extending from Voltaire as the sun to the tart she gave him at dinner, suffused with a provocative egotism, and relying too upon that stand-by of the ingratiating stranger, the reference to incidents already mutually experienced and to accurately remembered sayings of his hosts. How anxiously Boswell tried to make himself part of the château life, spreading the tentacles of his personality into every nook and cranny; beating down his melancholy, he rushed off to Voltaire's church, explored Voltaire's library, perambulated Voltaire's garden, demanded a volume of the plays so that he could read *Mahomet* in its author's home, asked for the philosopher's writing paper so that he could scribble letters, including one to that disapproving father of his, and then copied out his own *Ode on Ambition* with an inscription to his host.

After leaving the château he was still in pursuit of Voltaire and it was this pursuit which began, if at first hardly perceptibly, to undermine his admiration for Rousseau. Was it true that Voltaire relaxed his deistic principles when seriously ill and in fear of death? He spoke to Voltaire's doctor who, having denied this, went on to tell him all the unpleasant things which had just appeared in the *Sentiment des Citoyens*, including the suggestion that Rousseau's complaint was caused by venereal disease. He was, he says, prepared to discount this, in view of Dr Tronchin's closeness to the Genevan government, but it left its mark. For the rest, he was now happy. 'What a singular being do I find myself!...am I not well received everywhere? Am I not particularly taken notice of by men of the most distinguished genius? And why? I have neither profound knowledge, strong judgement, nor constant gaiety. But I have a noble soul which still shines forth, a certain degree of knowledge, a multiplicity of ideas of all kinds, an original humour and turn of expression, and, I really believe, a remarkable knowledge of human nature' (29th December). Furthermore Lord Auchinleck had given his consent to an extension of the tour. Boswell was about to cross the Alps. 'I set out for Italy tomorrow...I beg you to give me your advice as to how to conduct myself so as to profit most in that country of the fine arts. I love antiques. I love paintings. I shall have the best opportunities for perfecting myself in both. I have a real taste for music. I sing tolerably well. I play on the flute a little, but I think it beneath me...' (to Rousseau, 31st December, 1764).

As he approaches Mont Cenis and that 'alps-machine' we have already met in connection with Walpole and Gray, let us pause and reflect upon this Singular Being. What sort of traveller has he proved himself? Certainly he has been honest, even ruthlessly and shamelessly so; the emendations between memoranda and journal, the very few excisions, have shown nothing of the idealising or dramatising fabrication so common with William Beckford. He has been concerned, of course, to portray everything in relation to himself, his Journal being a private affair and dedicated to the growth of his own mind, but his egotism has had a paradoxical quality: temperamentally insecure, unsure of his own opinions and in many of his attitudes so normal as to be almost ordinary, he has constantly described other people because they were so important to him, he needed them so much, a task which his splendid ear for dialogue has assisted not a little. He travelled, as he said, in *search of men*; he considered himself a student of human nature, which was, of course, the chief Augustan interest. The proper study of Mankind was still Man. There is an interesting passage in the Journal where he contrasts knowledge of human nature with knowledge of the world in terms of the florist and the expert on artificial flowers. 'So I know in general your men of the world to be artificial, but am not able to develop their different qualities. What is really Man I think I know pretty well' (29th December, 1764). It is certainly true that he could 'tune myself so to the tone of any bearable man I am with that he is as much at freedom as with another self, and, till I am gone, cannot imagine a stranger'. (One wonders if this useful but dangerous gift resulted, as it often does, in a certain resentment when these interlocutors later learned how much they had told him.)

Boswell's interest in people is expressed in hundreds of small touches in the Journal, where the humble and the bourgeois figure just as largely as the great. It is all surprisingly good-humoured. Unlike most neurotics who seek refuge in the journal form — and Boswell's journalising could become for him the purpose of his life, so that he didn't want more living than could be got onto its pages — he does not seem to have sought revenge for his disappointments and his precariously maintained ego by either analysing *les autres* with a brilliantly elaborate (and hence superior) accuracy or by etching caricatures in acid. He allows his occasional pique to become funny. Irritated by the small town of Coswig, because it was dirty and no doubt also because the Prince of Zerbst was absent from home, he went around asking every sentry how many troops the state could boast, although he knew this perfectly well, and as a result got himself arrested as a spy. (A gloss on the dangers of literary curiosity: Goethe was to have the same experience when he began to draw the tower of the old castle at Malcesine on Garda...it is the Tonio Kröger syndrome, experienced by myself when poking about Dudley in the Midlands, where I then lived, because the police could not understand, I suppose, such interest in a place not usually celebrated.) Annoyed by the snub at Mannheim, his reactions were too warm to be superior: he wrote two bad poems and one of those heavily ironic letters that one doesn't send. He rarely grew as contemptuous as in this description of a dance and supper held on a Genevan Sunday, a scene that was of special interest to him because Sundays in Scotland were truly gloomy and surely the same should be expected at the source of the doctrine. 'We supped in a great town hall, and ate and drank considerably. After which they pelted each other with the crumbs of their bread turned into little balls. This was rather rude in a large company and in presence of a stranger. I however threw with the rest, partly to indulge my whim...They were monstrously familiar, the men pawing the sweaty hands of the women, and kissing them too, as the minister (for a clergyman was present) slobbered the greasy, unwashen hands of a married woman...I was disgusted much, and only consoled myself that I beheld a nauseous example of the manners of republicans.' Very Boswellian that: a whim to throw bread, a baronial repugnance to the rest of the proceedings. More usual is kindness, as when he was given a damp alcove to sleep in at Leipzig but only moved his bed onto the floor of the main apartment when the good hosts of the house had gone to bed; a young man's brash but imaginative impromptus, such as the occasion when the Court at Dresden being in mourning and himself without a black coat, he stuck a cockade in his hat and presented himself as wearing the uniform of an outlandish officer; a boyish interest in food: 'I shall not forget the luscious venison with currant jelly...I supped on a dozen of larks'; and moments of pure animal happiness, 'quite drunk with high spirits' after sitting up all night, and 'lying on the floor did me much good. I sprang up cheerful' and 'this morning I was in delicious spirits. I stood calm in the chamber, while the sun shone sweet on me...'

Boswell expected a great deal from his foreign travel; no young man can have expected more. He wanted to grow up, to prove himself strong and manly and, as we have seen, to achieve a balanced, consistent character. Writing to Temple from Ferney he already felt himself 'a very different man' and went on, 'I have got a character which I am proud of.' He also wanted to educate himself, for he felt his training at Edinburgh and Glasgow, and during the two years of partial disgrace when his father had superintended his studies, to have been 'unhappy' and 'narrow'. The archaeologizing he was to embark on so enthusiastically in Italy would complete what he had learned at Utrecht, agreeably supplemented as this had been by the experience of German thought and manners before the altogether transcendent courtship to Voltaire and discipleship of Rousseau. He had learned to talk and write French; he would now acquire sufficient Italian to compose 'reflections' in that language and also to curse a tardy boatman with no less than, *'Bestia bugerone! Non voglio esser piu coglionato!'* In March, 1765, he was to undertake a 'Course in Antiquities and Arts' about Rome with a Scottish antiquary, during which he insisted that they both spoke in Latin: 'We have harangued on Roman antiquities in the language of the Romans themselves.' He writes to Rousseau in a general sketch of his Italian tour (Lucca, 3rd October, 1765) that 'the study of antiquities, of pictures, of architecture, and of the other arts which are found in such perfection at Rome occupied me in a wise and elegant manner. You must know that I have a great taste for virtue. It entertains me agreeably during many hours when without it my mind would be a prey to ennui.' Personally I doubt whether he had much taste although he claimed to have acquired it 'to a certain degree'. He was not a Burlington or a Goethe. His staccato notes, for the Journal is often missing, do not tell us much about his capacity for appreciation; from the Vatican he notes, 'Apollo: baddish knees; Laocoon's sons too much formed: men in miniature' while at Cardinal Albani's villa, where his guide was none other than the Abbé Winckelmann, he produces the pleasant image, 'Garden like spread periwig', but most of his comments are those of routine enthusiasm. It is significant that his remarks to Rousseau switch immediately from *virtu* to 'traits of Character' as more likely to promote 'philosophical reflections'. It was the general illustriousness of the Italian past which excited him, as it excited many in a classical age. Could we say more of Byron? Yet he was genuinely liked by the antiquarian scholar, Andrew Lumisden, who took him to the hills above Tivoli, the still little-visited site of Horace's Sabine farm, a pilgrimage deserving the preliminary injunction, 'Horace jaunt...At villa be in enthusiasm', a wish satisfactorily fulfilled: 'Saw ruins; fell on knees and uttered some enthusiastic words.'

Education and, more generally, growing up had for Boswell a particular meaning. He knew only too well that he suffered from lassitude and depression. He was a hypochondriac or, as we should say, a neurotic; he had been pretty near to juvenile delinquency. He had a father problem and a sex problem and a problem about religion. He had a problem about his career and a problem about marriage. The tensions caused by these, in association with whatever temperamental disposition lay behind or beyond them, formed the egregiously volatile personality which was to be cured or at least matured by Europe. He respected and needed to love a father who lacked the ability to express himself affectionately to any of his children, and with whom he found it difficult to get along. (In Scotland Boswell had been rebellious, idolising the theatre, chasing actresses and endlessly publishing poems, pamphlets and letters which were exhibitionistic and indiscreet. In 1760 he had run away to London. He still lay under the threat of disinheritance.) All his travel beyond Holland was wheedled out of a grudging and suspicious parent. Towards the end of his stay in Italy, after the brilliant Corsican trip, he would receive such dry and scolding sentiments as these: 'Your conduct astonishes and amazes me. You solicited liberty to go for four months to Italy. I opposed it as altogether useless; but upon your pressing importunity, contrary to my own opinion, I agreed to it, and therefore allowed you one month more...[and then, finding his son was in Siena]...and this in order, as you write, to learn the Italian language. As you don't say where you are to go after this, or what your scheme is, I must suppose you intend fixing in Italy, where that language can only be of use to you; for in this country it is no better than Arabic' (dated 1st October, 1765; received at the end of November).

He required just as much to square his religious needs (the Calvinism of his birth had wavered towards Methodism, certain 'Pythagorean' theories and then the Roman Church before settling for an Anglicanism modified by Rousseau's Savoyard Vicar) with his strong appetites; he was guilty because of his dissipations with their consequent bouts of gonorrhoea and, even more, because of an adulterous relationship in Scotland which had abused the friendship of both the woman's father and her husband (this matter he discussed with Rousseau) and he was anxious because he tended to lack potency with women of his own class, preferring adventures with prostitutes. Could he settle down with Zélide? Could he be content as a lawyer based on terribly raw and provincial Auchinleck? Didn't his genius demand the freedom of an oriental sultan who was also an M.P. and moved gaily and graciously in London society? Was he damned? Didn't the new rationalism permit him to be natural and human? Wasn't religion the warmth, the worship he felt so keenly in St Peter's? Such questions preyed on a mind that found itself frequently, and genuinely, 'hipped'. No subject is discussed more often in the Journal than the 'fiend' of melancholia. And in the extraordinarily international society of Europe in the eighteenth century, amongst the officers and the antiquaries, the Dominicans and the Jacobites, the free thinkers and the free-lovers, the princes and the prostitutes, Boswell often found fellow sufferers prepared to discuss the great question.

It is usual to speak of the 'modernity' of Boswell. Our own auto-biographical and psycho-analytical period, with its insistence on the complexity and irrationality of the self, and its desire for the exposure of all the facts, including the discreditable ones, can obviously find much of interest in Boswell's journalising. Indeed, the century in which he lived — so orderly and rational in its general structure, so social, easy and yet concerned with propriety and decorum in many of its manners — can now be seen, like the Greece of the fifth century, to hold within its checks and balances, perhaps even to emphasise by its belief in 'rules', the existence of darker, wilder material. For the most part, admittedly, the material is concealed (but often at high tension) beneath an urbane and polished surface. The terrible misanthropy of Swift, the cripple's malice of Pope, the deeply surging melancholia of Johnson, the secret emotional life of Gray, the real oddity behind the deliciously affected oddity of Sterne, the instability of Collins and of Cowper — these tensions are generally transmuted or sublimated into socially-committed, rationally organised works. Pope speaks out from his inner heart in only a few lines; you must turn to the private meditations of Johnson to find the quaking silence behind the thunder; and Gray's

Elegy perhaps only faintly disturbs as it shifts towards the close into a region of ambiguous identity, where something like narcissism or homosexuality dampens the lines into wilting sentiment. Most of the eighteenth century 'sentimentalism', of course, carries no ascertainable threat. We read Thomsons' *Seasons* or Cowper's *The Task* for their mixture of period charm (patriotic self-congratulation, moralisation, pastoral mellowness) and of occasional objective, concrete, quasi-scientific images drawn from nature.

Boswell's difference is that he spoke out, that he made his day to day life the subject of his writing. I suspect that many young men in a variety of ages have been pretty much the same as he. 'Modernity' is a shaky criterion; the more we know of past times the more 'modern' much of their life becomes. That Boswell had difficulties with his father, that he feared the dullness of a particular job in a provincial setting, liked to be considered an intellectual while also enjoying the bright lights and thinking much of the chase and conquest of women must be something of a perennial predicament. T. S. Eliot put the case of all young men who are uncertain of themselves when, in *Portrait of a Lady*, the baffled, ironically posturing youth declares as he emerges from a cloying relationship with an older woman:

> And I must borrow every changing shape
> To find expression...dance, dance
> Like a dancing bear,
> Cry like a parrot, chatter like an ape.
> Let us take the air in a tobacco trance—

What is perhaps rather more modern is not Boswell's situation in itself but the frankness with which he confesses to muddle, conflict, fantasy and foolishness: the readiness with which, either consciously or unconsciously, he enlists the comic sense and makes of himself an anti-hero. He is 'tragic' only in the sense that the protagonist of some modern play about a salesman losing his grip, or an ageing vaudeville actor, or a businessman cheating himself and his family with a dream he will never realise, is tragic—or, more truly, pathetic. And, even in his latter drink-sodden and violence-ridden days, as Lord Lonsdale's buffoon and the errant, remorseful husband of Margaret Montgomerie, he is still the symbol of irresponsible life and, for better or worse, youthfulness. Another important quality, which differentiates him from similar romantics and makes him endearing today, is that he is blessedly non-literary. Long descriptions, experimental effusions, attempts to sob

River Arno and Ponte S. Trinita, Florence, 18th century

Beckford by George Romney

or charm his way into the reader's heart, in view of his limitations how dreadful these would have been! But the journal is plain, comparatively staccato, with no fine writing. Compared to the two other self-absorbed personalities with whom I am dealing in this book, Beckford and Byron, he is the rankest amateur. Beckford and Byron are in a sense elusive personalities because they are overshadowed by the formal structures of both their legend and their art. They are all identity but their identity is distributed between a variety of relatively autonomous and coherent artefacts which shade off into myth. Beckford is *Vathek* and Fonthill. Byron is *Childe Harold*, *Don Juan*, the martyr in Greece. Boswell, on the other hand, stumbles amongst the raw materials of existence, flushed and sweaty with life. The wonderful thing is that he, too, created a masterpiece at least as enduring as theirs.

Boswell's emphasis on the personal calls out the subjective element in all of us. Our tribute to him is to be ourselves. I must confess that I am drawn to him because I am myself an autobiographer and a writer of personal books of travel; I, too, have suffered from a neurosis, a problem about identity, and variations of his other difficulties. I have, for instance, *wanted* to win the friendship of a father-figure by writing such a letter as his to Rousseau; certainly I have often employed the calculating strategy of his letter to Mme Denis and Voltaire. I have experienced an 'enthusiasm of affection' which I contrasted with the dull emotions of other people and 'felt myself greatly improved' upon a former self, and, having one evening 'raged in the cause of pride' and scorned contentment in favour of the 'fiery', soon afterwards resolved: 'Let me then be master of myself. Let me be mild and agreeable.' And how well I know the attempt to catch and fix experience represented in Boswell's mountain walks at Môtiers or the famous moment on the threshold of consummating the affair with Mrs Lewis at the Black Lion, Fleet Street, when Boswell went out into the yard: 'The night was very dark and very cold. I experienced for some minutes the rigour of the season, and called into my mind a transition from such dreary thoughts to the most gay and delicious feelings...I came softly into the room, and in a sweet delirium slipped into bed' (*London Journal*, 12th January, 1763). But then so many threads, whose web is a kind of confirmation, even a kind of security, connect me to Boswell. When I see him on the Bay of Naples, Capri on the horizon and none other than the terrible John Wilkes by his side, and when I hear that witty political exile declaring: 'Dissipation and profligacy...renew the mind. I wrote my best *North Briton* in bed with Betsy Green', I cannot but reflect that

3

Capri was my first Mediterranean love, the object of my first solitary journey away from home, and that it was a proposed study of *John Wilkes and the American Revolution* which suddenly and almost inexplicably whisked me away from family, home and England itself when I was awarded a fellowship at Columbia University in 1938, a foreign trip which was in fact to last for nine years and to close my childhood behind me.

A degree of identification makes it easier, or at least less objectionable, for a person such as myself to speculate on what in Boswell's travel-writing one would like to be different. The appearance of Rousseau's and Voltaire's apartments, their books and pictures, their furniture, a revealing detail here and there, a surprise, an amusing discrepancy, I feel that I would have been on the lookout for such things. And then, for all Boswell's priding himself on being a physiognomist, how little he tells us about faces and expressions: the moment when Frederick the Great failed to resemble iron, or when the Margrave looked blank or annoyed or tender...the mannerisms, the personal quirks of a Jacob or a Thérèse, a Wilkes or a Mountstewart...And to such omissions I must add, of course, the fact that so much beautiful architecture (the height of German Baroque and Rococo) and the composition of so many gracious and elegant scenes form no part of his reporting. I must admit that at his age, caught in the flurry and adventure of sheer living and bereft of the discipline which made him scribble notes and then write them up, I should probably have been too lazy to get most of it down although, I, too, was a great journaliser; but I should, I think, have been aware of these things and retained their outline in memory. Often I wrote my journal not at the peak of living but during its duller moments. I have frequently regretted my failure to describe the evening I spent as Winston Churchill's host at Oxford in 1937; the snorts from the bedroom where the statesman was getting into his dinner-jacket ('Where's my shirt, you bloody fool?')...the pugnacious silence behind the grasped whisky and wobbling cigar... and then the quick, the disconcerting and to youthful eyes almost senile mellowing into linked arms and grandfatherly commendation as the two of us marched down Cornmarket Street after dinner at the Carlton Club. Much later, too, when I forced myself Boswell-like into an interview with T. S. Eliot, I failed to record the conversation and to weave into the autumnal atmosphere of that office in Russell Square the facts I *had* noted: the archdeaconly poet's garish socks and cheap packet of pseudo-American cigarettes. For atmosphere and wickedly caught detail we must leave Boswell for Beckford and Byron. Theirs is a different language altogether: the language of easy confidence, bubbling charm, humour and wit. And a character who knows in himself the Boswellian failings, the music-hall rowdiness and slapstick under the vulgar spotlight, must yearn after the ballet and the drama of which the two later travellers are respectively the embodiment.

It is the rich spectrum of experience in Boswell which I have declared the prime virtue of his Journals. Italy proves no different. Mont Cenis itself occasions little emotion, except: 'The prospect was horridly grand' and 'I have drank some of the snow, that I might say, "I have climbed the rudest heights—and drank the Alpine snow" ' (how true that is to my own experience) but then neither will the mountains of Corsica; more surprisingly perhaps, Italy does not receive one of those customary encomiums about the classical past and the 'deliciousness' of climate and flora for quite a time (but Boswell arrived in January). The dominant features of the busy Italian months are the two periods of furious gallantry at Turin immediately on arrival, and at Siena the following September: the archaeologizing at Rome; the encounter with Wilkes at Rome and Naples; and the tour with Bute's son, Lord Mountstewart, to Venice, Padua and Milan. Each of these has its characteristic flavour. At Turin Boswell pursued three countesses (one over fifty) and failed to make a conquest, partly because he laid so much emphasis on his animal impetuosity and his determination to get quick results. He was convinced that 'the manners here were so openly debauched that adultery was carried on without the least disguise'— which may have been true but didn't exclude the practice of *finesse*. At Siena, where he felt really at home, for the citizens were less formal and reserved than at, say, Florence, he courted the aristocratic Porzia Sansedoni because she had been the mistress of his young friend Mountstewart and he hoped to soften her with the extraordinary proposal that going to bed would somehow confirm and celebrate their mutual love for the absent milord—'How beautiful would be the mixture of tender feelings between the three of us!'—although in the end it was Moma Piccolomini (another married woman with several children) who succumbed to him and indeed offered him a love too deep for his acceptance. Her utterances had truth, wit and fire: 'The good in you amazes me as much as the bad' and, when he read her the *Nouvelle Héloïse*, 'You and that Rousseau of yours are just alike. You talk all the time about virtue and then go and do wrong'. He left her without commitment. 'You took her to bed and with wild courage did it fine. Both happy. She begged return from Livorno. But you was reserved...You was like Spanish cavalier and pronounced eternal friendship' (29th September, 1765).

As for archaeological studies in Rome, these had their curious aspects. While he visited the ruins, attended Catholic ceremonies, collected objects of vertu and was granted an audience of the Pope, all with intense seriousness, Boswell still contemplated evenings of carnal indulgence. In July he assured his young friend Johnston 'the climate of Italy affects me much. It inflamed my hot desires, and now it keeps my blood so warm that I have all day long such spirits as a man has after having taken a cheerful glass.' In October he told Rousseau, in the course of his general letter, that in Rome he had 'sallied forth of an evening like an imperious lion...I remembered the rakish deeds of Horace and other amorous Roman poets, and I thought that one might well allow one's self a little indulgence in a city where there are prostitutes licensed by the Cardinal Vicar.' During the first and rather disappointing visit to Rome his careful expense sheets show 14 paoli or 7 shillings paid to a *fille charmante* on 19th February, followed by 10 shillings for *des filles* the next day and then two girls worth respectively 1/6 and 2/- on the 21st and 22nd, after which an enigmatic MONSTRE (10 paoli) appears on the 24th. After this, remorseful, he left for Naples: 'Fine night's rest lulled by romantic Italian sea...For once in your life you are perfectly satisfied with self.' On his return to Rome the adventures continued although not without misgivings. At the beginning of May he suffered from both gonorrhoea and crabs. 'Shaved; ludicrous distress...Swear conduct. Remember family.'

This, however, was raking rather than real dissipation. British tourists apparently thought Boswell studious and aloof; avoiding their taverns and ribaldry, he had almost the appearance of having gone native. As for Wilkes, he was then an outlaw and they ignored him out of principle. He needed a friend but evidently grew to like Boswell as so many intelligent and interesting people did. To him Boswell was an 'original genius', to Boswell he was an 'extraordinary'. The Journal notes catch the wisdom, cynicism and life-loving force of a man with whose principles and morals Boswell could never be in agreement, although he must have been pleased to find that his talents as a reporter were recognised and encouraged. When Boswell asked him 'What shall I do to get life over?' Wilkes replied, 'While there's all ancient and modern learning and all the arts and sciences, there's enough to life even if it lasted three thousand years.' And, upon this question being followed by the familiar worry about Fate and Free Will, there came the brusque answer, 'Let 'em alone' (14th March, 1765). Boswell admired Wilkes's blitheness and erudition, qualities so dear to Norman Douglas: 'I'm always happy. I thank God for good health, good spirits, and the love of books.' And then there were the sentiments which Boswell never dared to formulate into a philosophic theory: 'Thank heaven for having given me the love of woman. To many she gives not the noble passion of lust.' Such was the figure who dominated Boswell's three weeks' stay in 'swarming, intense' Naples, during which he climbed Vesuvius, visited the embryonic excavations of Pompeii and Herculaneum and cut at the grotto supposed to be Virgil's tomb 'a wreath of laurel and...a wreath of ivy'. (At the same spot Beckford was to scramble as acrobatically as a chamois.)

From Wilkes Boswell turned in the opposite political direction. To have been the boon companion of a notorious outlaw and then to join the party of a leading figure of the Establishment, the eldest son of the Earl of Bute, was a remarkable feat of social adaptability. Furthermore Boswell joined as a *steadying* influence, the idea being that he should encourage Mountstewart, who was four years younger, in his studies. What resulted was a series of disputes, some with the haughty young peer, whom Boswell fancied as a political patron and to whom he was alternately fawning and on his dignity—a characteristic pattern to be repeated in later years—but more with the Swiss tutor, Paul Henri Mallet, a genuine scholar who had in fact been ennobled by the King of Denmark and was therefore a real Baron (although he apparently never admitted this) while Boswell had merely adopted the title for the purpose of travelling. (Mallet was later to inspire the seventeen-year-old Beckford with his knowledge of Norse literature.) Further but less crucial resentment on Boswell's part was caused by the rough, 'familiar' Scots manner of the 'governor' of the party, the middle-aged Colonel Edmonstone. The fact was that Boswell knew in his heart that he was a provincial, unpolished in his ways and unused to extravagant living (as Jacob used to point out, he had a stingy streak) while at the same time he was equally imbued with family pride and a sense of his own importance. He couldn't bear Mountstewart calling him 'Jamie' and there were a number of disagreements about the route to be taken, Boswell wanting to sight-see and Mountstewart indolently preferring to stay in the chaise and to go the shortest way. Meanwhile Mallet attacked not only Rousseau and Johnson but also Boswell's newly confident philosophy and culture: 'You know no one branch of learn-ing. You never read. I don't mean to make you angry, but among young men of education I have never found a single one who had as few ideas as you do.' Surely the ability of many of us to identify with Boswell, however uncomfortably and however much under the in-fluence of the more middle-class side of our natures, is nowhere more obvious than on this trip, during which sarcastic letters were exchanged and sulky silences prevailed. The climax was reached at Venice when Boswell (reluctantly, he declared) took Mountstewart to a brothel and they both caught venereal disease. This was, as Boswell said, 'a fine piece of witless behaviour!' Edmonstone then turned against him. They went on to Milan but, although Mountstewart and Boswell were friendly for several days, at that city there was bad feeling and their last dinner was an angry one. Boswell's pride had forced him to tell the youth, 'You have behaved ill to me...I'm glad we now quarrel', although he regretted the loss of a glamorous friend of whom he had grown fond. Hence the special attraction of Porzia Sansedoni.

For some time Boswell had 'wished for something more than just the common course of what is called the tour of Europe'. Rousseau had inspired him with the idea of Corsica and on the 11th October he set sail for an island that was almost unvisited. 'At present, I account myself, my petty pleasures and petty anxieties, as nothing...I am all vigour, all nobility. If I perish in the expedition, think of your Spanish Scot with affection, and we shall meet in the paradise of imaginative souls...Death is nothing to me' (to Rousseau on the date of sailing). He spent only six weeks on Corsica, and only six days with Paoli himself, although he contrived by a vagueness about dates to make this period seem longer, but no experience was more important to him. He dis-covered *his* country, the equivalent of Beckford's Portugal and Byron's Albania and Greece. His published account was to make him famous. He became for ever afterwards 'Corsica Boswell'. And yet the section of his book (published 1768) devoted to the actual visit amounts to no more than sixty or so pages, the rest being given up to an historical and geographical survey. Dr Johnson was to note the difference between the two parts: 'Your *History* is like other histories, but your *Journal* is in a very high degree curious and delightful. There is between the *History* and the *Journal* that difference which will always be found between notions borrowed from without and notions generated with-in' (*Life*, 9th September, 1769). Boswell's reporting was also praised by Gray although the poet had no high opinion of Boswell's mental

equipment and described the work in a letter to Walpole as 'a dialogue
between a green-goose and a hero...The pamphlet proves what I have
always maintained, that any fool may write a most valuable book by
chance, if he will only tell us what he heard and saw with veracity'
(25th February, 1768). Since Boswell had no eye for mountains and
maquis or at least no ability to express his sensations, and took his very
arduous journeying with nonchalance, the modern reader may find
these pages rather flatter than the author's more personal work.

But here are the 'frank, open, lively, and bold' peasants and soldiers
with their ferocious dogs, their hospitality, their bristling armoury
of weapons, their hatred of the office of hangman, their jealousy of
their women folk — 'if I attempted to debauch any of their women I
might expect instant death' — their cattle-baiting and game of rough
draughts played with bits of stone and wood on a chalked floor, their
primitive religiosity, their crowding-round with endless questions,
often critical of Britain's policy, and their coming and going as they
pleased. It is a picture of vivid friendliness which cannot but remind
one of Greece today, or of parts of Portugal. Boswell travels on foot
or by ass and mule, sometimes with women carrying his baggage.
Chestnuts are knocked down for him to eat 'with great relish'. And
when these make him and his party thirsty: 'we lay down by the side of
the first brook, put our mouths to the stream and drank sufficiently.'
He remembers Horace. 'It was just being for a while one of the "prisca
gens mortalium" who ran about in the woods eating acorns and drinking water.' Uncorrupted by civilisation these sturdy insurrectionaries
may be, but does he admire them most for being still in a state of nature
or for their feudal simplicity? How far is he *philosophe*, how far Baron?

Suspected, to his pleasure, of being some sort of ambassador or
accredited agent he thus comes to Pasquale Paoli at the remote town
of Sollacaro, travelling one hundred miles by way of the nationalist
capital of Corte in eight days. Paoli has for ten years been the father of
his long-insurgent people, resisting the oppressive Genoese overlords,
manoeuvring with the French who are also playing a part in the island's
affairs. He is the first entirely satisfactory great man that Boswell has
encountered and even Johnson will not supersede him: a philospher
and a man of action with a firm Catholic belief in his God-given
mission and a self-declared 'unspeakable pride' entirely wedded to love
of country. At first very suspicious of Boswell he is quickly won over
and soon becomes the recipient of Boswellian confessions. His own
words have the ring of both wisdom and grandeur: 'We are now to

our country like the prophet Elisha stretched over the dead child of the
Shunammite, eye to eye, nose to nose, mouth to mouth. It begins to
recover warmth and to revive. I hope it shall yet regain full health and
vigour.'

Boswell claimed that after his friendship with Paoli he need never
again feel anxious in the presence of the great. But as he now starts
home by way of Genoa and Marseilles, Avignon, Lyons, Paris his
figure is as comic as ever. He suffers from in-grown toenails; he quarrels
ever more incessantly with Jacob, who eats too much, claims he's too
stingy and too familiar and inquisitive — 'You want to know everything
to the very bottom' — and resents Boswell's mistreatment of the dog
Paoli has given him, a creature lacking in the subordination and affection required by his exacting master; and he begins to plant a series of
news-stories about his Corsican trip, under false date-lines, in the
London press. 'We think we now know the true motives of the late
mysterious expedition into Corsica...' (supposedly from Florence);
'There is no truth whatever in the rumours that Mr Boswell is really a
desperate adventurer named Macdonald. He is a gentleman of fortune
on his travels, a friend of the celebrated Rousseau...'(supposedly from
Turin). And so on. At Paris, which brings a further encounter with
Wilkes and a renewed assault upon Zélide, Boswell calls on the 'lean,
genteel' Walpole, who dislikes him and tells Gray that he 'forced himself upon me at Paris in spite of my teeth and my doors.' At Paris, too,
Boswell learns that his mother is dead, a bereavement responded to by
tears, prayers, visits to brothels and the singing of tranquillising Italian
airs. He is now twenty-five. In the arms of his ex-hero's middle-aged
mistress he is wafted home. And, on his arrival, Dr Johnson hugs him
like a sack.

Few of the succeeding years will yield the zest and promise of that
wonderful journey.

The Enchanted Garden

William Beckford in Italy and Portugal

I

Introduction, By Way of Ludwig of Bavaria

I WAS AT FÜSSEN, looking for Wittelsbach castles. Füssen is on the borders of Austrian Tyrol and the termination of the Romantische Strasse running down from Würzburg through Rothenburg, Dinkelsbühl and Donauwörth; a road so eminently picturesque that I had somehow failed to take it.

I'd been to Regensburg, once Ratisbon, on the northernmost bend of the Danube: a nobly grim city where the Imperial Diet used to meet. I'd gone there to visit Valhalla. In the delicate business of taking up preliminary positions before the assault on Greece, it had seemed best this year to reserve the splendours of Baroque and Rococo for my return journey; the nineteenth-century extravagances of the Wittelsbachs would do me nicely on the way down. Besides, Ludwig I had been a Philhellene; his son Otto, transformed to Otho, was the first king of liberated Greece and it was his Bavarian architects who built the Royal Palace and the University in Athens; indeed Schinkel, the designer of *Die Zauberflöte*, proposed establishing Otto on the Acropolis itself, an idea which fortunately came to nothing. What more appropriate, then, than to inspect a sort of Parthenon on the banks of the Danube? For such Valhalla is, a huge white temple approached through trees and across meadows, very virginal and crisp in that lush setting but terraced above the river in a conventional and imperious way, with immense stairs and flanking walls cut into the hillside.

It was almost empty when I got there. I found the interior excessively shiny; polished and of course cleaner and colder than the rather similar buildings on Odos Venizelou in Athens. The walls are porphyry, I suppose: not quite liver-coloured, not quite raspberries and cream. The roof is a gold trellis inset with blue panels and stars. Below it projecting cornices are supported by pairs of caryatids, gold filleted and with gold tunics over white and blue. At ground level plinths stand by the wall, each with its winged Victory and row of intensely white busts; these plinths are the colour of amber or honey, their surfaces as grained and slick as the petrified wood you buy in Arizona. White chairs or thrones stand by their sides, embellished with birds or griffons, and there are also free-standing ceremonial pillars with flat tops which seem to be awaiting a bowl of incense or a great torch or candle. Other busts rise from marble ledges on the walls. The decoration is brightly Ionic. Above the frieze with its egg-and-dart and palmette borders stand white plaques inscribed in gold: *Hengist*, simply, or *Der Dichter Des Nibelungenlieds*. The founder king has his throne at one end between two columns; an alert, lean-featured man in a swirling toga, he bends forward as though to engage the tiers of frozen faces in some Socratic discourse. He has none of the stiffness and prettiness of Ludwig the Second.

As for the busts themselves, they represent a kind of universal Teutonism from Charlemagne and Barbarossa to Gluck and Röntgen. Here are our Alcuin and Alfred the Great, to represent the Anglo-Saxon branch of the family; here, on what I should have taken to be quite another wave-length, is Alaric the Goth...*fiel in Italien ein und eroberte Rom* (as the explanatory booklet has it); elsewhere there are surprises like Peter Paul Rubens and Anthony van Dyck as well as the obvious choices: Dr Martin Luther, J.S.Bach and Walter von der Vogelweide. Despite their bald eye-balls, most of the heads are treated with some degree of realism. A surprising number of men, (I recall only one woman) wear their hair in long snaky ringlets, a style usually combined with a bristling moustache with waxed ends and a pursed-up mouth, the style of D'Artagnan. A few are wreathed in laurel, while Johann van Eyck wears a turban, Erasmus a species of bonnet and Hans von Hallwyl a sort of crash-helmet with a peak and a central ridge. Goethe has hyacinthine curls above a long cold face and poor Winckelmann a receding hair-line but compensatory tufts above the ears.

Mostly middle-aged or elderly, each figure pays no attention to his neighbours but poses in senatorial stillness as though he awaited with the confidence of a gifted servant, or probed with the severity of a distinguished schoolmaster, the verdict of posterity. I wouldn't call them a particularly prepossessing bunch. Perhaps the sculptors tended to make those blind eyes too small and narrow and to screw up those chins into a resolution too suggestive of obstinacy. Their expressions are marked enough; often, indeed, they come perilously near to caricature. And marble is too smoothly white to make facial quirks acceptable: a more living surface is needed, clay or bronze. Yet at least these bloodless creatures do not disturb their airy setting. (Even Bismarck looks small and worried, with a distinct resemblance to Thomas Hardy.) History, in fact, has ceased to ferment and, although one notices the absence of some famous Jews — Heine, for example, or Mendelssohn — one cannot help feeling that there is something charming, if a trifle silly, about a Valhalla which is trying to be Greek, and soft opulent Ionian Greek at that.

Soon I was strolling outside. In the colonnades of the peristyle I recalled the dramatic shadows made by the eroded columns of the Hephaesteion, or of the Temple of Apollo at Bassae, for here the sun was hidden behind soft clouds, the surface of the stone was perfect but without crystalline life, and the landscape full of melancholy. One liked the Germans best when they turned to the south. The tendency of their temperament to run to extremes — echoing, defining and underlining in their unappeased, intensely serious way some of our English characteristics, which we express with a dilettante lightness and casualness that they must find irritatingly amateur — is seen at its best in scholarship, notably archaeology, and in travel through lands which they feel will complete them. Travelling thus, they do not conquer; they are conquered. One thinks of the single-minded energy of Winckelmann and Schliemann with their earnest intensity, their *Innerlichkeit*. And of the way Hölderlin dreamed, and of how Goethe, for all his fame and position, laid himself open to the disturbing, liberating influences of classical Italy. The Philhellenic aspect of German culture is very different from the 'medieval renaissance' cultivated by modern nationalism, just as the buildings and gardens that the old German states established in the eighteenth century, where Baroque and Rococo reflected the grace and glitter of the south, are very different from the mists and dark pinewoods so often surrounding them. English history seems gentle, almost insipid, compared to German.

I first visited Germany in 1937, during an Oxford Long Vacation. I went with the Cadogan brothers and a young don from Merton. The Cadogans had their boots made in Germany, spoke the language and seemed fairly impressed by the Nazis; occasionally, I think, they asked me not to be rude to a policeman or a sentry or a precinct and once, as we passed a plaque on a street in Munich, they suggested I salute. The don seemed as yet untravelled and prim (he is now a Professor and, I suppose, as worldly as the next man); in France he would demand of a policeman: 'Where is the centre of life?', due to a misunderstanding about the pronunciation of the word *ville*, and when he heard me ask someone for 'fire' for my cigarette, he dissolved into giggles at the solecism. We stayed at good hotels, ate well, went sightseeing with Germanic diligence, and I at least felt that there hung about us a faint aura of the *milord*. (It was rather posh, I felt, to go to Germany for your boots.) But I remember very little except the summer feverishness, so many swastika flags on the Rhine, occasional nervous glances at the harvest—a good harvest, Vernon Bartlett said, and Mme Genevieve Tabouis agreed with him, might mean war—and dark beer that gave you diarrhoea when you first took it. The autobahn was thrilling to drive along; there were huge green sweeps of meadow and hill; then dark forests and road signs with delicate drawings of the deer one must watch out for; and soon one of the Cadogans announced in a hushed voice, 'Dachau', and I shivered. At Munich we visited the exquisitely elaborate Residenz Theatre to hear *Don Giovanni* but we were also entertained to coffee in the basement canteen of the Brown House: 'The Führer has no quarrel with England...The Führer wants peace... Communism, now, that is different, that is the enemy of us both.' Very different from Nymphenburg or the Residenz was Hitler's exhibition of Pure German Art which, perversely, I insisted on seeing, although I ignored the excellent display of so-called Decadent Art also being shown at the same time. It was quite like the Royal Academy, only without 'problem pictures': muscular men and bosomy girls in harvest scenes (again one thought nervously of the implications of such splendid crops) and autumn woods reflected in lakes and here and there a medieval knight or a bearded burgher. There were various sculptures illustrating Strength Through Joy. Emerging, I straightened my back and swung my arms vigorously to show any passing Germans that I possessed a modicum of military potential. I had done exactly the same thing to convince my housemaster at Sherborne that I was not wilting from self-abuse.

Of all that grand tour in miniature, which went on to Austria, Hungary and Italy, I seem to remember one thing above the rest. It was a Sunday morning at Heidelberg or Nuremberg: the former I think. Everyone was in holiday clothes and suffused with the rather feverish gaiety of that summer, feverish and buxom, feverish and heavy, the plodding mothers, the be-ribboned and giggling maidens, the larking youths, the stocky fathers of families in their feathered hats, green and grey jackets of Loden cloth and oily lederhosen, the shrewd smokers of elaborately carved pipes, the withered, mannish old women with their dowdy clothes and shiny walking-sticks, and here and there the elegant stiffness of an officer in the uniform of the S.S. or the smooth apricot legs, diminutive shorts and eager young face of some member of the Hitler Jugend. All this shiny super-normal crowd was parading up the streets into the castle. And then suddenly I saw him, moving amongst them with a terrible eye-swivelling, shoulder-shrugging, aggressive yet flinching and almost jeering self-consciousness, as though he were an entirely different creature, who swam where they waddled, or danced where they trooped and clogged, or played flute or oboe to their tubas and cornets — odd as a gypsy, a dwarf, the most effeminate queer, and odder still for being a consciousness, a quivering knower and mocker of himself and his fate, who, with a kind of flaunting indecency, actually dared to make himself and me and everybody else uncomfortable by pretending to be normal and by playing the ridiculous, far too clever game of survival. He swam, he smiled, he insinuated himself, checked, balanced, swayed to one side, glided along, and all the time his eyes were bright with blustering it out and brightest with the joke of his indiscreet, his obviously doomed but at this moment, such was human tolerance, just viable presence.

He didn't just look Jewish; he was a *Der Stürmer* caricature of a Jew. Crinkled hair, bony, swarthy face, a full protruding lower lip, emotional flickering eyes and, above all, a nose that would have looked excessive on Shylock or Fagin. For a moment our eyes met. And although one often hears nowadays that few people in England or elsewhere realised just how serious the Jewish position was before, say, the invasion of Austria, he clearly knew and so, a fairly innocent and blinkered undergraduate, did I. 'Get out,' I wanted to tell him, 'Escape.' I hated his air of ironic normalcy.

That crowded morning at Heidelberg couldn't have been less like the cool emptiness of Valhalla. Apart from being an interesting and 'amusing' artefact, a sort of folly which appealed to the imagination, the place felt dead. But then all Germany feels null to me now: a country of little interest (for I at least tell myself that I can find most of the art and architecture I need in neighbouring Austria), much bombed, sporadically picturesque in a way I scarcely appreciate and, in its commercial recovery, an object lesson in the nastier side of modern life. All over it the Americans spread like a fungus. In certain dark cafés you can see the boredom and neurosis furry and glimmering.

Having visited the sinister cities of Berlin and Hamburg I have no desire to repeat the experience. Frankfurt is bad enough. *Politically*, I can see Germany as an argument for a United Europe transcending outmoded nationalisms, but as a private person I generally motor through. Except for Würzburg, or Herrenhausen at Hanover, or the fountains at Augsburg, or an hour or two at Ulm and Munich. It would be stupid to claim one had no interest at all. And this summer it was the Wittelsbachs, not so much Ludwig the First, founder of Valhalla and subsequently exiled because of his infatuation for Lola Montez, but his grandson, Ludwig the Second. I expected this king, as one sort of German, to be sentimental, rather ridiculous and to some degree actually unpleasant. But he was also a man who tried to make poetry out of his life: a rebel who despised the bourgeois virtues and who befriended artists, or at least one artist, to a degree unprecedented amongst monarchs. In his way he became as alien as that Jew. But there was another, perhaps a very circuitous reason for my interest. I thought of words like the following: '*I am determined to enjoy my dreams, my fantasies and all my singularity, however irksome and discordant to the worldlings around me. In spite of them, I will be happy.*' These sentiments could have been Ludwig's but were actually those of William Beckford, a brilliant and perverse figure of the late Georgian period and of the Regency who shared, as we shall see, other of Ludwig's tastes. Perhaps I could learn something of the lonely eccentric who built Fonthill by visiting one of the dream castles of the equally lonely and eccentric Wittelsbach.

So it was that I drove out from Füssen to the castles of Hohenschwangau and Neuschwanstein. I hadn't realised that the two of them were so close together, compact and pinnacled, rising against the forested wall of the Allgäu Alps. For years I had held the memory of photographs in my mind; fantastic and remote, acrobatically aspiring, without those strong crude hints of Scottish Baronial or of the Château Frontenac at Quebec or even of another railway hotel, St Pancras, which now confronted me. I had allowed myself to remain vague as to their precise location but it was certainly Ludwig's Neuschwanstein which meant most to me, although divested of its sharpness and its newness, together with the knowledge that this Swan King had built others...Herrenchiemsee on the model of Versailles and situated on the broad lake I'd so often passed on the autobahn to Salzburg; Linderhof, too, the white arabesques of its façades reminiscent of the Petit Trianon; together with the re-decoration of Schloss Berg and a hunting-lodge retreat above Partenkirchen and heaven knows what else in the way of grottoes and eyries.

On this cool grey morning in late July I was a bit disappointed. The two castles rose side by side, very sharp and defined in a compactness so almost primly or pertly well-preserved, as though all the mystery had been squeezed out—as though they were just *that*, the photograph, and nothing more—and poised against a background of thundering picturesqueness with which they were not deeply involved, for they only climbed the outermost knolls of the Alps and the other way lay the green monotony of the Bavarian plain. A bit exhibitionistic and melodramatic, like a tourist who has clambered five hundred feet and pretends he has reached five thousand. Admittedly there was a small dark lake nearby, the Alpsee, and a smaller one visible when one ascended to a view, but the effect of these was rather diminished by the snail-smear of a much bigger lake in the plain. 'Here is mystery', said the small lakes, which would be a superfluous comment for the queer-coloured lakes around, say, the Fern Pass, where stillness and a kind of dark, malevolent purity achieve the glassiest finish and reproduce the enclosing shoreline with so lucid and tragic a finality that the human emotions can't anywhere get in. 'Here is fairyland,' piped the castles, but a fairyland spilled out of a Victorian children's book as one thought back to illustrations suffused with the warmth of memory rather than regarding the adult fact realised in genuine stone. 'Here is tourism,' exclaimed the hotel by the lake, and the car-park, and the booths and advertisements. 'Here is bourgeois Germany, where affluence can be quaint and the *gemütlich* grow heavy and dull to the point of cruelty,' the town of Füssen added, a statement reinforced by the big, green expanses of Bavaria. It was all fairly complicated. And somehow in the distance, beyond Neuschwanstein, scarcely heard as yet, the great waterfall roared 'Death and glory! Dream and self-dramatisation and glory and death!'

We were so hungry and cold that we sat in the car to have luncheon. We were in the Hohenschwangau car-park. The brownish castle rose ahead of us on a small precipice; the hotel was at our backs and the Alpsee two hundred yards away to the left. We ate leberwurst and Emmenthaler cheese with good bread we broke in our hands and we drank a Durnsteiner Grüner Veltliner 1963 we had bought on the way and which turned out to be a sparkling wine. We had pears and bananas for dessert. At the bottom of the castle precipice there was a small pool. In front of this stood a big Esso sign: *Pack den Tiger in den*

Tank. I recalled how at College various people were commenting on the symbolism of the tiger in Esso's advertising campaign—a Freudian here, a Jungian there, a sociologist, a lecturer in Religious Knowledge —producing various theories in the fanciful, fretful, frustrated college way when an elderly lady, a devotee of Jane Austen whom we thought out of earshot, suddenly provided the conclusive statement: 'It means power and passion and *thrust*!'

When we had finished eating we climbed up to the castle through the woods. Half-way along the path I saw a sign pointing in the other direction: *Alprosenweg* it read. But there were no roses, no obvious temptations to *stimmung*, only ravens croaking somewhere above us in the grey, heavy sky. We decided not to queue up for a conducted tour round Hohenschwangau. It wasn't Ludwig's creation, after all. If I had known, all the same, that this castle of the High Country of the Swan was basically very old, although re-built in about 1825 and then decorated with 'vivid, realistic paintings and frescoes' of the Lohengrin story, I might have made the effort of taking in two castles in one afternoon. A genuine medieval Ritterburg where Hiltbolt von Swanetou, the Minnesinger, had lived and where the Emperor Barbarossa had rested after his first journey to Rome and from which no one less than Lohengrin had set out on his adventures…! But the point of my visit was not really to enquire into Germanic history and legend. I was remembering Ludwig II's cry: 'When I can no longer build, I can no longer live', because of its similarity to Beckford's 'I grow rich and mean to build towers', together with his revealing, 'some people drink to forget their unhappiness. I do not drink, I build' and again: 'Blessed abbey, save and defend me from such riff-raff and riff-raffery as this! Grow, you forests, raise yourself, you walls, and make an everlasting barrier between me and them.' Such sentiments Ludwig quite obviously shared. And so I only pottered along the terrace, observing roses and phlox and dead spiraea and moss and mildew, but always conscious that Neuschwanstein rose back there to my left, much higher than the present castle and rather more withdrawn, too, from the road; a livid structure with green roofs, far too new and clean, but nevertheless itself and all that there was.

Now we drove to its car-park (the ticket gave you a discount at the adjoining café) and were advised to take the short-cut directly up the hill, avoiding the gentle curves of the carriage-road. I don't think I've ever been so conscious of a climb. It wasn't desultory impromptu scrambling about a Greek mountain, which you do for the joy of it and where you can pause to get your breath as often as you like, without even being aware of what you are doing; it was narrow paths and stairways, clearly defined, purposive; and I went up in a solemn, heavy plod, very dutiful and Teutonic. Suddenly I felt my age: I was one of the older ones, the puffers, and when I clutched the wooden handrail and stopped I realised that younger people understood and sympathised. They whistled and edged around me. They smiled, very faintly, and gave me a wide berth. Meanwhile some other middle-aged man, rather distinguished with his grey hair brushed back and regular features now a bit puffy and grey, managed to continue past me with a look of gentle superiority. I was disgruntled enough to catch in the faces passing me those hints of our northern sort of neurosis which are usually most apparent when one is returning from a long holiday in the south; do we English look like this to a foreigner, smug yet sad, commanding yet fatigued and baffled? In the Thirties Germany seemed to be a country of youth; now it was a place of survivors and ghosts... So much was ugly and dowdy: or sinister. You were either razor-sharp, platinum-flashing, incandescent as marsh-gas—a not quite believable spiv sharpening his knowledgeability to the point where it splintered, or a girl model posing in steely sexiness on the brink of some conventionally sulphurous hell in Düsseldorf or Cologne—or you were the blurred, squashy rubber-stamp of a middle-aged family man or woman. What official documents had these people stamped until their features bulged like Erhard's, withered like Adenauer's, rubbed into the few tough lines of a Strauss? The Nazi horror, the long tradition that the English and Germans were brothers or cousins, and then the brief period when the 'leaders' of my generation had found excitement and liberation in the Weimar Republic, these things clashed together in my mind.

In the end we got to the castle. 'The great Abbey...rose like an exhalation and passed away like a summer cloud,' the *Athenaeum* had once stated of Beckford's Fonthill; the point here, surely, was that every stone remained in place. We had to wait in a corridor. Another party was ahead of us. And we had to declare our native languages for the benefit of a multilingual guide. When he appeared he belonged to my sour characterisations on the ascent: a civil servant in his late fifties, or a retired schoolmaster, grey, null and incompetent, with an English I couldn't understand and a French that was no better. The only difference was that he was quite thin. He gabbled, he made cold little jokes, he rammed his inexplicable sentences home like a man closing a rifle bolt, he dropped a soggy answer to the very rare question like a bored soldier expelling a cigarette butt from his lower lip, and occasionally he pitied himself as he hurried ahead. *This way, this way, please*. But what did it matter? He wasn't going to tell us the truth about Ludwig. And the poor man certainly had to work for his living since floor after floor, as it seemed to me, had been too inferior, too nearly a basement for the Swan King; once more we had to climb and climb before we came to the quarters in which he had never really lived.

We had waited in a white corridor whose roof was beamed in light brown wood and whose windows and doors were picked out in light and dark grey, but soon we were passing under vaults with gaily painted ribs and past columns whose capitals seemed Turkish. As we struggled up and up, the walls pressed on us with an interminably repeated pattern of what I took to be stencil-work. Soon there was brown everywhere, the gravy-coloured and shiny wood of the grander type of Victorian rectory, but lovingly kept alive and here and there faintly touched by the spirit of William Morris; carved sideboards from Maples', pews from Keble College, bulging pilasters and fretted cornices from a pub in Euston Road, gloomy window-recesses one had encountered before in some Arthurian country house such as that celebrated in Evelyn Waugh's *A Handful of Dust*. The decorative system was certainly familiar although I had never seen it on so large and glossy a scale.

And to the brown wood was added colour, any amount of it, although somehow the brightness of these blues, greens and reds retained, paradoxically, a flatness, a medieval mustiness, an inability to inter-act and become meaningful, which is precisely the fault of the decoration of many pretentious nineteenth century churches I have seen, such as the Votivkirche in Vienna or the huge cathedral at Dakovo in Yugoslavia. There were jewelled collars to some of the pillars; there was much play with a swan motif and blue brocade; there was a hideous stove; there were candelabra and jewellery boxes which resembled stage-properties; the suite of rooms which looked out on the gorge of the Pölatt and the waterfall was temporarily interrupted by a bulging plaster grotto. Above all, there were the paintings. Ludwig had required these, here as elsewhere, to be illustrative and senti-mental. He wanted subject matter rather than significant form or tactile values or anything truly *mahlerisch*. And so it was Wagner everywhere, a story on every wall, *Lohengrin* and *Parsifal*, the *Meistersinger* and the *Ring*, acres of bright, almost new-looking but never truly alive romance and chivalry, all quickly painted to have the castle ready on time. The ceiling of the dressing-room relented for an acuter sentimentality: pink clouds and doves on a trellis. The Throne Room glittered with its deep blue columns supporting the gallery and an apse of gold palms and figures painted on gold; outside, from the terrace, you overlooked the Alpsee, Hohenschwangau and the smaller mountain lake of the Swan. Upstairs again, in a concert hall devoted to Parsifal, the stage set was of those forests and rocks which Ludwig loved to visit, in golden sledge or carriage and often at dead of night.

These bigger rooms were certainly cheerful—it is difficult to be entirely negative towards masses of blue and gold—but as for evidences of taste these were almost entirely lacking. Only the bedroom had some charm: Gothic panelled, with a bed all spires and pinnacles and a wash-basin in the form of a swan. I couldn't help contrasting Ludwig's castle with Beckford's abbey. There were obvious similarities. Both represented the working-out of a fantasy, had a strong element of the theatrical and were run up quickly because of the impatience of the owners, although not as quickly as those dreamers wished. Both rose on sites beloved from boyhood and in the neighbourhood of an older family residence. Both were medieval and, beyond this, enshrined a claim to glorious ancestry (Beckford was a descendant of Edward the Third, Ludwig a successor to Lohengrin) and both were conceived as arrogant and opulent retreats from a hostile world within which, as it turned out, the relationships tended to be fervent but limited to inferiors and servants. Finally, both had to be abandoned in unhappy, if very different, circumstances. But all the same, Fonthill Abbey was a more original and prodigious structure than Neuschwanstein. From the South Oriel of its St Michael's Gallery through the Octagon, King Edward's Gallery and the Vaulted Corridor to the five-sided Oratory at the north, it stretched for no less than 307 feet. The hammer-beam roof of the Great Western Hall rose 70 feet, the parapet of the Eastern Transept was 95 feet high while its octagonal turrets extended to 120 feet. But these dimensions, even the boast of having the highest tower in England, or of being enclosed by a wall reaching for eight miles, is of less importance than the pictures, books and precious objects which the building accumulated. Although Beckford's *heraldic* taste is difficult to judge—it is not something he displays elsewhere and one may entertain some doubts about the prevalence of crimson, scarlet and blue, the shields, badges, cinquefoils and stained glass—one can scarcely question that Fonthill's vistas were far simpler and nobler than Neuschwanstein's aerial suites, while Beckford's usual sensitivity ensured that there was always something of beauty to catch the eye in every direction.

The guide who gabbled so unintelligently did manage to tell us that Ludwig had occupied the castle for only six months. He did not add that he had then occupied the gate-house, whose peasant informality (calico and coconut matting) was also to his taste. It was, in fact, on June 9th, 1884, that a commission of doctors, psychiatrists and officials arrived at Hohenschwangau to take him into custody as insane. He was not there; when the news reached him he was at Neuschwanstein, pacing about the Minnesinger Hall and supposedly reciting from *Don Carlos* in a loud voice. The next morning the Commissioners presented themselves at his gates but by then he had rallied local support; he had always been popular with the mountain peasants, who liked his despotic familiarity towards them, and he could momentarily imagine himself in that role so beloved of romantic conservatives, a monarch at the head of his feudal folk in opposition to middle-class busybodies. The party failed to gain admission and the leading psychiatrist, Dr von Gudden, who was known to be carrying a strait-jacket, was nearly thrown into the waterfall. When it had retreated to Hohenschwangau some arrests were actually made but in the end everybody was allowed to disperse. A day or two later a new group of officials was sent by Prince Luitpold, the man who had assumed the Regency. This time there was no resistance. 'I did so enjoy being King' Ludwig is supposed to have said as he was led away. He was taken to Schloss Berg and behaved so reasonably that the next evening Dr von Gudden was only too delighted to accompany him on a walk to the lake. Both were discovered drowned and evidence pointed to a struggle in the water.

Before inquiring into what was wrong with Ludwig, what was the secret of his strange life, it seems only fair to admit that he adds a touch of colour and would-be beauty to the modern period. Heaven knows, it needs it. At the risk of sounding a familiar note, one cannot deny the fact that life grows increasingly utilitarian and conformist; machines and technology extend their influence over larger and larger areas; classes, which may have had distinctive values and an organic relationship with each other, melt into an undifferentiated suburban stodge; churches empty, monarchies collapse, rituals fade, landscape dwindles and—with the now evident failure of the modern movement in architecture from which so much was expected—standards of beauty and style disappear from our buildings and our streets, as they do also from our homes and gardens, our clothes and our manners.

Meanwhile the mass-media pre-digest the beautiful, the odd, the intelligent, the evil, until the sharp tang of what genuine life remains is edited to destruction: in the words of Yeats, 'the ceremony of innocence is drowned.' Instead of life you have documentaries, instead of people you have the 'personalities' of television. Pop-groups, whose members appear to be chosen for their frenetic but passionless hideousness, no longer shake their locks in some barnyard of darkest Thuringia, amongst the squawks of poultry and the reek of peasant sweat, but jerk their loins and strain their exiguous voices in front of millions, as the heroes of the age...Now condemnatory views such as these were held by Beckford as long as one hundred and twenty years ago. They are associated with romantic conservatism. But to my mind a belief in excellence or genius, an interest in, and a respect for, the oddities of human nature, and a desire to re-establish values and to hand these down to as large a part of the coming generation as possible, is just as much the duty of socialism. What matters is the liberation of the deepest resources of humanity, not their stultification at some superficial level which chances to be convenient for sociologists. It so happens, of course, that both Beckford and Ludwig were rich and well-born and that their protest against mediocrity took familiar romantic forms and expressed itself finally with misanthropic arrogance; they are still valuable as men who believed that life should be beautiful, although there is an enormous gulf between the civilised, shrewd Englishman and the muddled, finally lunatic German.

If both have their values as heroes of the imagination, men who sacrificed everything to making their personal vision of life concrete, visible, proclaimed, Beckford is clearly the more fortunate in being himself an artist with the result that, although his Abbey has almost entirely disappeared and his legend has dwindled, he can still be read with great enjoyment; indeed he can be read for qualities which extend far beyond his Gothicism and arrogant and misanthropic isolation while still embodying his intensely individual criticism of the world around him. Both remind us that romanticism, which in its English form has often been rendered by schoolmasters into something high-minded, morally earnest or yearningly ineffective, can be equally extravagant, daemonic or even frivolous, expressing itself in the gesture and the mask.

Ludwig's tragedy is, I suppose, that it is precisely the people he disliked and avoided who now appreciate Neuschwanstein with its subject-matter paintings and conventional air of fantasy. It was

Marianne Moore who described works of art as 'imaginary gardens with real toads in them'. Beckford's actual enchanted gardens had the real toads of startling, life-enhancing paintings and other objects, just as his literary garden gains by the concreteness of a botanical description or a monk vomiting in his cups or a barrel-full of ferrets. The elderly guide at Ludwig's Neuschwanstein might have set a shadowy toad of scandal and near-poetry hopping amongst us but, as an agent of tourism, he didn't; bereft of its creator, that 'imaginary garden' at the foot of the Alps becomes no more than a sterile essay in décor.

Ludwig is often described as a divinely beautiful youth. The portraits show a small, neat face, bright-eyed and with dimples to each side of smiling lips; the effect is peculiarly naked, as though the surface were everything. Dark hair waves gently from a central parting over an unusually flat head, with elaborate curls up-swept above the ears. As a child, he was dreamy and sensitive, prone to rages and often in rebellion against the strictness of his education. He read Schiller and winced at ugly footmen. In adolescence he discovered the writings of Richard Wagner; it was the *text* not the music of *Lohengrin* which captured him first and he was delighted to find in his uncle, Duke Max in Bavaria, a fellow admirer. Wagner's music was making slow headway in Munich, where the composer was regarded as a foreigner, an anti-clerical and a red, but on his sixteenth birthday Ludwig was allowed to attend a performance of *Lohengrin* and shortly afterwards he heard *Tannhäuser*, incidentally another figure associated with Hohenschwangau. Legation-Secretary von Leinfelder noted his raptures: 'It made an overwhelming impression on his nervous system, and at times during the performance his reactions were almost morbid...At the passage when Tannhäuser re-enters the Venusberg, Ludwig's body was thrown into such convulsions that I was afraid he might have an epileptic seizure.' (Beckford's appreciation of the 'divine' castrato, Pacchiarotti, was similarly intense but Beckford was himself both a musician and the friskiest of young persons: he was as likely to respond by singing and dancing as by becoming 'morbid'.) The music and spectacle of Wagnerian opera merely re-inforced for the young Ludwig the nobility of Wagner's ideas. In *The Work Of Art Of The Future* he read that 'the real trend of present-day life is toward a soulless utilitarianism' and again that 'music is the human heart. It is the perfect spiritual love, ennobling sensuous delight and humanising spiritual feeling'. Wagner was as contemptuous as himself of the 'beer-philistines'.

When he was eighteen Ludwig quite unexpectedly found himself king. He had little political training. Wagner's world of German legend combined with his own pride of ancestry and the love of landscape and country life which was common amongst the Wittelsbachs. But he was also fascinated by the concept of a Roi Soleil (witness the slavish copying of French models in Linderhof and Herrenchiemsee) and Louis XIV's imperious saying, '*Car tel est notre bon plaisir*', was often on his lips. In opposition to his easy-going father, Max II, and to his mother, Maria of Hohenzollern, with her democratic ideas and bourgeois habits, Ludwig soon saw himself as an absolutist: an Artist Prince, the mystical embodiment of virtuous kingship. Unfortunately he always preferred dreams to reality and was therefore no match for Bismarck who throughout this period was building up Prussian power at the expense of both Bavaria and Austria. Why bother with the details of administration and bureaucracy? Why demean oneself by haggling with councils and committees of 'beer-philistines'? One was young, one was beautiful, one wore glittering uniforms and performed imperious gestures with grace, one simply existed. *L'état, c'est moi.*

Ludwig immediately summoned Wagner, who was fifty, in debt, and worried about his work. Never did a monarch offer a struggling, perennially improvident artist more: complete freedom, a splendid villa on the Starnbergersee in close proximity to Schloss Berg, constant adulation and a handsome salary. Wagner was in ecstasy. 'No title, no functions, no obligations! The King is happy to have me, I am happy to be with him!' There was also love. Ludwig was infatuated with his Richard, as the composer noted with a surprise soon modified by gratification. 'He loves me with the ardour and devotion of first love... He wishes me to stay with him for ever...My happiness is so great that I am quite overcome by it!' Admittedly the sensitive youth's passions were a trifle alarming, while his constant visits to the Great Friend distracted him from his work on *Die Meistersinger*, which he was anxious to finish, or perhaps on some idea for *Der Ring des Nibelungen*. Nevertheless, 'here at last is a love-affair which brings no grief or pain.' Conceivably it could be a solution. 'Shall I be able to renounce women completely? With a deep sigh I confess I could almost wish it. One look at his dear picture helps me again! Oh, the lovely youth!'

For all his belief in 'splendid unrestraint' Wagner was a ruthless egotist whose calculating nature was only defeated by the excessive demands he made on other people. Having conquered the King (and it was a permanent conquest) he now in his turn summoned the von Bulows: with Cosima his relations were already so close that she had become pregnant. Public criticism grew. Ludwig was neglecting his duties and Wagner and his circle were taking over Bavarian music from the local worthies. Of all artists, the composer of grand opera is likely to be the most expensive: the huge orchestra, the imported singers, the endless rehearsals, the scenery and, in this case, the project for a new opera-house and a school of music. Besides, Wagner was notoriously extravagant. 'I need beauty, brilliance, light. The world must give me what I need. I cannot live on a modest organ stool like Master Bach.' Meetings between the two friends must indeed have been extraordinary: over-grown children who talked their heads off, narcissists drenched in perfume (Ludwig preferring *chypre* and Wagner *Rose de Bengale*), their surroundings glittering but usually in atrocious taste, the bond between them scarcely that of a deep appreciation of music (for Ludwig wasn't really musical), and with Ludwig suppressing his growing apprehensions about the relationship with Cosima. Since Ludwig enjoyed such exhibitionist acts as having the Great Friend receive the plaudits of the audience in the Residenz Theatre from the Royal Box, the nickname *Lolus* began to be heard in the beer-halls of Munich, masculine equivalent of the Lola whose scandal had forced the abdication of Ludwig I.

When Wagner began to interfere in politics, to the extent of intriguing for the dismissal of Ministers he did not like, Ludwig had to give way to the demands of the government and press. Tearfully, before the second year of his reign was over, he asked Wagner to absent himself for a while. Wagner, for his part, sent a valedictory message to the papers: 'Seek, Germans, Roman strength and Greek beauty.' Was he recalling Valhalla?

Wagner remained the guiding star of Ludwig's life but there were plenty of other romantic friendships, signified by letters of extravagant effusiveness. Prince Paul von Thurn und Taxis, for instance, had inspired Ludwig before Wagner's arrival and was to solace him when the composer had gone. A certain wooden but good-looking Baron de Variecourt was to be another candidate for the impossible ideal. There were the middle-class actors, Emil Rohde and Josef Kainz; the latter, who became very distinguished indeed, probably owed a good deal to Ludwig's sympathy. Most important of all was Richard Hornig ('Richard, Beloved of Heart') who was of yeoman origin and occupied a position sometimes described as that of a 'groom', sometimes 'master of horse', but which was clearly much more than either. The relationship with Hornig, beginning with trysts in that Amalienburg pavilion of

which I am personally so fond, developed into stability and even cosiness, for the King used to visit him and his wife once a week at their
small house at Seeleiten. Only Wagner continued so constant a friend,
but Wagner was usually at a distance while poor Hornig had to keep
his eyes open and listen and occasionally make a suggestion or an
encouraging remark during the sleepless nights when his master-
friend paced up and down.

Wagner's loss increased the King's tendency to isolation. 'The King
does not receive anybody now,' an observer wrote. 'With Prince Taxis
and head groom Volk he lives on the Roseninsel and has fire-work
displays.' Ludwig wished to abdicate in favour of his brother Otto,
although the boy showed marked signs of insanity. He wrote a long
confessional letter to Cosima, exposing the erotic side of his feelings
towards his 'Only one': 'My true, my sacred mission is to be with him,
his faithful, loving friend, and never leave him.' Yet he continued to
reign and to play some part in foreign affairs. Compromising with
reality, he became engaged to his friend Duke Max's daughter, Sophie,
a member of the relaxed, *ungeniert* court circle at Possenhofen, where
the cows ate the roses and the dogs sat on your lap at dinner, but he
could not go through with the marriage. 'Heaven be praised; the
horror has not come to pass,' he finally exclaimed, although his behaviour lost him for a time the friendship of the only member of the
circle who was capable of understanding him, Sophie's elder sister
Sisi, the Empress Elizabeth of Austria. She was as restless as he, and as
romantic—'Life will be meaningless to me when I am no longer
desirable,' she cried—and feeling herself betrayed by a conventional,
duty-ridden but still loving Emperor who apparently infected her with
venereal disease, she oscillated wildly between Homer and the stud
book, the hunting-field and the Greek islands, her tasteless Achilleion
at Corfu being as much an Enchanted Garden as Ludwig's Linderhof
or Roseninsel. Ludwig's engagement or attempts to cultivate relationships with actresses could not hide the fact that he was homosexual.
When he realised exactly what was happening between Wagner and
Cosima—his betrayal, as he saw it—his attitude hardened. As he
planned yet another building, yet another glittering retreat, the stories
that made his legend grew. There were the night rides in a gilded
carriage or a golden sledge, surrounded by be-plumed outriders, from
which he emerged in a hunter's simple costume 'to walk about the
forest like Haroun al Raschid'. There was the love of the artificial and
the theatrical, the grotto at Linderhof and the artificial moon with

which he embellished his bedroom at Hohenschwangau. There was the dressing-up in the costume of Louis XIV and, thus attired, attending plays of which he was the only spectator: 'I also think the play is bad—but still, it breathes the odour of Versailles.' There were the symbols of a fastidiousness that became paranoiac: the ministers listened to from behind a silken screen, for they might be ugly, and then the servants forced to wear masks and crawl towards him on the floor.

Certain of these stories achieve the disturbing power of symbols. There was the night, for instance, when he declared that he would go to Innsbruck and for hour upon hour rode his horse round the circle of the Riding School. There was the ruddy peasant lad he brought into the gallery of mirrors at Linderhof, accompanied by a chamois; the boy disconcerted by the utterly unfamiliar aspect of his surroundings and the animal going beserk amongst the precious objects. Now, some say, he enjoyed the sight of half-naked lackeys dancing in mountain meadows, or of the peasants he dressed in Moorish costumes, or of others entirely nude. There was always the quick explosion of passion followed by remorse, a dismissal, and then a new favourite amongst the grooms and palace servants. The 'Secret Diary' is full of resolutions and falls from grace. The guilt is greater, or at least more conscious, than Beckford's. 'When I can no longer build, I can no longer live'—but where was he to get the money for his schemes? He appealed to the Rothschilds in Paris, to Bismarck. When he dreamed of a final paradise far from his country, Richard Hornig asked him, 'How will you pay for it?' and he answered, 'With Bavaria...'

The Commissioners arrived.

Some of this tragic, symbolic but also preposterous story is applicable to Beckford. Beckford considered himself betrayed by William Courtenay, to whom he had expressed himself as enthusiastically as Ludwig did to Wagner, and in his case the beer-philistines (or, rather, the aristocratic tipplers of port wine) were even more virulent. No one would have understood the reference to Haroun al Raschid better than he. The glittering carriage, the golden sledge had played their part in alarmed reactions to his own behaviour. And where Ludwig had delighted in a theatrical moon, he had enjoyed a theatrical sun. So, at least, I told myself as I drove back to Füssen.

My companion and I arrived there tired and cold. Entering the restaurant of the Gasthof Mohren we discovered a round table by the door which was the only one without a red-checkered tablecloth. It was too early to eat, we thought, and so we sat down at this table and ordered beer. Soon one after another of the local burgers joined us; clearly it was their table, not so much of a restaurant as of a café, and we felt a little uncomfortable at their rather heavy attempts to be polite and to talk English to intruders. The grocer from the Lebensmittel across the road, the pharmacist, the baker, an official at the bank — one by one they turned up, expectedly heavy men with creased, rather greyly noble faces, and to them when they asked me about myself I explained that, yes, I was on holiday but that I was also a writer and that I had just visited Neuschwanstein, about which I was determined to be a little less enthusiastic than they. *Wunderschön*...well, not exactly. Amusing, would that do? Someone explained the adjective to the others and there was a slight hiatus of incomprehension until I added *fantastic*, which went down all right. Did my books sell? one of them asked — he had recently been staying in London at the Imperial Hotel, an excellent hostelry — and I did my best to reassure him. Might they inquire my name? And, with all the hopelessness that this usually brings out in me, I gave it to them, flat but rather over-loud. Had we travelled along the Romantische Strasse? Alas no, that was a pleasure still to be anticipated, but Würzburg I loved: the Schloss amongst the grey-green vineyards across the river, the bridge with its Baroque saints, the swirling dormers and elegantly canopied windows of the 'Zum Falken' house, the Residenz by Balthasar Neumann. The old Germany, I began. Ach, the old Germany! Had I seen the Rhine and the Lorelei, the castles, the vineyards — and the Black Forest, had I seen that?

They were pleasant people but they did not make me forget my Heidelberg Jew of 1937 or the fact that Ludwig, who to them was a tourist attraction, had been in flight from them during most of his life. The next morning, as I went to cash a traveller's cheque, they waved from their shops.

II

WILLIAM BECKFORD's first piece of travel-writing was a description of his visit to Italy in 1780 when he was still a minor. This he originally called *Dreams, Waking Thoughts, and Incidents*, of which five hundred large quarto copies with illustrations by Cipriani were ready for publication in March of 1783 when, on family counsels, the edition was suppressed. Some fifty years later the old Caliph, now retired to Bath, decided to revise his youthful work and to add a second volume drawn from the richer, denser notes and letters produced by his sojourn in

Portugal and Spain in 1787. He was encouraged by the fact that the publisher Richard Bentley was about to include the original oriental tale, *Vathek*, in his Standard Library where it would be accompanied by *The Castle of Otranto*, that bit of nonsense from the pen of the pseudo-Gothiciser, Horace Walpole (whose Strawberry Hill Beckford was to rifle at the sale of 1842). Most of his other writings he deemed unfinished, unpublishable or perhaps too precious to see the light of day. The hoarded *Episodes* designed to accompany *Vathek* belonged, it would seem, to both the first and the third of these categories; they were written in French and they had never been translated. His recent cantankerous animadversions on the subject of the decline of the British Nobility, where Smithsons now actually masqueraded as Dukes of Northumberland, belonged to the second; the *Liber Veritatis* was too libellous to print. But the travel diaries, with the help of a little padding and a good deal of suppression of unpleasant facts and facets, were a different matter. Not that Beckford allowed himself to appear unduly concerned: 'Upon the subject of publication I am as cool as the very freshest cucumber that ever issued from Kew' and again, 'incense and rotten eggs become all alike to me the moment we part with the work.'

News of the success of this venture soon reached the legendary septuagenarian. It was pleasant to be praised. Although by now he quite enjoyed his role of wizard-misogynist, abiding neither looking-glasses nor chamber-maids, indulging (as the citizens of Bath believed) in orgies requiring the assistance of dwarfs, he had for years been isolated from society, excluded from politics and refused the peerage he considered his due. Only in the sale-room was his power felt; only books and bibelots surrendered to his Arabian spells; only Old Masters bowed to the imperious summons of a Feudal Baron. Strolling amongst the roses and exotic shrubs and trees of the garden he had built upon the top of Lansdown Hill, where nature must reign undisturbed by the restriction of formal avenues and parterres, and entering that other essential embodiment of his nature, the great tower, from which he could see as far as the now abandoned Fonthill Abbey, the Caliph continued to muse on days long past. Always in love with youth, he now reconstructed from the frailest notes and jottings the twelve days, the forty-thousand words, that were to make his masterpiece, the *Recollections Of An Excursion To The Monasteries Of Alcobaça And Batalha*, a trip he had taken in 1794. Once again he had a success. Leigh Hunt was full of praise; the *Spectator* spoke of 'Champagne of the first growth'. Although not even this could ultimately satisfy so restless a nature, these were mellower years. Past eighty he still had his health — he who had so often complained of minor ailments, 'were it not for the swelling on my eye, my gums, and an extreme terror of the dew, I should enjoy myself tolerably', indispositions which led him to wonder about the efficacy of a lemon purgative or a bath followed by seltzer-water in whey or a douche of rum-oil for his hair, he in fact lived until 1844, dying in his eighty-fifth year. And we may presume the sun shone on him, although not with the Italian or Portuguese heat he had been wont to contrast with the 'medicine-coloured sky' of England, that 'rosbifish isle', where there wasn't enough light to see your own pen and 'aromatic breezes', 'delicious gales' and 'a balsamic serenity in the air' were rarely, if enthusiastically, encountered.

But why had the youthful travel book been withdrawn? Was it because of the author's imminent marriage? Certainly its opening was eccentric. The romantic note of personality had been struck in the first lines: 'Shall I tell you my dreams? — To give an account of my time, is doing, I assure you, but little better. Never did there exist a more ideal being. A fragrant mist hovers before my eyes, and, through its medium, I see objects so faint and hazy, that both their colours and forms are apt to delude me. This is a rare confession, say the wise, for a traveller to make: pretty accounts will such a one give of outlandish countries: his correspondents must reap great benefit, no doubt, from such purblind observations...' But he disclaimed, he went on, the vanity of having opinions and would be contented if a single person, suggested by a cryptic dash but evidently the imaginary recipient of the letters forming the book, should enjoy his 'visionary way of gazing'. To the modern reader, satiated with chattily factual accounts of expeditions by undergraduates or routine guides by journalists, this flourish of subjectivism may be positively welcome. What good travel book is not also a journey through the writer's interior landscape? He will in any case find it difficult to understand what objections Beckford's family could have had to the amusing, sensitive, if perhaps rather capricious narrative, from which personal revelations had been carefully omitted. Without any real evidence to go on it is difficult to know just what his contemporaries, and especially his elders, thought wrong with the youthful Beckford but clearly he could put people's backs up and indeed enjoyed discomforting the fusty, and perhaps at this stage one need say no more than that he was an artist — and, as an artist, born into the wrong class, if not the wrong country, and born many years too soon.

He was the son of the Wilkes-ite William Beckford, Alderman for
Billingsgate and twice Lord Mayor of London, whose family was of
recent lineage but had gained enormous wealth in Jamaica, and of
Maria Hamilton, granddaughter of the sixth Earl of Abercorn and
descended in three lines from Edward the Third. Thus on his father's
side he was *arriviste* and comparatively *nouveau riche*, on his mother's
related to half the aristocracy; one parent was a loud-mouthed slightly
ridiculous Radical with a strong colonial accent, the other a determined
snob. The great Lord Chatham was his godfather. His youth, for his
father died in 1770, was watched over by the Lord Chancellor, Lord
Thurlow, by his aunt Lady Effingham and by the formidably possessive
mother he nicknamed the Begum as well as by a group of official
guardians, Lords Chatham, Lyttleton and Camden. He was brought
up by tutors and knew few boys of his own age; as he told Benjamin
West years afterwards, 'incense was offered to him, and flowers strewed
in his way, wherever he went...being brought up so private he had not
experienced those checks which are useful.' The eight-year-old Mozart
taught him his five-finger exercises at the Beckford house in Soho
Square; in old age he claimed to have provided the air of *Non piu andrai*
for *Le Nozze di Figaro*. Sir William Chambers, the creator of Somerset
House, gave him lessons in architecture. More important, he came
under the influence of a former drawing-master at Eton who now
directed an academy at Bath. This was Alexander Cozens, who claimed
to be an illegitimate son of Peter the Great and who had certainly lived
in St Petersburg, where he had won favour at Court with a new method
of painting (coaxing picturesque landscapes out of ink-blots); much
travelled, and versed in Oriental and Arabic studies, if not also in black
magic, Cozens became 'Arch-angel' to the young William and, although
on one occasion his tutor, the Rev. John Lettice, wrote to Lord
Chatham that certain suspect oriental drawings and stories had been
burned by the boy's own hand, it seems clear that his considerable
imagination continued to be fed with forbidden fruit while his more
normal studies in Latin, Greek and the philosophy of William Locke
continued.

In 1777 Lettice took Beckford to his Hamilton cousins at Geneva.
The following year in Switzerland seems almost to have completed the
formation of the romantic writer. Romanticism may be impossible to
define but it has clearly something to do with individualism and self-
consciousness and a belief in the uniqueness of subjective feeling,
nourished as this is by the forces of the unconscious. It opposes set

forms, rules and limits. It sets a high value on the imaginative and the visionary and also on the organic: a work of art, for instance, develops naturally in obedience to its own interior laws. Arriving in England by way of sentimental reflective poetry, Whig principles, the cult of the barbaric, celtic, medieval — night thoughts, philosophic melancholy, ruins, groves and grottoes — it was to develop in all sorts of directions: the semi-Proustian autobiography of Wordsworth with its cult of the child and of the spirit informing natural objects; Coleridge's sense of the exotic; Byron's early combination of interesting maladjustment and colourful travelogue; Shelley's ethereal communism, and so on. Its greatest excesses were reserved for the continent. There *la princesse lointaine* was wooed most assiduously and the *femme fatale* sharpened her finger-nails on the palpitating flesh of her devotees. Towards the end of the nineteenth century Huysmans was to create his entirely subjective hero, Villiers de l'Isle Adam to condemn the vulgarity of life by having his Count Axel and Sara commit suicide at the moment of their greatest happiness, and George Moore to feed a living animal to the python he kept, voluptuously, in his room. But already, as Beckford arrived in Switzerland, the German *Sturm und Drang* movement had flowered and was in decline: that little group in Frankfurt and Strasburg who believed in *Gemut* and Genius and Energy and outraging the *kleinstädtisch*, the provincial French-emulating decorum-seeking bourgeoisie, with their cries of 'Remember that these are our years of passion and foolishness' and 'We are heroes twirled by every puff of love' and again 'Feeling may err but it can only be corrected by feeling', of which the most permanent expression was the young Goethe's *Die Leiden des jungen Werthers* (1774). In a sense Beckford was not only an early romantic, he was a romantic in the extreme continental manner.

For him this was a time of wide study in languages, Italian, Spanish and Portuguese, and also in law, philosophy and physics, while his reading ranged from Dante, Petrarch, Tasso and Ariosto to the now fashionable melancholy of Gray and of Goethe's *Young Werther*, with Rousseau doubtless in the background, as well as daydream-inducing accounts of China, Persia and the New World. At seventeen Beckford made the acquaintance of the Genevan group of intellectuals presided over by Voltaire. But the atmosphere of the *philosophes* was not his. He explained this to Cozens, the recipient of many an effusion at the time: 'To pay and receive fulsome compliments from the learned, to talk with modesty and precision, to sport an opinion gracefully, to adore Buffon and d'Alembert, to delight in mathematics, logick, geometry,

4

and the rule of Right, the *mal morale* and the *mal physique*, to despise poetry and venerable antiquity, murder taste, abhor imagination, detest all the charms of eloquence unless capable of mathematical demonstration, and more than all to be vigorously incredulous, is to gain the reputation of good sound sense.' He preferred a family named Huber who, although agnostics, were followers of nature and the arts and generally vivacious and unpredictable; he told Cozens how much he enjoyed their capricious versatility, falconry at one moment, philosophy the next, then music, engraving, writing, reminiscences of travel and, of course, revelations of exquisite sensibility.

A letter to his half-sister, now married, carries something of the aesthetic doctrine of a Walter Pater and has a remarkable note of authority for one only just eighteen: 'Let me, I conjure you, advise as much dissipation as possible, that is as much distraction as conveniently lies in your way. Arouse your imagination continually, give it full scope, and let buildings, pictures and characters fleet before your eyes. Vary the scene—I mean of your reflections. Occupy yourself very much. Draw, read entertaining works, write, have recourse to music, go to Mass—do anything but be melancholy.' He himself would often retreat to the rocks of Mount Salève (where centuries before Petrarch had begun, if only tentatively, the cult of alps) and here he would indulge his capacity to dream: 'How I should delight to wander with you thro' remote forests and pitch our tents by moonlight in a wilderness...' he would write to his Archangel, or again: 'On the summit of a lofty mountain, I gaze at an assemblage of substantial vapours which hover above, beneath and around me...' Out of such moods he created, in his tapestry-hung bedchamber at the Château de Nyon, the strange subterranean world of his 'Centrical History' (published only in 1929 as *The Vision*) about which he could adopt a commonsensical tone in a letter to Cozens, to whom he sent at least portions of what possibly remained an unfinished work; the extant manuscript runs to 25,000 words. 'You ought to be extremely cautious to whom you show the long story...They would probably exclaim—what can these high flown descriptions of grottoes and glittering forms and beings and Brahmins mean! and the dwarfs too—a charming set of little fellows who, to use a Newmarket expression, are literally got down in the Devil's Ditch and nowhere.' Dwarfs, indeed, were to play an unjustifiably important role in his legend.

The Begum must have become anxious about her adolescent son's proclivities. She imagined him in training for a statesmanlike role in the Whig oligarchy but he was as uninterested in politics as he was in sport, gaming and wenching. She went out to Switzerland, found her suspicions confirmed and so bore him home in the hope that she could immerse him in the affairs of society. However, Sir John Soane's mansion of Fonthill, classical in spirit if ostentatious in some of its decorations (it was nicknamed 'Splendens') boasted an Egyptian Hall which was only too capable of influencing the young man's imagination, while the surrounding landscape was too poetical and picturesque to induce a sober calm. And when a therapeutic round of great houses was prescribed, it took him finally to Powderham Castle near Exeter, the seat of the Courtenays, and so to what would prove a momentous occasion: namely his first meeting with the eleven-year-old son of the house, a Hylas pampered by innumerable sisters.

William, or 'Kitty', Courtenay, a schoolboy at Westminster, became the object of Beckford's devotion, while his aunt, Charlotte, was to be for a time a confidant and ally. There exists a long reverie in which Beckford described his feeling for the child: 'That dear form—which never fails to haunt me at sunset...I first saw sporting amongst the deer—first appeared in the beams of the evening sun. Therefore that moment is become so sacred. From my infancy I loved it but now I can neither read nor think of it—without the wildest and most extravagant raptures—nor can I look at a woody landscape of Claude Lorrain's whose deer are represented amongst the trees and the whole is suffused with the soft colours of declining day—without emotion—a faint vibration—a reflected light—of those very emotions I felt upon seeing him in such a scene as I have sketched.' Such unusually disjointed sentences are an indication, if such were needed, that Beckford was in earnest. He rhapsodised also to Cozens about 'that child who, I can assure you, has five times the sense, taste and discernment of the whole circle together...in which I am at present fated to move.' For his own good he rhapsodised too much. But, as a child of nature and Rousseau, why should he disguise such ideal feelings? He had already declared himself in a letter or reverie of December, 1778: 'I am determined to enjoy my dreams, my fantasies and all my singularity, however irksome and discordant to the worldlings around me. In spite of them, I will be happy...' He was also beginning to get to know his cousin, Louisa Beckford, the bored, fragile wife of a country squire and several years older than himself; their own intimate relationship would later be woven around the figure of 'little William'. His family seems already to have become disturbed and so, after a brief visit to London in June of 1780, where he was presented to the King and became acquainted with the musical circles which were to be so important to him and in particular with the *castrato*, Pacchiarotti, who was himself about to return to Italy, Beckford was sent off in the company of Mr Lettice on his Grand Tour.

We have in fact reached the occasion of *Waking Thoughts* and may be now in a better position to understand why its displays of sensibility and emotion, for all their guardedness, were not likely to be appreciated by the Begum or other interested parties, not excluding Lord Courtenay and his incessantly pregnant wife, who was, incidentally, an ex-barmaid with the far from euphonious name of Fanny Clack. Beckford simply wasn't turning out as a godson of Chatham should. With his soft brown hair, eager grey eyes, straight, slightly tilted nose, full petulant mouth, slim build and graceful bearing, he was handsome enough, as the Reynolds portrait shows. (The Romney of approximately the same date catches him in more arrogant mood, chin and mouth full but very firm and the family nose accentuated; the Hoppner reveals him in middle-age, faded, pensive and feminine, but with a melancholy that rasps.) He played the harpsichord and piano well, sang pleasantly in a light tenor which could easily become a soprano, danced with vivacity and had some talent for musical composition in the rather sugary style of Sacchini and Piccini. He had already proved that he could write — the soulful mysteries of *The Vision* had been counterbalanced by a humorous *jeu d'esprit*, the *Biographical Memoirs Of Extraordinary Painters*, which was published anonymously by his tutor early in 1780. He could flirt and use flirtation and intimacy as a conspiratorial stratagem against the Philistines. He was a devastatingly effective mimic. He invented peculiarly telling nicknames for those he disliked. But was this enough? Was this, in any sense, the right line of conduct for a Hamilton and a Lord Mayor's son?

It suffices for us that his first piece of travel-writing reads freshly today. If there is rather too much gush and fancy, and a good deal too little solid fact, especially in the early pages when he is touring the Low Countries and reacting against their dullness and ugliness, there is also a crisp ability to startle and shock; he belongs to the modern school of travellers — although the strain is, I suspect, perennial — in his concern with his own personality and his ability to dislike the places he visits and to be thoroughly rude about their inhabitants. (Both the fancifulness and the rudeness were toned down by the Beckford of 1833, whose Advertisement proclaimed that the letters were written 'in the bloom and heyday of youthful spirits and youthful confidence, at a period when the old order of things existed with all its picturesque pomps and absurdities' — his tongue was evidently in his cheek here; the book, he insisted, was light reading and wouldn't Homer's gods, when they returned from their customary scenes of havoc and carnage, have preferred to political manifestos and protocols the tales of Mother Goose?)

Like most good writing from the past, Beckford's impresses us from time to time with its modernity not only of attitude and choice of subject-matter but even of style, while also reminding us of writers in the intermediate years. Robert Louis Stevenson or some other picturesquely familiar essayist seems prefigured in phrasing like this, written about the ramparts at Ostend on 21st June, 1780: 'There, at least, thought I to myself, I may range undisturbed, and talk with my old friends the breezes, and address my discourse to the waves, and be as romantic and whimsical as I please.' A few pages later, in a description of Flemish landscape, the tone is measured and Augustan: 'All is still and peaceful in these fertile lowlands: the eye meets nothing but round unmeaning faces at every door, and harmless stupidity smiling at every window.' Not long after, though, Beckford describes an exhibition of natural history at the Hague with something of the irony of a Norman Douglas: 'One of the rarest articles it contains is the representation in wax of a human head, most dexterously flayed indeed. Rapturous encomiums have been bestowed by amateurs on this performance. A German professor could hardly believe it artificial; and, prompted by the love of truth, set his teeth in this delicious morsel, to be convinced of its reality.' At one moment he is conversational and timeless: 'I like this old town of Venice, and find every day some new amusement in rambling about its innumerable canals and alleys'; at another briskly succinct: 'The architect seems to have turned his building [the Duomo in Florence] inside out; nothing in art being more ornamental than the exterior, and few churches so simple within'; at a third 'Gothick': 'Dark clouds were driving athwart the sky, and the setting moon was flushed with the deepest crimson. A wan gleam covered the sea.' (Naples, 8th November, 1780).

Beckford travelled from Ostend to Ghent, Antwerp, the Hague, Haarlem, Utrecht, Maestricht, and so to Aix-la-Chapelle and Cologne. He was full of the classical, southern aim of his journey and the reader is immediately startled by references to Greece and Sicily and comparisons of Hymettus or Enna to such things as the 'vile Flemish dialect' and the 'unclassic' nature of his surroundings. Declaring himself 'resolved to grumble', he has no wish to 'slop through the Low Countries'. The countryside is neat, he admits; nature is fertile, the people seem happy, Antwerp is extraordinarily quiet; indeed it reminds him of the petrified city of Arabian fabulists. The churches tend to be dull, full of 'blubbering Magdalens and coarse Madonnas' for Rubens is not at this stage to his taste; the 'gigantic coarseness of his pencil' might do very well if it limited itself to Barabbas and the thieves 'but, when I find him lost in the flounces of the Virgin's drapery, or bewildered in the graces of St Catherine's smile, pardon me, if I withhold my adoration.' As for the work of all those realists in the galleries, the dew-drops on Van Huysem's flowers, 'the imitations of art rather than of nature in the likenesses of joint stools and the portraits of tankards' and, in particular, 'a most sublime thistle by Snyders, of the heroic size, and so faithfully imitated that I dare say no ass could see it unmoved', what have such things to do with romance, the visionary light and those slight but expressive vaguenesses achieved by Cozens with his ink-blots? Admittedly the weather is delightful, the landscape brings to mind something Chinese—Canton or Nsang Po—until tobacco-smoke rolls through the inns of scurvy Meerdyke where the people are 'the most uncouth bipeds in the universe'. The canals are 'sluggish puddles' but their stink must be congenial to the Dutch since they often build their cafés directly above them. In view of the fact that much of the land was once water, it is logical to imagine that the inhabitants were formerly fish. 'A certain oysterishness of eye and flabbiness of complexion are almost proofs sufficient of this aquatic descent.' Thus, anxious to enjoy the pastoral scene of hay-making between Leyden and Haarlem and in the act of approaching the nymphs at their bucolic tasks, he comes upon 'faces that would have dishonoured a flounder' and hears 'accents that would have confounded a hog'. In this mood he does no more than sigh, 'Well, thank Heavens! Amsterdam is behind us' and, on reaching Utrecht, finds 'nothing very remarkable' to capture his attention.

Aix-la-Chapelle brings him on the 7th of July to the threshold of Germany. He arrives late in the evening and sees 'the mouldering turrets of that once illustrious capital, by the help of a candle and a lantern', perceiving not the least trace of Charlemagne and his Paladins which does, indeed, seem careless of him, for the elaborate Rathaus faces a sizeable square with a statue of the Emperor in its middle and a few yards away rises the most ancient and curious of cathedrals,

centred upon an octagon of mistily ascending tiers, hung with lamps
and darkly rich with marbles and mosaics. He is, however, all for the
Rhine, which he reaches at 'Dusseldorp', while preferring boating
amongst its quivering osiers to the town which he finds infested with
bugs — 'the most unconscionable vermin ever engendered' — and with
brawny concubines and fat luxurious souls in torment by Rubens.
'Many wild ideas thronged into my mind the moment I beheld this
celebrated river.' Neither Cologne, 'clouds of dust' and a collection of
holy relics, nor Bonn, where the twilight outside his hotel window
shows the Elector's palace opposite in what he considers far too
favourable a light, can compare with 'the azure irregular mountains'
and the fancies they prompt: 'I shot swiftly from rock to rock, and
built castles in the style of Piranesi upon most of their pinnacles.'
Admittedly his pacing of a colonnade at Bonn has an alleviating
feature; he notices, in fact, 'the prevalence of a delicious perfume' and
soon he finds the entrance to an orangery, beyond whose trees there
'rises a romantic assemblage of distant mountains' and where he can
be entirely alone, lulled by the fluttering of moths and the tinkling
of fountains. 'These undecided sounds, corresponding with the dim-
ness and haze of the scenery, threw me into a pensive state of mind,
neither gay nor dismal.' What a beautiful use of the word *undecided*, we
may exclaim, as we prepare ourselves for the recollections of childhood
to follow, and the reflections upon the awful veil of futurity.

It is no wonder that one of the family's ostensible reasons for
declaring against the publication of the book was that it was rude to
the Dutch. The reader learns practically nothing about several cities of
considerable interest. Worse still from the conservative point of view,
this young puppy of twenty seems to consider his reading in classical
and oriental authors, about which he is insufficiently specific and whose
delights he shares across the reader's shoulder with his imaginary
friend, of equal importance with the sights he encounters, or would
encounter more fully if only he didn't so often arrive in the dark and
conduct his researches amongst buildings either closed or invisible.
Furthermore he stresses the importance not only of his reveries but of
his actual dreams, waking regretfully in Antwerp from a vision of a
tent, no less, on the mountains of Sanaa, amongst coffee-trees in bloom!
Having reached the shabby decayed town of Brie he falls gratefully
asleep when 'a dream bore me off to Persepolis...' Why go at all if you
don't enjoy it? He anticipates the question and answers simply that he
cannot fly direct to the summit of Aetna, although he would dearly

like to. But surely, when all is said, there is something in this single-minded honesty to be recommended. Beckford, as we shall see, can write observantly of places he enjoys, despite quirks of taste and strange omissions (but Goethe's omissions are notable too); for the moment he has given us thirty-five pages of entertaining and enlivening prejudice and he has exploded a certain amount of bourgeois smugness.

'All impatience to reach that delightful classic region which already possesses, as I have said, the better half of my spirit,' he continues south. Between Bonn and Coblenz he hires a skiff, lands at a hayfield and exclaims, 'What a spot for a tent!' He likes Mannheim a good deal better than poor Boswell did. At Ulm he ignores the tallest spire in Europe but greets the Danube, plucking a purple iris from its banks and enjoying a vision of American Indians performing their cere-monial dances on similarly green and boundless lawns. The stately fountains of Augsburg please him; descending a flight of stairs, he imagines he is about to entertain the Queen of Sheba. On the approach to Munich he is depressed by the formality, not the first mention of this aesthetic *bête noir*, with which the avenues are drawn across a dreary plain.

It is surprising to find him as critical of the palace and pavilions of Nymphenburg as Walpole and Gray were of Versailles. Much in that wonderful place seems exactly suited to his youthful spirit but no, he will have nothing of it; presumably the geometrical precision of the outer façade and gardens puts him off—there is indeed something stiff about those flanking villas, symmetrically matched—although he also wanders in the woods beyond the main pavilion, where a green casual-ness and spontaneity contrast with the central vista, to find the Amalienburg no more than tinsel. To my mind the Amalienburg, so simple without, such a glory of silver filigree thrown upon walls of pale blue and deep yellow within, is one of the loveliest buildings in the world. Nevertheless, it is not to Beckford's taste. Southern Bavaria means to him the mountains of the Tyrol, with a foreground of orchards, forests and chalets. He is all for 'awful groves' and, encounter-ing a thunderstorm on the way to the Wallersee, he remarks, 'Perhaps the Norwegian forests alone, equal these in grandeur and extent.' He finds a typical *genre* scene on a mountainside: wooden hut, picturesquely dressed peasants, flock of goats and beautiful children to offer him a jug of milk and a platter of fresh-picked strawberries. But, not under-standing their dialect, he does not stay long.

It is a scene which exposes some of the limitations of Beckford's travel writing. Its charm is that of a painting, mellow in recollection and carefully framed; there is no sense of disturbance or immediacy, no tension between the artist and the experience he has appropriated only too fully. Furthermore he is on his own; no bear-leader, no servants, no details as to his own behaviour or the circumstances of the stopped carriage and horses are allowed to disrupt the solitariness of a dream. Furthermore he is still a good deal of an Augustan in his feeling for the generality and the type: charming Rousseau-esque peasants or, in a different mood, 'lubbers', 'hags' and 'slobbering grey-beards'. The friendly relations which Boswell and Byron established with members of the working-class are absent from most, if not all, his published writing, although much later in writing to Franchi he will sigh after 'Master Saunders, the celebrated equestrian infant-phenomenon' and imagine the delights to be found in the sands of Hounslow: 'There, in a rude cottage surrounded by a few pines and a wall, I'd finish my days in the lap of platonism and devotion, educating the little rogue (?)!' He specialises in the lyricism of an Enchanted Garden where all is too easily dissolved into mood, or in witty cameos and satirical analyses. Even as a boy of twenty, he can do both these things extraordinarily well. There is the fantasy, the elegance of expression, with which he evokes one of his Edens: at Bassano, for instance, 'a level green where people walk and eat ices by moonlight.' And there is the fun, admittedly a little cruel, which he has with the lady musicians at the Mendicanti in Venice: 'Some that have grown old and Amazonian, who have abandoned their fiddles and their lovers, take vigorously to the kettle-drum, and one poor limping lady, who has been crossed in love, now makes an admirable figure on the bassoon.'

He is now on the point of reaching Italy at last. He can't bear to pause long at Innsbruck, proceeds to Steinach and is soon entranced by the poppy-fields and then the fire-flies on the banks of the Adige. So eager is he now that from Bolzano to Trento he travels by night. On July 31st, some five weeks after leaving Ostend, he writes: 'My heart beat quick when I saw some hills, not very distant, which I was told lay in the Venetian State, and I thought an age, at least, had elapsed before we were passing their base.' Changing horses at Tremolino, he enters 'my long-desired Italy' through a tremendous pass, haunted by eagles, with the Brenta foaming and thundering below. 'It was now I beheld groves of olives, and vines clustering the summits of the tallest elms; pomegranates in every garden, and vases of citron and orange

4*

before every door. The softness and transparency of the air soon told me I was arrived in happier climates; and I felt sensations of joy and novelty run through my veins, upon beholding this smiling land of groves and verdure stretched before me.'

For two hot August days he pauses at Bassano, rejoicing in the absence of officials and soldiers and in the freedom and happiness of people under Venetian rule, meeting the notables and sharing with them his adoration for the divine Pachiarotti. Then it is time for Venice itself. He takes a gondola at Mestre — that craft which Shelley is to describe as being 'of a most romantic and picturesque appearance; I can only compare them to a moth of which a coffin might have been the chrysalis' — and, stretched beneath the awning, gives himself up to 'the freshness of the gales, and the sight of the waters'. It is near to sunset: Murano, San Michele, San Giorgio in Alga detach themselves from the 'grand cluster' and then the convent of San Secondo drifts past: 'here, meditation may indulge her reveries in the midst of the surges, and walk in cloisters, alone vocal with the whispers of the pine'. Soon he has reached the Grand Canal, passed the Palazzo Pesaro and landed at the Leone Bianco where the hotel, with its huge interior gallery 'painted with grotesques in a very good style', is much to his taste. He retires to a balcony whence he watches the glow of innumerable tapers in the windows and the tracks of oily ruffled light cast by the lanterns of the gondolas. An illuminated barge appears through the arch of the Rialto. It is filled with musicians whose serenade penetrates every awning and tracery, every screened garden and arcaded court, and whose airs are caught up and echoed by the gondoliers into the far distance, until the melody seems to line the air, to breathe from the intricate glimmering stone and finally to weave itself about his sleep.

Whatever one may feel with regard to Beckford's attitude to Holland or Germany, there can be no question that his first impressions of Venice are a movingly poetic addition to the literature of discovery. The next morning he is woken at five by 'a loud din of voices and a splashing of water'. Rushing out to his balcony he watches the floating fruit and vegetable market and is interested to notice, amongst the crowds of shoppers, various jaded members of the aristocracy on their way home from the casinos. He orders a gondola, buys bread and grapes — nearly all the food mentioned by Beckford is either simple (chestnuts, milk, wild strawberries) or light but exquisite (ortolans, quails, sherbets) — and is borne away to the marble steps of S. Maria della Salute, the great church which Longhena built to honour the Virgin after she had remitted the plague of 1630 and which Ruskin, who loathed everything in Venice that was not the purest Gothic, admitted to have from a distance 'a good stage effect'. Beckford gazes, 'delighted with its superb frontispiece and dome, relieved by a clear blue sky' and then, as the bronze doors open, is able to 'expatiate' the interior in solitude except for a single old priest trimming the lamps at an altar still wrapped in shadows. Thence he is wafted to the spacious platform from which S. Giorgio Maggiore rises, 'by far the most perfect and beautiful edifice my eyes ever beheld. When my first transport was a little subsided... I planted my umbrella on the margin of the sea, and reclining under its shade, viewed the vast range of palaces, of porticos, of towers, opening on every side and extending out of sight.' His thoughts become historical; he recollects the grandeur of past ages and contrasts the splendid fleets the Republic once owned with the solitary galeass now anchored by the Doge's Palace. Removed from the buzz of the town he eats his grapes and reads Metastasio before entering the church and admiring once again the genius of Palladio, after which he inspects the adjoining convent and its refectory. He is amused that the monks have evidently plenty to eat and that they are encouraged to make excursions across the intervening water, which he takes to be a matter of Venetian policy, since they thus reveal themselves as 'being mere flesh and blood, and that of the frailest composition'. If only the rest of poor Italy would come to regard the papal tiara, 'with all its host of idle fears and scaring phantoms, as the offspring of a distempered dream!'

Soon he finds himself, he knows not how, in front of the Redentore, 'a structure so simple and elegant, that I thought myself entering an antique temple, and looked about for the statue of the God of Delphi, or some other graceful divinity.' However, it is now midday; he begs to be transported to some woody island, the haunt of tranquillity and shade, and although his gondoliers shoot off at a brisk pace he wishes to fly even faster and so transfers himself to a six-oared craft. 'A pale greenish light ran along the shores of the distant continent, whose mountains seemed to catch the motion of my boat, and to fly with equal celerity. I had not much time to contemplate the beautiful effects on the waters—the emerald and purple hues which gleamed along their surface.' He gains the gardens of the Carthusian convent and the shade of a bay-tree on a hillock with some pines nearby. 'I listened to the conversation they held, with a wind just flown from Greece, and charged, as well as I could understand their airy language, with many affectionate remembrances from their relations on Mount Ida.' The fathers soon hurry out with a picnic luncheon (unspecified except for fruit and wine) and a desire to discuss English politics, but Beckford gets rid of them by pretending not to understand their language. Only the plaintive murmuring of the men left waiting in the boat, 'who wondered not a little, I dare say, of what the deuce was become of me', finally disturbs his sentimental reverie. The sun is about to go down 'in all its sacred calm'.

He is rowed slowly to the Piazza and is soon busy with references to tournaments and festivals once held in the square ('What a magnificent idea!' he boyishly exclaims) and then to an examination of Sansovino's bronze pedestals for the standards opposite the church, together with the finely 'enriched' and 'finished' loggieta as compared with the awe-inspiring but 'barbarous' campanile with its 'uncouth' and 'heavy' termination (isn't one inclined to agree?); yet even here, where his book comes close to the traditional guide, 'the dusk prevented my remarking the various sculptures with which the Loggietta is crowded'. Indeed he has scarcely entered the courtyard of the Doge's Palace and gazed upon the Scala dei Giganti when, like other less privileged travellers, the police tell him that the palace is closing for the night: a pity, he feels, for 'the twilight, which bats and owls love not better than I do, enlarged every portico, lengthened every colonnade, and increased the dimensions of the whole, just as imagination dictated.' Still, he *hurries* away obediently; or so he tells us on one page for, by the next, his admiration of the twilight and anticipation of the moon have so transported him, at least in the act of writing, that he declares the police think him distracted: 'True enough, I was stalking proudly about like an actor in an ancient Grecian tragedy, lifting up my hands to the consecrated faces and images around, expecting the reply of his attendant Chorus, and declaiming the first verse of Oedipus Tyrannus'. He concludes this first day in Venice with a witty description of the *mores* of the Venetians, their enervation by coffee-drinking, gondola-gliding and sexual intrigues.

In these Venetian pages Beckford comes alive and the way he composes the fruit-market, the three great churches, the distant views, the race across the water and the tranquillity of the garden into a single picture is certainly effective and characteristically full of those elements of experience which suited his temperament so well: atmospherics, they might be called, the interweaving of music and colours and perfumes together with movements of the air and changes of the light. There is also a scholarly accompaniment, both historical and literary, as well as a touch of the Enlightenment when he speaks of the Church, one or two nice bits of irony and a more successful attempt than usual to suggest an endearing eccentricity in the narrator himself. That umbrella of his helps, and so does the use of 'deuce' to include for once the opinion of his servants. The greater detail assigned to the Piazza comes well after this impressionism; the even more detailed description of Venetian life makes a satisfactory close. One must, I suppose, add that — dusk or no dusk — not very much of the real appearance of things emerges and not a single character comes into focus. A modern Beckford might very well be careless about the particulars of the buildings, ('I leave that sort of thing to H. V. Morton or Baedeker') but he would certainly desire first of all an experience of the Italians. He would want to describe his gondoliers, possessing them visually, even if, unlike Beckford, he didn't speak their tongue; and, at least on his *first* day, he would be unlikely to get rid of the hospitable monks just because he wanted to listen to the wind in the trees.

As for his touristic range, by the end of his stay of five weeks Beckford has done pretty well. He has revisited the Doge's Palace where too many paintings by Veronese and Tintoretto have exhausted him although he has behaved, he assures us, with 'exemplary resignation'; what he really enjoyed — and I for one have had precisely the same experience — was his emergence at the end of the great suite of rooms into the light from the sea. He has seen the interior of St Mark's but has been driven away by 'the vile stench which exhales from every recess and corner' so that in fact a mere mention of marbles and mosaics is all he can give us. He has bathed at the Lido, a dreary sun-burned shore 'all of a hop with toads and locusts' and quite deserted by human beings; his method of bathing is sympathetic and perhaps expressive of a character which was often so energetic on land: 'The tide rolled over me as I lay floating about, buoyed up by the water, and carried me wheresoever it listed...my ears were filled with murmuring undecided sounds; my limbs, stretched languidly on the surge, rose or sunk just as it swelled or subsided. In this passive state I remained.' This is the most physical that Beckford will ever get, I think, for bathing enables cerebral narcissists, whose sensuality is suppressed, to free themselves a little. He has also visited Torcello, accompanied by hired musicians, and as he wound through those reedy serpentine canals into that somnolent outpost he has been impressed by an aromatic weed on the banks which serves to quell the musky odour arising (or so he is told) from the numberless serpents on the island: guardians it would seem

of quantities of buried treasure. The lovely circular church of Santa
Fosca has scarcely impressed him, although it transports the fancy to
'the twilight glimmering period when it was raised', and the cathedral
itself he has found beautiful only for its floor of variegated marble, the
rest apparently savouring of 'the grossest barbarism'. But then all his
descriptions of Venice ignore the Gothic, Romanesque and Byzantine.
There is no reference to such buildings as the Ca d'Oro, no account of
the delicate white sculptures at the corners of the Doge's Palace, nor is
his feeling for the exotic stimulated by the red porphyry crusaders from
Acre. At this stage he is clearly a classicist, but, even so, the wonderful
Libreria Vecchia doesn't get a line. Nevertheless, a modern visitor
could do worse than follow his itinerary.

Beckford is sensible in his desire to meet foreigners from those lands
immemorially associated with Venice, and then far more in evidence
than they are now; solemn Turks and lively Greeks engage his attention; but the only individual who really makes an impression on the
reader is, of all things, a Laplander kept as a curiosity by a scholar.
Beckford goes with this man to view a collection of medals and has the
opportunity of observing his lack of charm. 'What a perfect void! Cold
and silent as the polar regions, not one passion ever throbbed in his
bosom; not one bright ray of fancy ever glittered in his mind; without
love or anger, pleasure or pain, his days fleet smoothly along: all things
considered, I must confess I envied such comfortable apathy.'

In real life Beckford's stay at Venice contained scenes as stormy as
any that assailed Lord Byron in the Palazzo Mocenigo, and scandals no
less savoury than those that drove the unfortunate Baron Corvo to the
outermost lagoons in his rat-infested gondola. His Swiss friends, the
Hubers, had given him an introduction to the Contessa Giustiniana
Wynne d'Orsini-Rosenberg, a former associate of Casanova and now
a woman of the world who held a salon, wrote, philosophised and
gambled in the company of her *cavaliere servente*, an ex-diplomat and
adventurer called Count Bartolommeo Benincasa. The Contessa
devoted herself to showing Beckford the town and indulging his
passion for music; she introduced him to young people, amongst whom
were two sisters and a brother identifiable only as the family C——
(but possibly the Cornari); one at least of the sisters fell violently in
love with him, declared herself and, on being politely refused,
attempted to poison her husband but mistakenly drank a near-fatal dose
herself; meanwhile he and the brother were deeply involved with each
other. To Beckford the young C—— was 'the pagan idol' although, in

a footnote to one of his letters added years afterwards, he was careful
to explain, 'it was a passion of the mind resembling those generous
attachments we venerate in ancient history, and holy writ. What David
felt towards the brother of his heart, the son of Saul, I expressed towards the person here alluded to.' When he left Venice on September
4th the boy came with him at least as far as Fiesso; the night was filled
with the music so beloved of Venetians, 'everyone seemed to catch the
flame, and to listen with reciprocal delight'; and, to the strains of
Gluck's *Orfeo*, Beckford fell into a 'strange delirium which had nearly
proved fatal not only to me but to one to whom I felt the most enthusiastic friendship.' The Contessa accompanied him to Padua, whose
University had long been a favourite with English travellers, and to the
Euganean Hills, where Petrarch of course had to be worshipped, but the
memory of the pagan idol remained with him much longer, occasioning
transports and regrets at leaving, letters of advice from Benincasa and
a good deal of straight talk from the first Lady Hamilton when he got
to Naples. But Venice lay on his way home and apparently there were
further adventures there: a 'fatal journey...into perils and misfortunes'
was the way he put it to Lady Hamilton but to another correspondent
he was less remorseful: 'Having been burnt out at Venice by certain
fascinating eyes, the very precise Meteors which dazzled me on the
bank of the Brenta...'

The rest of Beckford's journey was as imaginative and as idio-
syncratic. He travelled by way of Vicenza, Verona, Modena, Florence,
Lucca — with an excursion to the Campo Santo at Pisa and to the sea-
shore at Leghorn — and then back to Florence, where he was held up
by news of heat and fevers at Rome. Towards the end of October he
reached that city and shortly afterwards moved down to Naples. On
January 20th, 1781, he was at Augsburg again.

There are plenty of good things in these pages, plenty of omissions
too, some caused by the very real melancholy consequent upon leaving
Venice and the pagan idol, others quite normally by the sheer amount
to be seen, still others by that youthful carelessness and self-centredness
which, within reason, can be considered one of the virtues of the book;
Beckford's idiosyncrasy is often attractively displayed and can fill in
many of the gaps. At Vicenza, for instance, he adores the Teatro
Olimpico: 'It is impossible to conceive a structure more truly classical,
or to point out a single ornament which has not the best antique
authority.' He goes there on an overcast morning, 'full of the spirit of
Aeschylus', and vents his evil temper in reciting 'some of the most

tremendous verses of his furies' but we hear nothing beyond this: nothing of the little statue-strewn garden in front of the entrance, or of the balconied Chiericati palace opposite, or of the mossy, weedy river Bacchiglione by its side with, across the bridge, the gothic balcony of the Palazzo Regaù. Lovers of Vicenza must regret that he has not told them of his feelings in the noble, bland and shining *piazza* where the eye soars at once about Palladio's basilica, with its great hump of ribbed green roof (what a Nissen hut would be like in Heaven) and its galleries and stairs—all watched by the sculptured figure of the architect himself who, finger to beard, gives a look of acute professional concentration upon the girdle he has thus made for a medieval building —before it is riveted into an enthusiastic calm by the rose-flushed columns of the Loggia del Capitanio, where overweening power has exploded and become stylised and almost picturesque, and then wanders, less certainly, along the extended façade of the Monte di Pietà which is broken in the centre by the baroque church of San Vicenzo. A lover of towers, he says nothing of the tall red-brown campanile rising by the end of the basilica, only twenty-two feet wide and yet almost two hundred and seventy feet high; an amateur of gardens, he ignores the Querini Park or the Salvi Gardens, with the pool and the loggia at its side, *hilaritatio ac genio dictata*, dedicated to laughter and ease, a place which Coryat had declared 'so delectable and pleasant that it seemeth a second Paradise' (and who loved second Paradises more than Beckford?). There is no reference to the Palladian palaces rising all over the town, nor to the villas just outside, the Rotunda, the Ai Nani.

At Verona (and here, as in Germany or Venice, twilight is drawing on) he has to dispense with a loquacious guide, 'one of those diligent, plausible young men, to whom, God help me! I have so capital an aversion...and [who] flourished away upon cloacas and vomitoriums with eternal fluency' before he can reach the Roman amphitheatre, the 'awful ruins', where he enjoys being enclosed in total solitude and experiences many a *frisson* in the vaulted colonnades. 'Red and fatal were the tints of the western sky and something more than common seemed to issue from the withering herbage of the walls', he declares before he flees up the arcade and arrives positively panting on the square. One can see the point, especially during a hurried journey (but was Beckford in such a rush?) of concentrating on a single aspect of a town; modern travellers will, I think, be grateful for the incident of the officious guide; and one must add that, on emerging from the amphitheatre, Beckford discovers the Scaliger castle (I presume the one by the Adige, since he also notes a triumphal arch attributed to Vitruvius, although the wonderful sweep of the river is not mentioned), but, as he returns, he sees only 'the outline of several palaces' and has recourse to the old excuse, 'it was too dusky to examine their details'. To my mind the river bank is incomplete without at least San Zeno, while the wide space around the amphitheatre must be balanced by the red-brown, rust-smeared, endearingly shabby or darkly austere buildings of the Piazza dell' Erbe and the Piazza dei Signori behind it. The first is narrow, near claustrophobic; from its dense, over-lapping umbrellas, flat and shell-like, there struggle upward an antique column, a tribune and a fountain supporting a Roman maiden with a spiked crown. The Piazza dei Signori, presided over by Dante, is a miracle of medievalism: vast expanses of the richest, gloomiest red brick, sometimes striped by courses of white stone; jagged fish-tail castellations; towers, arches and courtyards; and, as a partial relief, the elegant saffron-coloured Loggia del Consiglio together with a distant glimpse of the lacy Scaliger tombs...The next morning Beckford is off to Mantua, where he dines 'in dudgeon', since 'the beating of drums, and the sight of German whiskers, finished what croaking frogs and stagnant ditches had begun'. But neither gay Vicenza nor grim Verona has brought out that capacity to form a generalised and atmospheric picture which we have seen in Venice and will see again in Portugal.

After a wearying 'jumble over the Appenines' he reaches Florence late at night. 'The serene moonlight on the pale grey tints of the olives, gives an elysian, visionary appearance to the landscape', but he must still explore the bridges of the Arno. Next morning he bustles about the galleries, impressed by various paintings but even more concerned with the sculpture, the antique bronzes, candelabra, urns and sacred utensils, cases of diminutive deities and tutelary lares. Nor does he omit the Venus de Medici with its 'warm ivory hue' and 'a faint ruddy cast in the hair' although, to be sure, the athletic energy of many of the figures alarms him: 'Such wearisome attitudes I can view with admiration, but never with pleasure'; and what he is really searching for is an ideal representation of Morpheus, the god of sleep: 'Sleeping figures with me always produce the finest illusion...I can gaze whole hours upon them with complacency.' He briefly abandons Florence for Lucca, where he gets into trouble by taking Pacchiarotti riding in the hills, with the result that the great singer catches a cold. At Pisa he shows himself favourable to Gothic, at least when it is in conjunction with 'pagan sarcophagi' and 'fifty other contradictory ornaments' so that the general effect is airy, capricious, exotic, and he feels himself in fairy-land. At Livorno he buys branches of coral and then fills his carriage with jasmine. Back at Pisa he takes his 'usual portion of ice and pome-granate seeds' before hurrying off to a performance of *Quinto Fabio* at the Lucca opera.

In Florence again he inspects the great piazza, finding John of Bologna's fountain 'admirably wrought' and Cellini's Perseus 'in-comparably designed and executed'; in the courtyard of the Signory he sees a bronze image 'that looks quite strange and cabalistic'. Although he comes to dislike 'the chit-chat and nothingness of Florence' (where he clearly found few friends) and regards the opera as 'addressed to the sight alone', especially in view of the unfortunate first soprano ('you never behold such a porpoise') his description is both lively and reasonably thorough. Michelangelo gets his tribute in the summatory chapter which concludes the tour. But the faded sweetness and high-mindedness of the Florence discovered by the Victorians and still filtering through to us today, the city of Giotto and Fra Angelico and Botticelli and Della Robbia which lingers amongst the clouds of dust and the stutter of the motor-scooters, is obviously not Beckford's. As so often, he is at his most poetic during his many retirements to the Boboli Gardens; the pavilion there reminds him of a Turkish kiosk and he enjoys the springs, the fountains, the statue of Ganymede, 'full of that graceful languor so peculiarly Grecian', and the combination of roses, aloes, bays and oaks. 'Really this garden is enough to bewilder an enthusiastic spirit.'

The arrival at Rome, even more than at Athens, was a prime subject for the romantic imagination. Beckford gives us a mixture of feelings and reflections. He is already travelling when dawn breaks over the Lago di Vico and he broods on the past history and pageantry of the great plain: 'the splendid tumult is passed away: silence and desolation remain.' It is a familiar note. Shepherds' huts stand here and there on the banks of a stream, 'propped up with broken pedestals and marble friezes'. He enters one that is empty and begins 'writing upon the sand and murmuring a melancholy song'. The weather depresses him: 'You are well acquainted how greatly I depend upon skies and sunshine.' The road is bad. From ridge to ridge the promised view of the city fails to materialise. These shepherds, he tells himself, are poor, oppressed by the papal government, but who can say they fared better in the days of luxurious pomp? When the city finally does come into view, he is excited in a characteristic way: he leaps out of his carriage, dips his hands into a marble cistern shaded by cypress and pine and, lifting them, implores the protection of sylvan Genii. His body is full of adrenalin and his head of literature. 'I wished to have run wild in the fresh fields and copses above the Vatican, there to have remained, till fauns might peep out of their concealments, and satyrs begin to touch their flutes...for the place looks still so wondrous classical.' By the time he reaches the walls the day is almost over, the long perspective of the streets and palaces glows with the vivid red of sunset. St Peter's is a miracle of freshness: it could have been built yesterday. Although he gains admittance, it is (dare one say this again?) about to close.

His stay in Rome is short, from October 29th to November 1st, and perhaps in excuse for this he adopts a strategy familiar to other traveller-writers; he wants 'no antiquary to go prattling from fragment to fragment' and is resolved 'to view nothing at all in a scientific way, but straggle and wander about, just as the spirit chuses'. The Pantheon rather disappoints him; and he is furious to find the 'holy trumpery' of chapels and cells in the Colosseum. But St Peter's yield him a womb image, a fantasy of secure withdrawal, which prefigures the famous Christmas party of 1781–2. He imagines building a small tabernacle for winter habitation under the dome, the climax of the various yearnings for tents we have encountered already, but will only be truly happy if he can provide a similar one for his friend. They will live in an enclosed, an entirely artificial world, whose sky will be the vast arches glowing with golden ornaments, 'so lofty as to lose all glitter and gaudiness'. They will take their evening walk on fields of marble and instead of visiting a copse or a grotto they will stroll amongst screens and candelabra or descend to a crypt. 'Sometimes, instead of climbing a mountain, we should ascend the cupola, and look down on our little encampment below.' Meanwhile music will breathe from subterranean chapels or monuments, fine as the music of the spheres, into the dome. 'No priests, no cardinals; God forbid! We would have all the space to ourselves, and to such creatures too as resemble us.' The curtains will be of transparent yellow silk to suggest, in winter, the glow of perpetual summertime. It will be all very like the palace of the Chinese emperor, Ki. 'Was it not a fantastic idea? For my part, I should like of all things to immure myself, after his example, with those I love; forget the divisions of time, have a moon at command, and a theatrical sun to rise, and set, at pleasure.'

These phrases, in the 'cabalistic' style he loves to display to Cozens,

are full of significance for his life. The glow of the curtains he was to
find at Ramalhao in Portugal or to imagine in relation to the mosquito-
netting around the beloved form of a certain 'sprite': 'Oh that it were
decent and proper for me to lay this spirit, not in the Red Sea, but on a
bed of rose leaves, defended from mosquitoes by awnings of gauze,
and cooled by an almost imperceptible rain of iced perfumed water'
(*Journal*, Portugal, 1787); the theatrical sun was to be ingeniously produced by Loutherbourg's *Eidophusikon*, an apparatus for atmospheric
panoramas and apparently one of the delights of the Christmas party
of 1781—a year later a London magazine wrote of plans to have an
artificial sun in a pavilion specially built at Fonthill; and, as for being
immured, was there not to be the great wall about Fonthill?

From Rome he proceeded to the Hamiltons'[1] villa on the slopes of
Vesuvius, with Pompeii nearby and a reverie on the Rites of Isis; food
for Flaubert and Wilde in 'every form of creeping thing, and abominable
beast, every Egyptian pollution, which the true prophet had seen in
vision, among the secret idolatries of the temples at Jerusalem.' Naples
meant also the tomb of Virgil and brought with it, in the rocks above
the Mare Morto, a gothic tale supposedly told Beckford by a dis-
tinguished-looking old woman, not quite a witch, to whose thrilling:
'Your features are wonderfully like those of an unfortunate young
person, who, in this retirement...' he secretly responded, like a born
writer, with: 'Now I come upon the verge of an adventure! O Quixote!
O Sylvio di Rosalven! how would ye have strutted in such a situation!'

His literary journey was over, to be supplemented by a few letters
from his second Italian visit in 1782, when he also worked on the
summarising chapter with its analyses, and 'sensible' patriotic opinions,
and general air of a correspondent for *The Times* or *The Guardian*. But
Chatham once described him as a creature of air and fire and it is surely
this often delightful, sometimes jejune waywardness and sensitivity
which we dwell on as we close the book; he has flitted through dark
towns like some luminous moth; he has expanded in gardens and
galleries in the happier shape of a butterfly, an image he uses of himself
in the Florentine galleries: 'I ran childishly by the ample ranks of
sculpture, like a butterfly in a parterre'; he has thrilled and trembled on
the heights of the Rhine or in the lagoons of Venice or on the slopes of
Vallombrosa; slopping through the Low Countries, he has drooped
and, in certain situations, he has buzzed and even bitten. But we
shouldn't forget that this exotic creature loved to rise early and to ride

[1] Sir William Hamilton, Envoy to the Court of Naples, was his cousin.

fast. Outside Rome, mounting a horse I flew before them, and seemed to catch inspiration from the breezes.' (At the age of eighty-three, when his white horse Deborah bolted with him in Hyde Park, he succeeded in checking the animal.) He was all energy. Clambering about the shrubbery above Virgil's tomb, 'no squirrel ever scampered from bough to bough more venturously...I hazarded my neck on the top of one of the pines.'

III

BECKFORD RETURNED to England on 14th April, 1781. In October he would succeed to his inheritance. He seemed popular in London, where invitations to parties arrived by the score; retired to Fonthill, he began working on his diaries and notes. The intimacy with Louisa was growing. Arabic and oriental lore could now be consulted without interference from his elders. Alexander Cozens could be a guest. Everything seemed so promising, except that there wasn't really very much for a man of his position and temperament to do: the army he disliked, the church was reserved for younger sons, the professions belonged to the middle-classes...he could be a hunting and shooting squire (which God forbid) or he could try politics (but surely not yet: 'Age will soon draw on, and the gay texture be shrivelled. Then will I mump, growl, snarl, bite, and be political').

This period began with two parties: the official coming of age at the end of September, 1781, when the ceremonies extended over three days: 'Above ten thousand people all neatly dressed covered the lawn' to watch the display of fireworks, and a specially commissioned opera was performed; and the 'romantic villegiatura', the 'zennina', the private, youthful, voluptuous, cabalistic house-party of the Christmas following. It was there that the first real seeds of scandal were sown, and a sort of reckless feverishness, hardly distinguishable from youthful gaiety, can be detected in the complicated events that followed: the ever closer, more effusive and conspiratorial intimacy with Louisa, the wife of Beckford's cousin, who eventually became his mistress; the gallivantings in London, where it was at the faintly bohemian houses of the members of what would now be called café society that Beckford made his 'vivid sensation', was never 'quiet a single instant' and could, in retrospect, remark, 'what a strange exotic animal I was in those days...I seemed like the antique Mercury, perpetually on tiptoe as if on the point of darting into the air'; the writing, in French, of *Vathek*;

and, above all, the intense cultivation of 'Kitty' (little William) Courtenay. Beckford's family not only heard rumours but repeated them; looking askance at his artistic activities—he had set the far from respectable Lady Craven's pastoral to music and was stage-managing its performance in Lady Queensberry's London mansion: a brilliant social occasion, as it turned out—they began to mutter that he must give up Sophia and that he ought to marry. In response he tried evasion. Lady Craven's *répétition générale* had been on 13th April, 1782; a month later he set out on his second Italian journey with the Hamiltons' villa at Portici as his destination; this time he took with him Cozens' brilliant artist son, John Robert, to provide sketches. His *equipage* was so splendid, and the speed of his progress so great, that many people, including greedy innkeepers, believed he was the Emperor of Austria travelling incognito. But already a sort of doom was upon him. A foreign observer noted the paradox: 'His destiny appears brilliant, for he has a great fortune and talents supposed to be marvellous, and he is young and his own master...Yet a fever consumes his powers, and up to now nothing stops its progress.' No healthy peasant but would congratulate himself at not being Beckford.

On his return in November he spent some quiet scholarly weeks at Fonthill, drawing the narrative of *Vathek* together and revising *Waking Thoughts*. Although Louisa was now abroad for her health, he was in greater danger than before. Not only had 'Kitty's' aunt Charlotte turned against him, she had married Alexander Wedderburn, Lord Loughborough, a puritanical and ambitious Scots lawyer who supported the dissection in public of the bodies of murderers and the burning of women coiners; he was now Chief Justice of Common Pleas. His dislike of Beckford was instant, a fact that both Beckford and Kitty realised: 'We both live in horror of that malicious fiend.' In March, 1783, he agreed to the suppression of *Waking Thoughts*, Cipriani drawings and all. In May he was married to Lady Margaret Gordon, daughter of the Earl of Aboyne, the girl with whom he had led the opening *cotillon* at his coming of age. The couple spent a long honeymoon in Switzerland and then in Paris, during which the Begum made further moves to ensure that Beckford and Louisa did not meet. Paris on the brink of revolution was 'a glaring, noisy, racketing place, Lucifer's own metropolis' and, since his wife was pregnant, Beckford racketed most successfully and outrageously with a couple of English girls who shared his loathing of 'fustitude'. In March 1784 Lady Margaret and he returned to England. Beckford began to show an interest in politics, got himself elected M.P. for Wells and then secured the promise of a barony; it was gazetted in October. Even more important to him was his plan to have 'little William' transferred from Westminster School to the care of a private tutor of his own choice, namely the Rev. Samuel Henley, the translator and subsequently the betrayer of *Vathek*. 'How I tremble lest that plant which nature has formed so delicately should be committed to bungling hands,' he had written from Geneva the previous year. 'K's little lovely person' must be preserved at all costs, especially as he now found him, with an odd change of tone, lacking in manliness, 'quite lost in flowers and foolery at present...*Still more* girlish and trifling' and full of 'milinary dispositions' with regard to balloon hats or silvered sashes. However, this project had fallen through before Beckford took the fatal step of going with his wife for a month's visit to Powderham Castle where to known enemies of his own class there was now added the tutor Lord Courtenay had selected in Henley's stead. It was this tutor who found Beckford locked in a bedroom with 'Kitty' and reported an incident of sexual malpractice. After fermenting in family circles for several weeks, the scandal, at Loughborough's instigation, broke in the London newspapers in November. 'The rumour concerning a *Grammatical mistake of Mr. B*—— and the *Hon. Mr. C*——, in regard to the genders, we hope for the honour of Nature originates in *Calumny!*' Thus the *Morning Herald* of November 29th. A week later its tone was fiercer as it referred to 'the detestable scene lately acted in *Wiltshire*, by a pair of fashionable *male lovers*', a scene made even worse by 'the ocular demonstration of their infamy, to the young and beautiful wife of one of the monsters', whatever that meant.

At twenty-four, Beckford was ruined. Whatever we may think of the free manners of British society during the eighteenth century, there is no doubt of the almost entire ostracism he was to endure for the next half century. When Fonthill Abbey was being built one can recall no guests of anywhere near his own class, except for Lady Craven and Lord Nelson, who consented to stay with him and visit it; others sneaked in for a look but only when the Caliph was away. The barony was withdrawn. And, although Beckford bravely turned back from Dover where he was supposed to take ship and bore the matter out for a while, long years of exile became a necessity. But what was Beckford guilty of? How far, with several known mistresses and a wife he loved and by whom, except for miscarriages, he would have had four children in three years, can he be considered a homosexual?

Of his recent biographers, Professor Guy Chapman, who thought that no more than sentimental and romantic attachments were involved when he wrote his book in 1932, changed his mind in the revised edition twenty years later. On the other hand Mr Boyd Alexander, while recognising a constant stream of homosexual reference throughout Beckford's life, and also attempting to estimate the psychological importance of his dreams and nightmares and of his working his autobiography into the Arabian tales, is inclined to think that Beckford was 'framed' by Loughborough in the instance of William Courtenay. Both would agree that Beckford was far more a dreamer and a talker than a doer. His life, like that of Ludwig of Bavaria, became a flight from reality. Women fell in love with him, some men, notably the Marquis of Marialva, became strongly emotional friends, but Beckford never seemed able to give himself after the first rush of enthusiasm: preferring his moods and dreams, he failed both the Marquis and Franchi at the crises of their lives. Repudiating 'Kitty', whom a different kind of man might have tried to help, rescue or simply understand, despite the 'betrayal', he nevertheless returned to him in fantasy as the original Portuguese Journal shows: 'Methought I was walking with William Courtenay on the declivity of green hills scattered over with orange trees in bloom. Our eyes were bathed in tears of affection and forgiveness, our hands were joined, and we seemed to have entirely forgotten the miseries we had occasioned each other', although this didn't in the least prevent his referring a few days later, when contemplating his own career, to 'that cowardly effeminate fool'.

I personally find the letters he wrote to Franchi in middle age typically those of a gossipy, coy and amusing 'queen'. Although I admit there is no reason to suppose that he wanted or got more than mental titillation, I cannot see what else one can make of a reference to 'purse trouble and the trouble which is a hundred times worse than all others — boy trouble' or to those arch references to a certain Cooper, 'The eclipse of dear Cooper distresses me — the good, sweet and amiable creature. With such a companion I would have experienced all the innocent delights of married life...' (25th June, 1808). There is also the record of his sympathy for those caught in the raid on the White Swan in Vere Street in 1810, 'Poor sods — what a fine ordeal, what a procession, what a pilgrimage, what a song and dance, what a rosary!' and for the wretched Eglerton, sentenced to be hanged for sodomy in 1816, 'I should like to know what deity they fancy they are placating with these shocking human sacrifices.'

If Beckford was a sexual fantasist, it is still possible that there was a period when, as psychologists put it, he worked these fantasies out, as he did those other dreams of his in the 'enchantment' of a transmuted building or a peculiarly elaborate fête. But what were his erotic fantasies? The answer, it seems to me, can be generally covered by the words childlike and 'Indian'. He yearned for *le paradis des amours enfantins* and he yearned for an exotic Eden. Behind these concepts one may discern something else, something much more difficult to be sure of: the degree to which a self-centred being, whom a sense of genius and of enormous wealth made consciously superior, was concerned with power – and power that could be used recklessly and destructively. In his oriental tales, notably the *Episodes of Vathek*, Beckford dealt with dark subjects: the homosexual relationship of two princes, Alasi and Firouz (later changed out of prudence to a girl, but a girl who wears male dress); the exploitation of one by the other, and finally their mutual damnation; the story of a murderous necrophiliac, a self-divided character who hardens from remorse to despair as he sinks into the Halls of Eblis; and an unfinished tale of a princess's unhealthy affection for her twin brother, who is an echo of both the youthful Beckford and of Courtenay and whose father is clearly the Alderman. If Beckford was aware of the sterility in certain human relationships and of a sense of fascinating doom, we know that he was equally fascinated by the stories of oriental despotism he read. And in his own life he could be despotic as he was with his elder daughter[1] or with the people in Jamaica to whom he had to return an estate illegally appropriated by his family sixty years before, and which he had razed of trees, crops and buildings before he gave it back. How far did his Caliph-like omnipotence or some doom-driven Satanism affect the childlike side of his character?

He had fallen in love with 'Kitty' when the boy was still a child. Children clearly attracted Beckford; when anticipating his first encounter with Policarpio's young friend, Gregorio Franchi, he commented that he had himself 'all the fancies and levity of a child'. There is certainly nothing coarse about his description of the twelve-year-old Mohammed in Madrid: 'I thought myself in a dream – nay, I still think myself so, and expect to wake. What is there in me to attract the affection of these infidels at first sight, I cannot imagine.' In view of this, the supposed assault, which would seem to have been buggery and which was discovered by 'Kitty's' cries or screams, strikes one as uncharacteristic; violence in a locked bedroom, rather than tenderness in an

[1] He disapproved of her Marriage to an impecunious soldier.

arbour, sounds thoroughly un-Beckfordian, although one must note Beckford's recent expression of fatherly sternness towards the boy's effeminacy, including a reference to the value of the rod at Westminster; and also his explanation of the incident between them to the family council, which was that 'Kitty' had been acting as a go-between for Charlotte's continuing passion towards him, had foolishly dropped an incriminating letter and was being *chastised* by Beckford for this stupidity! Furthermore, the event in itself was evidently not regarded as sufficiently grave to justify instant exposure: it took several weeks before 'Kitty' was induced to make some sort of confession.

Here we come back to the great Christmas party of 1781. Nothing in his life meant more to him than this. Sixty years later he wrote a lyrical description of it in the fly-leaves of a book: 'I seem even at this long distance to be warmed by the genial artificial light Loutherbourg [the stage designer at Drury Lane] had created throughout the whole of what absolutely appeared a necromantic region.' It was a house-party of youth, for the older members of the family were away; 'no fallen mouths or furrowed foreheads were permitted to meet our eye. Our society was extremely youthful and lovely to look upon.' And, as a winter fête, occurring at that season when the outside world relaxes its hold upon all but the most refined senses and even they must, through the creative mind and imagination, make a world of their own, when ice must be answered by fire and summers of southern perfection spun out of mirrors, carpets and hangings on the twin breaths of perfume and music and when, too, the naked simplicity of the landscape, sometimes misty and glimmering, sometimes defined in gauntly geometrical shapes, now stamped with the petrified nervous systems of trees and now transformed into the enlivening, light-refractive extravagance of frost and snow, promotes and secretly nourishes the re-birth of childhood affections, of the sense of wonder, of fantasies played out as Christmas charades – as such a winter fête it must appeal to us today as the ideal romantic occasion. Beckford spoke of serenity and geniality 'while all without was bleak and dark and howling'. Not for nothing do we remember that the last great romantic novel, Alain-Fournier's *Le Grand Meaulnes*, is concerned with the winter fête of children at the most remote of châteaux.

To this party Beckford invited Louisa, who told him it would be impolitic not to include her husband also, especially as he had other engagements and could not accept: 'He is in high spirits, surrounded by hounds, foxes, and foxhunters. Every hour of the day do I curse the

fetters which bind me to a being so unlike myself.' Her close friend
Sophia Musters, married but infatuated with Louisa's brother, George
Pitt, was asked too, as was Pitt himself. Then there were the Hamilton
cousins from Harrow, attended by their tutor, Henley. Beckford himself drove down with Cozens and the thirteen-year-old 'Kitty'. Later
he would write to Cozens: 'That night in particular haunts my imagination, when we arrived from Salisbury and seemed transported to a
warm illuminated palace raised by spells in some lonely wilderness.' In
several other letters he returned to this theme of enchanted arrival,
combined with the previous evening at Staines: 'Don't you remember
the soft tints that coloured the Thames...?' when Cozens had evidently
had a peculiarly important talk with 'Kitty', whose subject we do not
know.

These generally very youthful people were entertained by the
miraculous lighting-effects of the 'mystagogue', Count Loutherbourg,
although there was, of course, a place for 'gloom', and they were
soothed by surges of organ music, the lighter brilliance of orchestral
pieces, sometimes a chant and frequently the voices of Pacchiarotti,
Tenducci and Rauzzini (for once in amicable harmony) as the guests
wandered about, 'too often hand in hand', to pause by tables 'covered
with delicious consommations and tempting dishes, masked by the
fragrance of a bright mass of flowers, the heliotrope, the basil and the
rose' while incense poured up to the gilded vault in fragrant clouds. 'The
glowing haze, the mystic look, the endless intricacy of the vaulted
labyrinth produced an effect so bewildering that it became impossible
for anyone to define exactly where at the moment he was wandering —
so perplexing was the confusion so many different storeys and galleries
gave rise to. It was the realisation of romance in all its fervours, in all its
extravagance. The delirium of seductive influences may be conceived
but too easily.'

All this, with its 'innocent affecting sounds', appears harmless
enough; even the note of rebellion against an older generation is an
expected one. 'I seem already to hear the shrill pipings and whistlings
of an approaching storm...Let us seize the pleasuring hour, my beloved
Louisa. Let us enjoy uncontrolled delights before they are declared
High Treason.' On the other hand, there are stranger notes. 'Stay a
week — and then, Louisa, we must lie in wait for souls together' he had
written as preparations for the party went forward: Louisa copied the
letter but when he was covering his tracks Beckford seems to have torn
the pages out with the exception of this cryptic sentence. And her reply,

only partially obliterated, began: 'William—my lovely infernal! how gloriously you write of iniquities.' Subsequent to the party she continued to hint at certain practices or rites which involved the use of children. 'I wish to God my William (in this case her own son, then five years of age) was old enough for it. He grows every day more and more beautiful and will in time answer your purpose to perfection' (6th February, 1782) and again: 'Do you point out the victims. It shall be my care to lure them into your snares, and you shall find them at your return panting on your altars' (20th March) and once more: 'I honour your dauntless assurances, truly worthy of a descendant of the great Lucifer. Your apartment adorned with the youthful victims you have sacrificed on his altars may perhaps ere long be sanctified by his presence, where, transformed in the mystick shape of a goat, he will receive in person our adorations' (21st April). More than a year later she cried: 'Come then, my lovely Daemon, if you still wish me to follow you, and by your presence blow up in my soul the dying embers of Paganism.'

Did there exist behind the genial warmth, the elegant cosiness of those winter days at Splendens some sort of black magic, some attempt to use the vain and impressionable 'Kitty' in a mediumistic way? Doubtless the key is Cozens; it is significant that all his letters to Beckford were destroyed by their recipient. And it is just conceivable that Beckford, so brilliant and so rebellious, and possessed of wealth vast enough to carry out all the fantasies to which he was addicted, may have become obsessed with the idea of power: not power in the ordinary sense but power allied to his conception of genius (and genii) where sensuous and aesthetic appreciation tended always to cross the frontier into a magical 'India', and imagination sought not only to interpret the world but to control or change it. (One cannot help thinking here of Coleridge's dream poem *Kubla Khan*; serenity and fertility co-existent with Alpine aspects of the tremendous and the horrid, magic expressing itself in terms of anxiety and violence both in the chasm and in the fantastically elaborate palace, and the dreamer emerging as an awesome shaman-artist who can re-make the world. It is only a step or two to Rimbaud's concept of the seer.) Thus the Christmas party may suggest that the relations between Beckford and 'Kitty' contained a more savage element—in the sense that one manipulated the other as a victim—than one would guess from the sentimental effusions and paternal solicitude of most of the letters. In any case it shows the ease with which Beckford turned his reverie in St

Peter's into reality in Wiltshire. It, and the *Vathek* to which it gave rise, help to explain the more permanent fantasy embodied in the Abbey, while its mystery, its hints of the sinister, are perhaps reflected in certain curious, not otherwise quite explicable moments during the trip to the Portuguese monasteries.

If Beckford's friendship with 'Kitty' was to some degree criminal, whether by way of black magic or homosexual seduction (and the latter charge may not have been refuted because evidence existed for the former) he never seems to have felt the expected guilt. (A less specific guiltiness is manifested in the dreams he recounts and in his stories; he was also to feel regret for not having fulfilled his promise.) As we have seen, he looked back upon the Christmas of 1781 with the greatest tenderness. And, now that he was ruined, he dismissed his little friend with the utmost contempt. In October, 1784, before the scandal came out into the open, he had written to Henley that 'Wm., poor wretch, is more to be pitied than any reptile that crawls the earth, and is mangled, bruised and smashed every day' but in February of the following year he told the same correspondent that 'a certain young person I once thought my friend has proved himself the meanest traitor and blackest enemy. You may guess who pulled the wires and made this miserable puppet dance to its destruction.'

IV

BECKFORD was a fighter and remarkably resilient. He could fall back on his writing; he did so in the winter after the scandal broke and, when he and his wife had finally fled to Switzerland, he concerned himself with the French publication of *Vathek* in the original text and tried to ensure that Henley's translation should not precede it and its accompanying Episodes, one problem being that the only manuscript of *Vathek* was in Henley's hands. He was still working on the *Episodes*, successors to the first oriental tale. In May, 1786, Lady Margaret died after giving birth to a second daughter. The English press renewed its attacks, suggesting that she had been the victim of a broken heart, but this time they were forced to withdraw and apologise while a body of the notables of Vevey prepared a testimonial to Beckford's treatment of her. For months he was disconsolate. And there was the further blow that Henley ignored his wishes and published *Vathek* with the implication that it was actually taken from an ancient manuscript and not an original work of the imagination, followed by various hints that, in so far as any contemporary authorship was concerned, the pen was Henley's. Beckford set himself all the more vigorously to ensuring the best possible French edition.

After slipping back briefly to England, Beckford planned a long trip to his estates in Jamaica or, if the climate proved too exacting, the colonies on the mainland although, perhaps, in the end, Madeira would be more pleasant. Lord Loughborough's malignity made it impossible for him to remain in England. Only the roughness of the sea forced him ashore at Lisbon. He arrived in Portugal by accident. He was to stay there between March and December of 1787 (when he left for Spain), to return in the autumn of 1793 and not leave again until October, 1795, and to pay a final visit from the end of 1798 to July, 1799. During his periods of exile abroad he also spent much time in Switzerland and Paris. Intermittently he returned to England where the great project of building Fonthill Abbey became more and more an obsession. In 1790 his idea had been no more than a romantic ruin; by 1796 it had developed into the project for an enormous residence.

Beckford's writing on Portugal is, as one would expect, far less concerned with his personal fantasies than the previous book. His pages are crowded with incident; he is constantly making expeditions to convents and *quintas*, where dusk no longer obscures the sculptures and decorations. He is also surrounded by people: languid, eccentric, aristocrats and clerics of every description, all of them held in the ornate, mellow, somewhat tarnished and even slightly ridiculous frame of a cohesive community, all of them faintly shadowed by forces he allows to remain enigmatic but which have evidently something to do with politics and religion; something crumbling, something catastrophic, the earthquake, the wreck of the Pombal regime, the dangers from Spain and France, the fact that Queen Maria I is sinking into imbecility.

Lisbon is loud with howling dogs, stung by clouds of dust, full of innumerable steps and stairs, 'a succession of villages awkwardly tacked together, and overpowered by massive convents'. Bells ring out, cannons roar, litanies are bellowed, and the rockets of yet another religious festival whizz by one's ear: some 'pompous' ceremony, no doubt, which brings this 'beastly mob of old hags, children and ragamuffins' beneath the windows, not to speak of those negroes in scarlet jackets and blowing French horns with unusual vehemence. No wonder the devout but sensitive tourist is inclined to sigh, 'I have had pretty nearly my fill of motets, and Kyrie eleisons, and incense, and

sweetmeats, and sermons'. Music of course is everywhere, although
not all of it is to Beckford's taste; at a royal party he can hear 'a sonata
on the dulcimer, accompanied on the jew's harp by a couple of dwarfs'
but the sonata is not his favourite form of music as is proved when a
doctor starts thumping his poor pianoforte—'a tall knock-kneed,
rhubarb-faced physician, in a gorgeous suit of glistening satin, one of
the most ungainly, conceited professors of the art of murdering'—and he
notices that this playing is scarcely improved by the toad-eating fiddler
who assists, since 'certain chromatic, squeaking tones of a fiddle, when
the performer turns up the whites of his eyes, wriggles a greasy chin,
and affects ecstasies, set my teeth on edge'. In any case he prefers
Haydn or Jommelli although, to be sure, he is becoming an addict to
modinhas from Brazil: 'Those who have never heard this original sort
of music, must and will remain ignorant of the most bewitching
melodies that ever existed since the days of the Sybarites. They consist
of languid interrupted measures, as if the breath was gone with excess
of rapture, and the soul panting to meet the kindred soul of some
beloved object. With a childish carelessness they steal into the heart,
before it has time to arm itself against their enervating influence; you
fancy you are swallowing milk, and are admitting the poison of
voluptuousness into the closest recesses of your existence.' If this
sounds a trifle sinister, he is also much affected by the singing of a
young girl at the Angeja Palace who, having mastered the technique
of Ferracuti, nevertheless 'gives a simplicity of expression to the most
difficult passages, that makes them appear the effusions of a young
romantic girl warbling to herself in the secret recesses of the forest.'
Infinitely preferable, this, to all the noise of Lisbon in June: 'The heat
seems not only to have new venomed the stings of fleas and mosquitoes,
but to have drawn out, the whole night long, all the human ephemerals
of Lisbon. They frisk, and dance, and tinkle their guitars from sunset
to sunrise.'

But how admirably the scene enables him to employ those gifts of
wit and irony, that elegant turn of phrase, which the years of misunderstanding and now of abuse have forged and tempered. How well
he conveys the vacuity of a court where the men spend half their time
looking out of the windows, 'their eyes wandering from object to
object, with a stare of royal vacancy'. How amusingly he evokes a
dozen little vices, the greed of 'five or six hags of supreme quality', for
instance, 'feeding like cormorants upon a variety of high-coloured and
high-seasoned dishes' or the frailty of that leading ecclesiastic, the

Archbishop-Confessor and Grand Inquisitor himself, as he too stands at a window of the palace: 'I am told the Confessor, although somewhat advanced in his career, is far from being insensible to the allurements of beauty, and pursues the young nymphs of the palace from window to window with juvenile alacrity.' How sharply he winces at the 'hypocritical cant' of many a 'seraphic discourse' launched in his direction. 'The whites of their eyes alone were visible, nor could Whitfield himself, the original Doctor Squintum...have squinted more scientifically.' Language can catch them all, from the groups to the individuals, from 'many strange, aboriginal figures of both sexes were assembled' to 'a little square friar, with greenish eyes' or 'a lay-brother, fat, round, buffoonical, and to the full as coarse and vulgar as any carter or muleteer' or indeed the Viceroy of Algarve himself, whose 'flow of eloquence was accompanied by the strangest, most buffoonical grimaces and slobberings I ever beheld, for the Viceroy having a perennial moistness of the mouth, drivels at every syllable.' Here is the Brazilian wife, fubsical and squat, of a nobleman of Irish extraction: 'Poor soul! to be sure, she is neither a Venus nor a Hebe, has a rough lip, and a manly voice, and I fear is somewhat inclined to be dropsical; but her smiles are frequent and fondling and she cleaves to her husband with great perseverance.'

And here is the touch of exotic poetry we have come to expect. It refers to the retinue of the old Marquis[1] of Marialva, the gourmandising and clock-loving father of Beckford's particular friend, just returned from a pilgrimage across the Tagus: 'He was hardly out of hearing before a confused rabble of watermen and servants with bird-cages, lanterns, baskets of fruit, and chaplets of flowers, came gambolling along to the great delight of a bevy of children; who, to look more like the inhabitants of Heaven than even Nature designed, had light fluttering wings attached to their rose-coloured shoulders. Some of the little theatrical angels were extremely beautiful, and had their hair most coquettishly ararnged in ringlets.' Innocence and irony are delicately mingled.

For that matter, his ability to build up an ironic picture, this time in a single sentence, is well-illustrated in his description of the sermon of a certain Fra João Jacinto who possessed a loud voice, 'great powers of elocution' and none of the usual 'canting nasal whine' (the mockery and the praise are almost equally distributed). The words following remind one of Logan Pearsall Smith: 'He treated kings, tetrarchs, and conquerors, the heroes and sages of antiquity, with ineffable contempt;

[1] More properly Marquez.

Belem Monastery

Sicilian Lettica by A. J. Strutt

The Road to Italy

reduced their palaces and fortifications to dust, their armies to pismires, their imperial vestments to cobwebs, and impressed all his audience, except the heretical squinters at the door, with the most thorough conviction of St Anthony's superiority over those objects of an erring and impious admiration.'

Parties and expeditions are endless: people are always ringing at Beckford's door ('This set shan't catch me at home again in a hurry') and some of these are foreign residents or even members of the British Factory, although behind the scenes of the published Portuguese Travel-Letters, as evidenced in the Journal, Beckford was far more disgruntled because of his rejection by the British Minister. Frequently he escaped to the countryside, of course: to the sea-shore at Belem and the nearby convent of San José de Ribamar; to Cintra, where he was lent the Quinta da Ramalhão, importing almost immediately a flock of sheep from Fonthill, replenishing the garden, assembling also a sextet of musicians to play in his lantern room. (In 1794 he would build his own house at the mouth of the Tagus and have for country retreat another Cintra villa, that of Monserrate, whose garden became even more famous.) Cintra produced the usual exclamations of delight: 'The scenery is truly Elysian,' 'Never did I behold so fine a day or a sky of such lovely azure'; he wanders amongst odiferous bay-trees, crooked corks, 'hanging shrubberies of arbutus, bay and myrtle', 'almonds, plum, and cherry, something like the groves of Tonga-Taboo, as represented in Cook's voyages'; he notices some capillaries and polypodiums of infinite delicacy: he is enchanted—as what southern traveller is not?— by stands of cane whose 'fresh green leaves, agitated by the feeblest wind, form a perpetual murmur'. On the precipitous coast near the village of Collares he comes upon a cave: 'The tide was beginning to ebb, and allowed us, not without some risk however to pass into a cavern of surprising loftiness, the sides of which were encrusted with beautiful limpets, and a variety of small shells grouped together. Against some rude and porous fragments, not far from the aperture through which we had crept, the waves swell with violence, rush into the air, form instantaneous canopies of foam, then fall down in a thousand trickling rills of silver. The flickering gleams of light thrown upon irregular arches admitting into darker and more retired grottoes, the mysterious, watery gloom, the echoing murmurs and almost musical sounds, occasioned by the conflict of winds and waters, the strong odour of an atmosphere composed of saline particles, produced altogether such a bewildering effect upon the senses, that I can easily

5

conceive a mind, poetically given, might be thrown into that kind of tone which inclines to the belief of supernatural appearances. I am not surprised, therefore, at the credulity of the ancients, and only wonder my own imagination did not deceive me in a similar manner.'

This passage seems to reach forward to the careful observation of Gerard Manley Hopkins' note-books while also retaining something of the 'scientific' atmosphere ('porous fragments...saline particles') to be found here and there in James Thomson's *Seasons*.

Other passages, equally good, deal with more characteristic subjects. There is for instance (in Letter XXIV of 29th August, 1787) the description of the cheerful funeral. An 'old consumptive English-woman', living at an inn in Sintra kept by 'a most flaming Irish Catholic', has undergone a deathbed conversion, which is 'a rapturous story' indeed. Although Beckford has no great taste for funerals, so gay an occasion obviously demands his presence. All is excitement in the room of the aged innocent. 'Acciaoli, whom I was before acquainted with, skipped about the room, rubbing his hands for joy, with a cunning leer on his jovial countenance, and snapping his fingers at Satan as much as to say, "I don't care a d--n for you. We have got one at least safe out of your clutches, and clear at this very moment of the smoke of your cauldrons." ' The humour is increased by the fact that some of those attending are really pretty sickened by the nearness of death, and not least the Grand Prior of Aviz, illegitimate brother of the senior Marquis of Marialva and Beckford's companion in the later visit to the monasteries. He has little relish for his position at the head of the open coffin with 'the corpse, dressed in virgin-white, lying snug in a sort of rose-coloured bandbox, with six silvered handles'; as for the younger Marquis of Marialva, he is red to the ears with disgust. Furthermore, rumour has it that the defunct lady had by no means suffered 'the cup of joy to pass untasted in this existence' but had 'lived many years on a very easy footing, not only with a stout English bachelor, but with several others, married and unmarried, of his particular acquaintance.' Nevertheless 'all the bells of Sintra struck up a cheerful peal and to their merry jinglings we hurried along through a dense cloud of dust, a rabble of children frolicking on either side, and their grandmothers hobbling after, telling their beads, and grinning from ear to ear at the triumph over the prince of darkness.'

In a priest-ridden state ecclesiastics and their devout adherents provide most of the humour. A notable absentee at this funeral is that hopeful young nobleman, the Conde de Vila Nova, who can be seen in all weathers, night and day, ringing his bell before the Sacrament as it is processed to some dying person. 'He is always in close attendance upon the Host, and passes the flower of his days in this singular species of danglement. No lover was ever more zealous of his mistress than this ingenious youth of his bell. He cannot endure any other person should give it vibration.' Not that flesh isn't frail. That young Bishop of Algarve, now, (brought up by the most Jansenistical of bigots) is discovered, when Beckford goes to take breakfast with the Marquis of Penalva, seated on the ground *à la façon de Batavie*, amongst a positive harem of senhoras, his 'small black, sleek, schoolboyish head and sallow countenance...overshadowed by an enormous pair of green spectacles. Truth obliges me to confess that the expression which beamed from the eyes under these formidable glasses, did not absolutely partake of the most decent, mild, or apostolic character.'

This humour extends to the miraculous. There are the Holy Crows at Lisbon, direct descendants of the birds who pursued the murderers of St Vincent and tore out their eyes, and now roosting in a cloister of the cathedral: 'O how plump and sleek, and glossy they are! My admiration of their size, their plumage, and their deep-toned croakings carried me, I fear, beyond the bounds of saintly decorum. I was just stretching out my hand to stroke their feathers, when the missionary checked me with a solemn forbidding look...' And later, at the Escurial in Spain, he will be given a glimpse of a bird of an altogether different colour. 'Forth stalked the prior, and drawing out from a remarkably large cabinet an equally capacious sliding shelf—(the source, I conjecture, of the potent odour I complained of)—displayed lying stretched out upon a quilted silken mattress, the most glorious specimen of plumage ever beheld in terrestrial regions—a feather from the wing of the Archangel Gabriel, full three feet long, and of a blushing hue more soft and delicate than that of the loveliest rose. I longed to ask at what precise moment this treasure beyond price had been dropped—whether from the air—on the open ground, or within the walls of the humble tenement at Nazareth; but I repressed all questions of an indiscreet tendency—the why and wherefore, the when and how, for what and to whom such a palpable manifestation of archangelic beauty and wingedness had been vouchsafed.'

The Portuguese Letters (which begin with a most amusing introductory account of days spent becalmed at Falmouth) have an obvious advantage over those from Italy. Instead of moving rapidly from place to place Beckford is able to saturate himself in the atmosphere and customs of a single small country which happens to be in an interesting state of decay. Characters start emerging and the narrator himself, no longer *un promeneur solitaire*, allows himself to be seen basking in a good deal of popularity. Like the Caliph or the English Baron he wanted to be, he is a figure of importance, invited by the Archbishop-Confessor to the most private, and rare, of luncheons (in reality it was probably an interview, friendly but brief), confided in by courtiers and diplomats, and granted the privilege of a mysterious meeting with the Prince Regent, Dom José, which is probably imaginary but is none the less convincing, especially as it makes the Regent appear to be an earnest bore. Instead of finding his classical reading echoed in Italy, as thousands of travellers have done, or attempting to link sunny landscapes with vague, oriental dreams, he can master Portugal, which he generally enjoys but sometimes dislikes. Occasionally lyrical and dream-like it is also a busy, intriguing, comical place and it seems the right background for a whimsical millionaire artist who enjoys possessing a certain amount of power but who can't really, scandal or no, pretend to be either a politician or a leader of country squires.

The omissions in the published letters remind us of how skilful a writer Beckford is, for he has created a good book despite the exclusion of almost all its plot. The reader who enjoys his Portugal and Spain will almost certainly wish to turn to the original *Journal*, although here too a good deal of excision and emendation has taken place, including the writing-up years afterwards of notes made on the spot. It is indeed a question which is the better book; and for those who like their Beckford in an undressed, conversational style worthy of Byron, and who can appreciate the ease with which now, at twenty-seven, he handles his foibles and eccentricities, the *Journal* may be preferable to the more polished work. Much of the material, of course, is shared by both.

The omitted 'plot' concerns two subjects which are to some extent inter-related. First, there is his struggle to 'kiss Queen Maria's hand' by persuading the British Minister, Robert Walpole, to present him in the way prescribed by diplomatic etiquette. His flamboyant piety wins him the notice and soon the admiration of the powerful Marialva family; the 'young' Marquis, Diogo, who is twenty-one years older than himself, forms a strangely deep attachment to him and prosecutes his cause with energy. A favourite of the Queen, and Master of the Horse, Marialva quickly secures Beckford's acceptance by most of the aristocracy and also stimulates a good deal of unofficial but benevolent interest in Royal circles. It is Marialva who arranges a meeting with

Mello, the Pombal-trained and anti-clerical, anti-traditionalist Prime Minister, whose diplomatic smoothness and insincerity cause Beckford to leave in a rage: 'I dashed into my carriage and whirled off in a twinkling', to which he adds characteristically: 'It is amazing how I enjoy getting into scrapes. To me a scrape is like a dram. It raises my spirits and brightens my imagination' (1st July, 1787). Marialva also tries to ensure that the Portuguese Ambassador in London win over the British Government, supported as he will surely be by representations from Beckford's family. He hopes, too, that Beckford may marry his daughter, Dona Henriqueta, a girl of fifteen unofficially engaged to the sixty-eight-year-old Duke of Lafoẽs, the 'Uncle to the Queen', and he even toys with the idea that one of Beckford's baby daughters should be affianced to his son, Dom Pedro. Indeed, why doesn't Beckford renounce Britain altogether, embrace the Catholic faith and become a Portuguese Duke?—a suggestion which brings out all Beckford's homesickness for the pines and lawns of Fonthill. 'It is too hot for fairies in Portugal.' When all these plans fail Beckford decides to leave.

Beckford's final comment on the Marialvas (17th October) is kindly, if egocentric: 'How grieved I am to quit this family. Not a blot in their conduct to me, affectionate, open, and disinterested.' Nevertheless he found the Marquis's attentions a trifle oppressive, 'The happiness of his life seems to consist in being with me' (5th August), while his intellectual range was far from wide, 'Here every night my great friend the Marquis bores me with zealous perseverance, and repeats the same professions of regard for my person, and zeal for the salvation of my soul' (16th July). Both father and son strike him as too frequently inactive and listless, with no proper occupation, 'I am worn to a skeleton with doing nothing…Not a book to be seen at the Marialvas', they never ever read' (17th July).

Yet, at the same time, Beckford shows a steady interest in Dom Pedro, Dona Henriqueta's fifteen-year-old brother. At one moment he is 'the proudest youth that ever sat by me, but I will humble him if Saint Anthony gives me health and spirits' (15th June); at the next they are dancing minuets: 'I could not help thinking how certain acquaintances of mine in England would laugh could they have seen me and a young boy of the first distinction, educated with more severity than anyone in Portugal, languishing away in a minuet and never taking our eyes off each other' — but then 'my singing, playing and capering subdues every Portuguese' (17th June); at a third he is taken by Dom

Pedro's 'serious and melancholy disposition', now further darkened by their visit to a Carthusian convent; and then again he declares: 'This wretch D. Pedro has infected me', for the deserted garden at Marvila is melancholy too, immediately upon which 'we filled the carriage with flowering sprays of jasmine pulled from mutilated statues, and we were all half intoxicated before we reached home with the delicious but overcoming fragrance. We found tea very refreshing...' (22nd June). Dom Pedro can be 'a sickly child' or 'the dismallest child I ever saw' or simply not a child at all. Then (25th July) 'He begins to grow childish and engaging' while two days later at the Cork convent, 'D. Pedro and I scampered madly home over the rough craggy pavement'. In late October they are both 'wild with spirits' for Beckford has given a party, everyone has got rather drunk and 'He loves me. I have tasted the sweetness of his lips; his dear eyes have confessed the secret of his bosom' (22nd October). However, the boy soon shows signs that he is not exclusively submissive to the whims of his admirer. Guzzling arbutus berries he appears not to mind that the Queen's requiring his presence countermands their evening together. 'I abhor from my soul such passive characters, and will attempt at least tearing out by the roots my affection for D. Pedro' (25th October). And Beckford gallops off.

The quest for Dom Pedro was accompanied, of course, by Beckford's appreciation of Gregorio Franchi, so gifted and so admiring, and here again the emphasis lies on the child-like, playful quality in affection. The first note is one of caution: 'I shall get into a scrape, if I don't care. How tired I am of keeping a Mask on my face. How tight it sticks – it makes me sore', but he soon grows freer: 'I think his eyes are grown larger than ever, and fix themselves so inveterately upon me that I cannot help colouring...These Portuguese youths are composed of more inflammable materials than other mortals. I could keep them spellbound for hours at my side, listening to the childish notes of my voice, and dissolving like snow in sunshine' (1st July). Or shortly afterwards, 'I returned home exactly at eight and passed the remainder of the even pleasantly enough in hearing Gregorio Franchi, who takes me to be not much older than himself, and imagines that I shall soon lose the high clear notes of my voice. I could not help smiling at this notion, but I am not surprised at it. My movements, gestures, attitudes become, whenever I please, as careless, sportive and supple as those of a child' (3rd July). This sort of attitude is expressed elsewhere towards Marialva's nephew, 'a lovely boy of thirteen' who finds him 'more youthful and condescending than he expected' (15th June). Such characters, who must not be 'passive', unless in relation to Beckford, can be soft and dreamy. 'I am extremely partial to youths who play on the harpsichord. 'Tis a sweet, soothing, effeminate employment' (12th November).

What emerges more clearly than in any other of his writings is Beckford's childlike vivacity, exuberance and nervous energy. He sings to his musician friends, he plays the piano for hours, he dances, he reads his mail on horseback, he jumps into cold tubs, and romps and 'courses' with children, scampers over rocks and retires to read Theocritus or to turn over albums of prints. Admittedly he is often bored. 'Feeling dull and spiritless I had recourse to the cold bath', ' 'Tis a wonder I do not expire with ennui, the life I lead is so stupid and uniform' and 'I rise, gape about me, wipe the dust off my books, receive begging epistles and sweetmeats from convents, dash into a tub of cold water...' On the other hand, he cannot hear a minuet 'without gliding about the room and throwing myself into theatrical attitudes'. He wonders why he sometimes behaves badly: visiting those 'good folks', the family of Paul Jorge, 'I know not what the deuce was the matter with me, but I spun round two or three times on my heel, and gave myself a thousand tosses, complained of heat and cold, wind and dust, and after a quarter of an hour's sidling and fidgetting left the whole family.' What motive could he have had? They must have thought him 'one of the proudest and most conceited puppies in the universe' (19th June). Puppy-like he abandons himself to physical movement: 'I kept cutting *entrechats à huit* and leaping over chairs and tables without intermission' when the Marquis arrives, shouts Bravo! and himself begins to caper (8th July). On the 20th August there is a strange scene in his lantern-like room at Ramalhão. The lamps and lustres are sparkling, Franchi is flourishing away at the pianoforte, Dr Verdeil is explaining Hogarth to the Marquis, the Abbade Xavier is snoozing and Beckford, too, falls into a deep reverie about Cozens and Lady Margaret. 'I woke from my trance in tears, and to dissipate the impression it left upon me, began dancing and coursing along the galleries. Marialva, who is never behindhand in any sort of exercise, followed my example. We hopped on one leg, leaped over handkerchiefs held four feet from the floor, and amused ourselves like schoolboys with these fooleries. Franchi must have thought it rare sport to be playing so familiarly with the Marquez *Estribeiro-mor* (Grand Master of Horse) and the *Fidalgo Rico* (Rich Gentleman).' I cannot recall any other writer having revealed so charmingly and gaily what is one side of certain refined and sometimes homosexual temperaments: sheer childish high spirits freely and inventively displayed.

The *Journal* is valuable for other things too. It shows, for instance, how much Beckford associated with other foreigners, people with plebeian names including members of the English Factory (the association of English merchants) such as Thomas Horne, his banker and agent, with whom there was a coolness for a time, and the two Miss Sills, Betty and Sophia, and 'poor old Collett', a martyr to rheumatism but so keenly interested in Beckford's not giving up his connection with England, and a certain old toothless Mr Connolly, and 'slender-waisted, wild-eyed' Miss Staits, 'by no means unpleasing or flinty-hearted', not to speak of the less desirable expatriates, a Mrs Aik (or Hake), the mistress of Mr Burn, dealer in cod-fish, and that 'fussocky' Presbyterian merchantess who is so named below. He often took his evening drive when he was at Lisbon with Thomas Horne, or visited his villa, and he also enjoyed the entertainments at the Dutch Consul's establishment, where Madame Gildemeester was a cut above the rest (with her French lover and her two toad-eating ladies, the toad active and the toad passive) and certainly enjoyed a 'slashing conversation'. It was at Miss Staits's party for 'all the Scrubs and Scrubesses of the English nation at Cintra' on the 22nd of August that Beckford, depressed by the dingy illuminations and the cadaverous smell of a dish of rotten prawns, addressed Mme Gildemeester in accents again not unsimilar to those of a Logan Pearsall Smith. ' "Alas!" said I to Mrs Gildemeester, "it is all over with us now, this is our first banquet in the infernal regions, we are all equalled and jumbled to-gether. There sits the pious Presbyterian Mrs Fussock and close to her those adulterous doves Mr Burn and his sultana. Here am I, miserable sinner, right opposite your righteous and much-enduring spouse, a little lower than our kind host, that pattern of conjugal meekness and resignation. Hark! Don't you hear a thumping noise? They are letting down a cargo of fat souls into a neighbouring tomb." '

This is Beckford in undress, willing to admit that 'blessed be the salts of Epsom', to sigh over 'a vile beverage of salts and rhubarb' and to be concerned about a 'cursed corn' which Dr Verdeil, his Swiss physician-friend, cuts away. His language is livelier than in the pub-lished book. There sonata-players set his teeth on edge, here it is his guts. He confesses 'I have written myself muzzy'. He has 'a new coat that stinks of the tailor enough to poison me'. He is alarmed because 'my bile is in a ferment, I squitter and feel the giddiness and nausea of sea-sickness'. He is furious with his *chef* because Verdeil and he sit down to 'a dish of cloth soup, wizzled chicken and flabby turbot'. He gives common-sensical information: 'I should think the Portuguese tolerably ingenious in making fireworks', and grows earthily observant, as when Verdeil 'remained at the entrance to the church, scraping the dirt of his boots against the angular bend of a Gothic column', and he even mentions money: 'Every day I remain at Lisbon costs me at least four guineas in mule money.'

V

IN THE *Letters* and the *Journal* we can see the background to the *Visit To The Monasteries*. Just as they contracted breathless rambling and 'jumbling' into the experience of a single country, so the final master-piece adds the discipline of time; the whole book covers only twelve days, from 3rd June, 1794, to 14th June. Sandwiched between the grandest of opening sentences, which declares that the trip was taken at the suggestion of Dom João, the new Prince Regent, and the most satisfactorily important, if mysterious, of conclusions, when Beckford has an audience with this same Regent and also overhears the screams of the lunatic monarch, the journey perambulates from *quinta* to con-vent, from vineyard to fishing-party, from siestas too prolonged for Beckford's energetic temperament to sumptuous banquets followed by stiff masculine minuets or hoydenish masculine plays. The background is spun out of many different threads: the glories of past history, represented in the grandeur and extravagance of architecture and decoration, but darkened here and there by memories of the tyrannical Pombal and threatened anew by French rationalism and the utilitarian concept of Man; the strange world of priests and monks and novices, at once extravagant in piety, 'pompous' in ceremonial, self-indulgent in practice (what with sharks'-fin soup from Macao, curries from Goa, music from Brazil) and beset by the grotesqueness of obsession as well as the prevalence of secret sins; and the atmosphere of the hot Portu-guese landscape with its orchards and grottoes, perfumes and nightin-gales, cypresses, corks and bays.

Into this background Beckford weaves his two ecclesiastical con-ductors, the indolent and timid Grand Prior of Aviz (Marialva's illegitimate uncle) and the ruddy-faced, effervescent Prior of San Vicente who takes charge of many of the arrangements; Franchi is

5*

there too, high-spirited enough under the influence of the Aljubarota wine to gallop and fall off and later to imitate the cuckoo, loudly, wantonly, in the presence of a lady who is not amused; and Beckford's French *chef*, M. Simon (*o grande Simão*) who makes a conquest of all the gourmandisers with his *omelette à la provençale*; and, since Verdeil has returned to Switzerland, a new medical man, Dr Errhardt, who enjoys a visit to the Infirmary, where he encounters a magnificent ulcer, with the same guttural gusto as everything else.

They were slow to start from Beckford's *quinta* at S. José de Ribamar at the mouth of the Tagus. 'We formed altogether a caravan which, camels and dromedaries excepted, would have cut no despicable figure even on the route of Mecca or Meschad-Ali.' The Grand Prior was the problem. In the earlier books Beckford had written of him with considerable fondness, praising his diligence in good works, appreciating his love of the ruined gardens at Marvila and even saying that he had a liking for the sun. Perhaps seven years had changed him. He was now the perennial source of comedy because of his dilatoriness, dread of any activity and terror of the heat. 'It was settled he should loll in his dormeuse or in my chaise just as he best pleased, and look at nothing calculated to excite the fatigue of reflection; topographical inquiries were to be waived completely, and no questions asked about who endowed such a church or raised such a palace. We are to proceed, or rather creep along, by short and facile stages, stopping to dine, and sup, and repose, as delectably as in the most commodious of homes.' Already, as Beckford handed him out of the old Marquis of Marialva's 'most sleepifying dormeuse', the Grand Prior was querulous. Had Errhardt got his medicine-chest? Had Franchi his pianoforte? And, oh dear, the chaise horses were snorting so, because of the nearness of Beckford's English mare...It was difficult for Beckford to stop this dawdling. They were not, he reminded them, setting out to explore the Kingdom of Prester John.

That night they stopped at the Prior of San Vicente's *quinta* at Tojal, 'half village, half hermitage'. The Grand Prior would not move again for two whole days. On the first, largely occupied by a fishing-party in the Trancão and an evening drive to the over-elaborate palace of the Patriarchal, Beckford enjoyed a siesta under a bay tree, 'one of the grandest objects of the vegetable world...clothed with luxurious boughs that glistened with health and vigour...I loitered away the sultry hours of midday most pleasantly under its deep, fragrant shade'. On the second, 'this superiorly fine and glowing morning', he over-

heard a violent altercation between the Grand Prior's secretary and San
Vicente's attendant, about the old man's laziness: 'his excellency has
made up his mind to take his fill of repose'. While agreeing that 'if ever
a decent excuse could be offered for perfect laziness, it was to be found
in the warm, enervating atmosphere, loaded with perfume, which
universally invested this pleasant umbrageous region', Beckford was
forced to admit that the Grand Prior was 'the most consummate
professor of "il dolce far niente" in all Portugal'. They had a picnic
breakfast by the river but he could 'hardly even be persuaded to
traverse a short avenue' leading to a pavilion on its bank and, despite
San Vicente's and Beckford's enthusiasm for eating on the grass, he
insisted on tables and chairs. Nevertheless the day was 'all warmth, and
chat, and idleness'.

On June 6th, the sky being now overcast, they travelled as far as
Cadafaiz. 'The wide latticed windows of the apartment allotted to me
commanded a view of a boundless vineyard in full luxuriant leaf,
divided by long broad tracts of thyme and camomile, admirably well
kept and nicely weeded' together with apricot trees from Damascus
and other orchards, all surrounded by hills and rocks. 'How often...did
I bless the hour when my steps were directed to Portugal!' On the fifth
day, after some difficulty with the carriages, they came in sight of
Alcobaça: 'The first sight of this regal monastery is very imposing; and
the picturesque, well-wooded and well-watered village, out of the
quiet bosom of which it appears to rise, relieves the mind from a sense
of oppression the huge domineering bulk of the conventual buildings
inspire.' Four hundred persons were drawn up to welcome them. 'It
was quite delectable to witness with what cooings and comfortings the
Lord Abbot of Alcobaça greeted his right reverend brethren of Aviz
and St Vincent's — turtle-doves were never more fondlesome, at least
in outward appearance.' The ecclesiastics went to worship; Beckford
repaired to the sepulchral chapel and it was there, in the midst of
'affecting reveries', that the three Priors broke in upon him. ' "To the
kitchen," they said in perfect unison — "to the kitchen, and that
immediately; you will then judge whether we have been wanting in
zeal to regale you".' This kitchen proved to be one of the climaxes of
the tour, although even its denizens would bow before the superior
genius of Beckford's M. Simon. It was, 'I verily believe, the most
distinguished temple of gluttony in all Europe...my eyes never beheld
in any modern convent of France, Italy or Germany, such an enormous
space devoted to culinary purposes.' A central rivulet was full of fish;

to one side rose loads of game and venison, to the other vegetables and fruit 'in endless variety' together with 'hillocks of wheaten flour whiter than any snow, rocks of sugar, jars of the purest oil, and pastry in vast abundance', which the lay brothers were pulling as they sang 'as blithely as larks in a corn-field'. Beckford was duly impressed. ' "There," said the Lord Abbot, "we shall not starve: God's bounties are great, it is fit we should enjoy them." ' But before the feast Beckford was shown to his room and his description of its mixture of simplicity and magnificence, especially the tables encased in rich velvet petticoats, enables his readers to join him in relaxation and anticipation: we identify as we read. He 'took a foot-bath as serenely as if I had been at Abraham's tent-door, and waited in a perfect refreshing calm till three thundering knocks at the outward portal announced the Abbot himself coming to lead me to the banquet-hall.'

It would be tempting to tell the whole of the story but one feels that the reader will wish to discover some things for himself. To indicate the flavour of this short work, to emphasise the brilliance with which Beckford builds up an incident here, a character there, is perhaps all that should be attempted. The next morning, for instance, the Grand Prior had a hangover but San Vicente 'made tea as skilfully as the most complete old dowager in Christendom'. Then the expedition continued. Batalha was a poorer monastery than Alcobaça and its monks watched with envious admiration 'whilst our sumpter-mules were unloading, and ham and pies and sausages were rolling out of plethoric hampers', not to mention the Grand Prior's gauze-curtained bed and fringed pillow, or San Vicente's superb coverlet. 'My more fortunate companions—no wretched cadets of the mortification family, but the true elder sons of fat mother church—could hardly conceal the sneers of conscious superiority.' Batalha produced two oddities; a senile patriot overcome with the glories of the past and the contents of a huge silver goblet, who was carried out from their enormous supper, 'chair and all, weeping, puking, and more than drivelling, with such maudlin tenderness that he actually marked his track with a flow of liquid sorrows'; and a prophetic night-walker, victim of Pombal's tyranny, who interrupted the song of a nightingale with his 'loud but melancholy voice' echoing through the arched avenues of a vast garden, *Woe to Portugal! Woe! Woe!*

Back at Alcobaça on June 9th, the seventh day, they partook of a meal memorable even amongst such a succession of masterpieces. It included 'a certain truffle cream so exquisite, that my Lord Abbot forestalled the usual grace at the termination of repasts, most piously to give thanks for it.' Errhardt arrived late, full of enthusiasm for something he had seen at the Infirmary: 'a sweet, simple perennial sore... which had contrived during a series of years to ebb and flow as regularly as the ocean'. Afterwards they attended an excruciating performance of *Dona Inez de Castro*, the heroine being played by 'one of the most ungain hobbledehoys I ever met with—no cow bereaved of her last-dropped young one ever uttered sounds more doleful...' Indeed Franchi had tried to persuade the youth to dispense with some of his female trappings, those ear-rings and that unmanageable train, but 'anything in the shape of metropolitan criticism wounded the awkward stripling's provincial amour-propre so deeply, that he threatened hysterics and an appeal to the Lord Abbot.'

Soon after, Beckford having made a return visit to Batalha by himself, they started home. Their journey seems now to have had a fantastic, at times a surrealist quality; to the sly lyricism of Ronald Firbank must be added the symbolic dream-world of Jean Cocteau. While the general tone remains light and playful, dark shadows and enigmatic depths appear between the brilliantly illuminated objects. Thus the Priors accused the Abbot of certain sexual irregularities in his establishment, a fact which mitigated the poignancy of his loss of M. Simon. Then, on their way, they were mysteriously summoned to the *quinta* of the Bird Lady, an eccentric crone devoted to kites, owls and buzzards as well as to peacocks and birds of paradise: an experience which hovered between the lyrical and the ludicrous. At one moment Beckford was delighted at 'one of the strangest scenes in fairyland' with the 'strange green light' glowing around arcaded parterres each containing a cage and a fountain, the whole effect being soft, perfumed and voluptuous; at the next the quaintness of the villa struck him, and also of the lady's three nephews of fourteen, fifteen and sixteen years, grouped on the steps to the verandah in obsolete court dress—'each with a little abdominal bulge that promised in the course of a very few years to become a paunch of considerable dignity'—and attended by 'a stripling page, a half-crazed buffoon, an ex-Jesuit, and a dwarf'; and then he fretted in the stuffiness of the villa's interior: 'It was some time before any sounds, except the whirring and whizzing of enormous cockchafers, and the flirting of fans almost as large as the vanes of a windmill, were audible.' On June 12th, the tenth day, they were back at Cadafaiz; on the next they celebrated the Feast of St Anthony, returning with the Grand Prior in a state of 'almost total exhaustion' and the rest of them 'as brown as mummies, and as dry as cinders' to find a royal summons to the Prince Regent at the Palace of Queluz; the final day took Beckford to the Palace.

June 14th was 'the very essence of summer'. While the Priors were closeted with the Prince ('an uncontrollable love of gossip is inherent in the character of royalty' and Dom João doubtless heard much about the irregularities at Alcobaça) Beckford wandered about the shabby, dusty apartments of the Lord in Waiting, where the courtiers resembled the furniture: 'walking chairs, animated screens, commodes and conveniences, to be used by sovereigns in any means they like best'. He had a boring luncheon with the Marquis of Angeja and the Conde de Vila Verde, The Marquis told him that the Prince was burdened 'by strange apprehensions and stranger dreams' but was called to the royal presence before he could explain further. 'Oppressed by a warm atmosphere, and lulled by the drone of humblebees' Beckford and the Conde both fell asleep. On awaking Beckford changed his clothes and was told by the Marquis that his audience would take place after nightfall; in the meantime a visit to the garden was suggested although it was apparently unusual for people to be allowed to wander there. Indeed, Beckford soon encountered a negro ex-gardener of his who, 'touching the extremities of my garments with his exuberant lips', expressed surprise at his presence 'where so few are permitted to enter'. When Beckford explained that he had the Prince's permission, the negro replied: 'Ah, sir, it is the Princess who reigns here almost exclusively.' The Princess was the Infanta Dona Carlota, a daughter of dangerously proprinquent Spain, and Beckford told himself that 'reports, I well knew, not generally to the good fame of this exalted personage, had been flying about, numerous as butterflies: some dark-coloured, like the wings of the death-head moth, and some brilliant and gay, like those of the fritillaria.' Having inspected a pavilion and become attracted by wandering lights — surely not those of fire-flies? — in the thickets, whom should Beckford stumble upon but Dom Pedro, his very dear friend of previous years, whose nearness to the Princess was thus revealed for the first time: he would become, perhaps this very night, her lover and would be later rumoured as the father of her child. He conducted Beckford to a mysterious fête in the trees: an amphitheatre of verdure deep in the odoriferous thickets, with thirty or so beautiful girls seated oriental-fashion on a velvet carpet. Abruptly Dona Carlota greeted and questioned him; abruptly she commanded that he confirm his reputation for swiftness by racing two 'Indian-looking girls of fourteen or fifteen' down an avenue of catalpas and orange trees to a statue 'rendered faintly visible by lamps gleaming through transparent vases.' After this he was made to dance a bolero with the Andalusian Antonita. All this gaiety was sharp, tense, capriciously controlled: and quiet, too, because it must not reach the tortured Queen.

Angeja then appeared and took him to the Prince, a sombre worried creature, bedevilled by his gay cold wife, preoccupied with his religious melancholic of a mother, and now shocked by intelligence of new excesses in France. As Beckford tells it, their conversation moved from gossip straight into mystery, political or ideological; it is a masterstroke, I think, to make it nightmarishly significant but unclear, as they walked in the long state gallery, 'a pompous, richly gilded apartment, set round with colossal vases of porcelain, as tall and formal as grenadiers.' This mystery persisted when Beckford found himself back in the shadowy ante-room, full of hopeless aspirants for favours, himself reflecting on the perils of despotism, and listening the while to Angeja's voice muttering intrigue or describing the Queen's hallucination of her father's image, a calcined mass of cinders on a pedestal of molten iron in a room of flame. Finally, like the shrieks at Berkeley Castle, the royal voice broke through. '*Ai Jesous! Ai Jesous!*' Beckford's eyes filled with tears. Angeja embraced him and personally escorted him to the door of the palace; 'nor did he cease gazing, I was afterwards told, upon the carriage which bore me away, till the sound of the wheels grew fainter and fainter, and even the torches which were borne before it became invisible.' It is a fine concluding sentence even if it does suggest that Beckford will somehow or other find a way of saving the Portuguese Royal Family, the Church and the State.

How much of this really happened? I find none of it inconceivable although it is surely the poetic and symbolic implications which are most interesting. The atmosphere is again reminiscent of *Kubla Khan*: a paradise hemmed in by anxiety, a Garden of Eden shaken by madness and ancestral voices prophesying war. It is easy enough to notice a general flavour of the eighteenth century without insisting pedantically on the enumeration of points: something of Alexander Pope's *Rape Of The Lock* in the comparisons of courtiers to furniture; a hint of *The Castle Of Otranto* in the Queen's lurid vision; a reminder of Marie Antoinette in the garden ceremonies; a fashionably 'enlightened' comment upon despotism—and even, in the description of the waiting aspirants, a thought that leads back to Dr Johnson cooling his heels in the ante-rooms of Lord Chesterfield. It is perhaps equally possible to find the passage pointing to the future: to Alain Fournier's château, Kipling's curious story, *They*, and T. S. Eliot's *Rose Garden*, to Swinburne and Aubrey Beardsley, to Kafka and Sansom. But, above everything else, it is surely in this dream-like sequence of events that Beckford manages to play the role of a gifted but somewhat startled child—the role, shall we say, which is associated with a writer like Denton Welch—commanded to show off his paces, to race and dance, by an unpredictable woman who has some form of secret alliance with his romantic friend, whose territory is hedged by taboos and whose royal caprices are nonetheless hushed (like a children's feast) by the necessity not to disturb the grown-ups, while almost simultaneously he is a man of the world, an English Baron, falling asleep to the drone of humble-bees but soon consulted by the highest power in the land. How close to *Alice In Wonderland* much of this seems!

Our own imaginations are touched, are opened up, by matters that have no easy explanation and are rounded off with no solution; suggestion is everything; the mystery is that of consciousness itself, alert but victimised, shifting for security into the stasis of art. Ludwig of Bavaria's crude strokes break out of legend into case-history but, being a good writer, Beckford can re-live a life that steps again and again across the threshold of a deeper reality so that, as we re-read him, we enter that enchanted garden which we have encountered in dreams and of which we may hope to find glimpses in places particularly responsive to our own temperaments.

But it was only when I myself visited the Palace of Queluz that I saw how much the actual pavilions and gardens still support and indeed extend Beckford's beautiful picture of more than a hundred years ago.

Childe Harold in Greece

Lord Byron's Youthful Journey

ONE WONDERS how much modern Greeks care about Lord Byron. The Cyprus problem and the dwindling of our national power and confidence have made us less popular in Greece than we once were. We seem, I suppose, unexciting compared to the Germans—terrible old enemies become naïve, earnest and moneyed friends—for whom we are nonetheless often mistaken, the eager cry of 'Deutsch?' sounding oddly in our ears and the little hiatus consequent upon our denial scarcely concealing a hint of disappointment and even of bored familiarity: 'Ah, so you are English...' To this the vast increase in tourism has contributed a general lowering of enthusiasm: the Greeks are a little less hospitable, a little more conscious of money, a little more genteel and bourgeois than they used to be.

It was as long ago as 1958 that I met at Parga, a village on the Epirus coast famous for its resistance to the Turks, the Athenian poet who disclaimed Byron altogether; he was no more than an insincere adventurer who shared with other British imperialists the vice of pederasty. Yet, a week later, I was escorted into the Heroon at Missolonghi by a small boy whose name was Veeron. The Heroon is a park devoted to national heroes; its palm trees and shrubberies of oleander provide a welcome relief from the mud flats and stinking marshes of that pathetically unlovely town, its other claim to interest being the proliferation of marble busts on pillars and plinths, all of the intensest whiteness—no detergent could do better, no toothpaste appear more astringently hygienic—their moustachio'd solemnity in the strongest contrast with the dark-eyed, oily-skinned, pilafi-stuffing, garlic-breathing, indefatigably vociferous Levantines that many of them must have been in real life. A silence truly unearthly possessed these politicians. An unnatural, almost introspective isolation separated these extroverted, once quarrelsome heads. A butterfly, inanely wandering, settled upon Prince Mavrocordato's nose. A lizard flickered to stillness on the plinth supporting the ferocious features of Kolokotronis. All the similar busts encountered in public gardens elsewhere, from the vaguely Regency esplanade of Corfu to a mere pocket-handkerchief of

shrubbery at Florina on the Yugoslav border, all those bloodless and
curiously null watchers of municipal hibiscus and canna-lilies and
plumbago, whom one stumbles upon only to ignore between the hedges
of Tripolis or in the park at Thebes, or who suddenly congeal before
one's eyes in the amorous moonlight of the thickets of the Zappeion,
received here their apotheosis, their ultimate expression. And amongst
them, elegant upon his pillar, the only full-length figure was that of
Lord Byron. A disdainful figure, perhaps: petulance on a monument.
'White as a chicken wing,' a girl had described his flesh when she laid
out the fever-stricken body, so unmercifully leeched and bled, at
Easter of 1824. And white he certainly remained. My escort pointed to
his namesake, his voice full of pride. 'Veeron!' he said.

But perhaps the Greeks today call their children by the poet's name
with no more thought than they give to the use of Epaminondas for a
boy or Penelope for a girl. After all, the one classical name to have
really permeated folk-lore is that of the Macedonian who ushered in the
decline or, at least the profound alteration, of Hellas, Alexander the
Great, just as it is the lesser immortals (centaurs and nymphs) who
appear in superstition as bogies. Still, the name of Byron is pretty indispensable to our English view of Greek travel. And its modern use
can also conjure up memories.

There was the time last summer when a friend and I were exploring
Mount Pelion, home of the centaurs and birthplace of Jason. Based on
a beach between Kala Nera and Afissos, where we set out our posses-
sions and slept at night, we made trips by car to the 'hanging villages'
of the mountain itself and also visited many areas of the lovely, un-
dulating peninsula which curls round the Gulf of Volos. On the way
back from the remote village of Platanias we kept looking for a place
where we could eat our lunch. Finally we saw big trees with a chapel
below them. The chapel turned its back on the road, its small porch
facing a spring which bubbled from a plinth into a scalloped stone cup
and then ran over into a rectangular trough near the ground. Some of
this water spilled into a trench at right angles to the trough. The ground
all about was either muddy or covered with a fine light-toned gravel
which the moisture kept shiny. One of the planes had friendly roots
swollen from the ground and twisted to make a perch. Beyond this
was the dazing presence of rough fields or bush with some sparse maize
near at hand. A splendid place for a picnic, we thought it, with tall
shade, the locked but friendly chapel and the gentle, almost imperceptible persistance of water. I established myself on the dusty tree-

roots, unpacking sausage, cucumber, tomatoes and a bottle of wine
from the khaki canvas bag. 'At last I can do some washing!' my friend
cried. Stripped to the waist he plunged shirts into the trough. I walked
over to the chapel and tried to peer first through a small window high
up on its side, then through the keyhole of the flaking, splintered
door.

Chapels intrigue me. I reflected that only the other day I had climbed
to the theatre at Thasos and then, following the ridge, continued the
ascent to the acropolis, grateful to be able to pause by the way at a tiny
chapel whose floor was cobbled in blue-grey stones drifted with pine-
needles. A home-made painting declared that the place was dedicated
to O *prognesis Elias* (who once would have been Helios, the sun-god).
It was a naïve affair, blobs of oil on cardboard, with the prophet framed
in a mountain from which he was differentiated chiefly by his orange
halo and by the extraordinary folds of his garment (Prussian blue
against the precipice's sticky black), for the painter had given this a
prodigious bulge from the navel to half-way down the thigh in a sort of
grotesque development of the *kolpos* of classical maidens, below which
his skirts flew out sideways in flat blunt nubs, all of which was no doubt
designed to express holy agitation and power. His right sleeve just
missed the mountain's edge but his hand stretched out beyond it, into
a patch of sky soon blackened by a tree like a brussels sprout, and flying
down to this exclamatory if not imperious hand from the two sides of
the picture, from green-choked tree and along the contour of the
mountain's peak, which fitted into the join between the bird's out-
thrust neck and wings, were the two projectile ravens, their scarlet
beaks smudged with the succouring food. Elsewhere, propped on a
ledge of the whitewashed wall, stood an icon almost impossible to
make out but to one of whose arms a pinkish paper hand had been
attached. Skimpy lace curtains, the usual paraphernalia (a cruse of oil,
a broom, several matchboxes, a few candles and much wax, a tray piled
with herbs, a jug, together with a lottery ticket and part of a plastic
comb) — this was about all, except for the peace and the all-important
shade, with the view down to agora and harbour (supposedly floored in
marble) and across to the tree-fringed shores of Thrace.

Even the smallest church is likely to have pious women somewhere
about it but it's rare to meet another human being in chapels such as
these. Their simplicity makes them an organic part of the landscape.
Sometimes they act quite obviously as a focus, as do the many chapels
on promontories and sea-washed rocks. Often they are just stumbled

upon: a shed, a shelter, declaring itself to have greater significance than the surrounding olives and very gently asserting, as would a small classical ruin, the qualities of space, direction, order in a landscape. In them the Holy Ghost is still very much a pigeon and the congregation a child who plays by himself.

At the fountain my friend had finished his washing. Since the trough was narrow and a bit muddy he had only done a couple of shirts which he now hung on the sunny side of the tree. We began to eat. We passed the knife between us. I was holding this knife and edging sliced sausage and cucumber on to the by now monotonous rusk when there was a cry, a clatter, a slither becoming a run and the cattle were upon us. They came down from the road, a cow and two bullocks. Behind them was a woman with a switch. Gentle in their clumsiness the beasts checked when they saw us; all shoulders and muzzle, they veered and swayed. The woman encouraged them. When they had moved past and turned to the fountain she greeted us. 'You're eating,' she said. 'Yes,' we answered her. She was a whiplash of a woman, brown-faced and sharp of feature, with a head-scarf and a big skirt bunched at the waist and swinging with the weight of many petticoats. 'Good eating,' she said.

The cow went to the trough at once, the bullocks were content with the channel at its side. I was looking at the woman with some anxiety because of the washing. Within a second of the cow's reaching the water I saw her whole body stiffen. She bent forward to release the terrible keenness of her glance. The cow raised its head, smelling the stone. The woman, no longer graceful, scuttled beside it. She began to whistle in short bursts, very soft and mild. She cared for it as did the woman we met on the cliff above our beach, who guided a goat and a sheep from one bit of grazing to the next, telling the goat of a thistle and the sheep of a tuft of grass. The cow lowered its head, vaguely skimming the water. It would not drink. The woman stooped over the trough and then there burst from her a wild high-pitched tirade. With the words piling round her she turned and advanced upon us, denouncing us from afar, her hand flung high, her head thrown back, but as yet it was not time for a closer confrontation and so she turned back, accumulating her indignation in an endless series of mutters interspersed now and then with the entirely different sound of the sweet, thin whistling. *Rooha* we heard — it was *rooha* again and again — and this was a word that neither of us recognised; we were waiting for *saponi* (soap) but it was a long time before her voice rose, her argument with the trees and dust, the proprieties of generations, the neighbours so far distant from this isolated place, became clear and menacing and *The xenee have been using Soap!!* was shrieked through the air.

In view of the stamped muddiness around the fountain both of us had been a bit uncertain as to whether it was the right place for laundry (we now guessed that *rooha* meant this) but my friend and I thought that the suds would quickly seep away; besides which the principal feature, the drinking cup, had been left untouched, and surely the propinquity of the chapel suggested that this was, so to speak, ecclesiastical water provided for man, and travellers most of all, and that to bring cattle there was at least as much a sacrilege as to wash clothes. Cleanliness, they said, was next to godliness.

The woman scooped the cup and trailed the water towards the cow's lips. Perhaps this would do the trick. But the cow did not respond. It was now that she drew nearer to us, no longer attacking the general concept of *xenee* but concerned with us in particular, so unnaturally lolling there by the tree; she waved her switch while I, pacifically, lowered my knife. 'I'm sorry,' I said uncomfortably. 'May I excuse myself' — which is the idiom used in Greece when one mentions a donkey or a cucumber, since both are such indecent things.

Nothing, however, would stop the flow of her scorn, magnificently delivered as it was, so that I understood her better than anyone else encountered on my travels hereabouts. '*Krema*,' she repeated; the cow will give no cream. She paid no attention to the bullocks. *Water*, she cried; only a *xenos* would suppose that water was of no importance in the summertime. Her man, she threatened; her man would settle a matter of this seriousness. And, over her stick, her wonderful eyes darted to the road and the hillside behind it. 'For God's sake don't argue with her. Let's make a move,' my friend whispered. 'I am a foreigner,' I said finally. 'I do not understand. I do not speak Greek.'

At this her passion reached its apogee, and incidentally flattered me enormously.

'You said "I'm sorry", you said "May I excuse myself"…how can you say you don't understand?' Once more she looked at the hillside. And now a figure really did detach itself from scrub throbbing in the intense sunlight. As we gathered up our belongings with a shameful efficiency her words rang clear. '*Veeron*,' she called, '*Veeron, bring your father here at once!*' Or so we interpreted a far more prolix volley of words, at which a rather large boy raced forward under an echoing treble scream, hung for a moment uncertain in a slither of stones and a puff of dust, and then doubled back towards the ridge in the wake of a series of stabbing calls.

Veeron was certainly a forthright lad. As I reversed on to the road and put my foot down on the accelerator, a stone smashed into the side of the car.

What a thing to happen to a Philhellene! And from Byron of all people.

No wonder one writes, as I see I did in an article more than a year before this incident, that to modern travellers the Greek Experience is complex, existentially challenging. Greece scares as well as delights; for all its natural beauty, and the charm of its climate for much of the year, it emerges as a tough, cruel country where no one is being sentimental if he thinks of the presence of gods; Zeus with his thunderbolt, Apollo with his death-dealing bow, Pan raging from his lair in the terrible noonday silence of high mountains and Poseidon whipping the whitecaps of *meltemi* across the Aegean. Greece demands loyalties and exacts involvement. It is not a country in which it is easy to be placid or neutral.

In this context the figure of the real Byron has a peculiar relevance. One reason for this is historical: his first visit came at a time when Philhellenism was rapidly developing from an interest in the ancient arts to a concern for the whole cultural and political situation of the country; his second was, of course, a noble if not particularly effective episode in the War of Liberation. At both periods Greece was confusingly and tantalizingly unformed, beset alike by promise and doubt, a place embodying in a quite practical form things which in a philosophical or symbolic sense still persist to this day, for how, and to what degree, can the mother of civilisations be resurrected in the modern world? To Byron the Greeks were classically beautiful but unclassically apathetic and even slave-minded; this was one aspect of the problem. No modern traveller of any sensitivity can have failed to recognise the tension between Greece as a western state of mind, thawed out of school books or still perhaps half-frozen in plaster casts, and the demands of a clamorous humanity. Are the modern Greeks in any significant sense descendants of the ancient? Some will doubtless have found in the crumbling or wavering of the 'classical ideal', in the shifting alliances between Classical and Byzantine and Turkish, in the hallucinatory re-assertion of the distant past in terms of sunshine and sensuality, with the gods becoming more real than actual human beings such as Pericles or Plato, a kind of invigorating and challenging truth.

To them Greece will be a perpetual re-discovery they must make for themselves. Unlike countries whose development has been continuous, with the result that they are rich in works of art and may indeed be felt as culturally overwhelming, Greece has the sort of emptiness which demands the individual imagination. And it is in this metaphysical sense quite as much as in his historical interest that a highly individual person like Byron has meaning for the modern traveller.

Byron is the most complex of the three odd and very personal writers who are the chief subjects of this study. With Boswell, after all, we know where we are; Boswell is in the most endearing way the middle-class provincial adolescent on the make, the insecure careerist who would conquer the world. Beckford, on the other hand, is, although much more mysterious, the kind of person about whom one has said a good deal when one has described him as a creature of arrogant artifice, an exotic sprite. Boswell is plain honest all through; Beckford is only honest as a man whose fantasies embody the search for the ideal and expose subconscious truth. One is all earth, the other a blend of genuine and tinsel fire. But what is Byron? A careless and even at times empty romantic poet, he is also a witty, highly intelligent man of the world. As exemplified by *Childe Harold*, his interests are usually robust: he enjoys history, especially the scenes of heroic action and patriotic defiance; he is moved by landscape; he loves to describe girls and the transports and dissatisfactions of love. But the shifts between boyish excitement and world-weary cynicism, the combination of energy with solitariness, ennui and despair, suggest the contradictions in his character. There is little about him that does not have two opposing aspects. He was athletic but lame, enormously handsome but inclined to corpulence (fifteen stone at the age of eighteen), a hard drinker who for days on end imbibed nothing but seltzer water. 'That beautiful pale face is my fate,' declared the insufferable Caroline Lamb, but the owner of the face had 'a sad Trick of biting his Nails'. A radical in politics, he had an almost mystical belief in the virtues of rank. A constant scribbler of verses, he often affected to regard his work with aristocratic indifference. Loyal and affectionate to his friends, he could be ruthless and callous to his women and their children. There was a strong strain of passivity in his role as a great lover, and it is arguable that he really preferred a succession of boys (Lord Clare, John Edleston, Nicolo Giraud, Loukas Chalidratsanos) to such passions as the Maid of Athens, Margarita Cogni, the Venetian baker's wife, or Teresa Guiccioli. His prose is down to earth; he writes to his mother from

Greece that 'it is astonishing how far money goes in this country' and he will later sum up his amorous conquests in Venice by claiming 'at least two hundred of one sort or another', something of a feat in view of the fact that it is 'a hot climate where they grow relaxed and doughy, and flumpity a short time after breeding'. His earlier poetry is deficient in such concreteness. Above all he was the copy-book romantic who found himself in the anti-romanticism of *Don Juan*. And yet even this statement seems only a half-truth. For Byron really was a daemonic force. In his total presence he stands for life as do the plays of *Hamlet* and *Lear*. He is a symbol. And, as is the case with symbols, we feel more about him than we can hope to understand.

To call upon such a figure in the ordinary course of travelling will seem unnecessary to many. The presence of dead writers may add nothing to the appreciation of the places they once visited. Beckford may not enhance Florence or Lisbon; Boswell may not bring an additional smile to a morning walk in Siena, or Gray momentarily illumine an evening in Rome. For those who regard their holidays abroad as in some sense an assault upon time, a reaching out towards the timelessness of a continuous present, the matter may be different; an intermediary from a different period, who looks both forward and back, is better known to us than the ancients and yet frees us from contemporary preoccupations, may help us in the process of dissolving barriers. What might be an absolute distinction (then and now), or what might, in a different mood, collapse into a sun-induced sentimental dream of complete union, is given gradation and perspective. And certainly in Greece, the most elemental of countries, we can do with a daemonic companion who was also an adventurous, high-spirited youth.

Byron spent exactly two years on the Grand Tour, from July 2nd, 1809, to July 14th, 1811. Owing to the Napoleonic wars he could not take Boswell's or Beckford's route through the Low Countries and Germany to the Alps and Italy. He and his friend John Cam Hobhouse sailed direct from Falmouth to Lisbon, a speedy journey of four and a half days during which he was 'seasick, and sick of the sea'. Often moody and changeable, Byron's feelings on departing veered between the melancholy of 'I leave England without regret—I shall return to it without pleasure. I am like Adam, the first convict sentenced to Transportation, but I have no Eve, and have eaten no apple but was sour as a crab' on the one hand, and the boyish high-spirits of his poem,

The Lisbon Packet, on the other. In this stanza he refers first to the three
servants:

> Fletcher! Murray! Bob! where are you?
>   Stretch'd along the deck like logs—
> Bear a hand, you jolly tar you!
>   Here's a rope's end for the dogs.
> Hobhouse muttering fearful curses,
>   As the hatchway down he rolls;
> Now his breakfast, now his verses,
>   Vomits forth—and damns our souls.

Byron's first adventures were therefore Iberian. While Hobhouse
complained about the poverty and dirt of the country, 'at least 100 years
behind the English in all the improvements of civilised and comfortable
life', Byron enjoyed Portugal. 'I am very happy here, because I loves
oranges, and talks bad Latin to the monks, who understand it, as it is
like their own,—and I goes into society (with my pocket pistols), and
I swims in the Tagus all across at once, and I rides on an ass or a mule,
and swears Portuguese, and have got a diarrhoea and bites from the
mosquitoes.' Already we have the essence of travelling expressed by
one of our best and raciest letter-writers: a good-humoured recognition
of difference, an honest acceptance of discomfort, a touch of self-
dramatisation—and who, amongst travellers such as this, does not learn
a few swear-words first? Soon *Childe Harold*, not begun until Greece,
will find the land 'delicious' and at least the prospect of Lisbon full of
'beauties', although admittedly 'The dingy denizens are reared in dirt'
and the entire Portuguese people form 'A nation swoln with ignor-
ance and pride'.

After some sight-seeing and a couple of visits to the theatre where,
in view of the wartime situation, with Sir Arthur Wellesley poised on
the frontier for his campaign in Spain, 'God Save The King' concluded
the proceedings, Byron and Hobhouse set off for nearby Cintra and
were so delighted that they stayed two nights. This umbrageous region
of misty pinnacles and voluptuous defiles is one of the miracles of
Portugal, not least because it rises from a landscape of windmills and
wind-swept downs. It is of course Beckford country and Byron was a
great admirer of the author of *Vathek*, which he considered the best
Oriental tale ever written by an Englishman. Only a few months before
he had unsuccessfully tried to catch a glimpse of 'the martyr to prejudice' whom he understood to be staying in the inn at which he was

changing horses. Very much later Samuel Rogers was to write to Byron with the news that he had been invited to the Abbey and had there listened to some 'unimaginable horrors' from the *Episodes*; Byron eagerly replied, 'Could you not beg of *him* for *me* a copy in Ms. of the remaining tales? I think I deserve this, as a strenuous and public admirer of the first one' (Venice, 3rd March, 1818). But Beckford was reluctant to let the most jealously guarded of all his documents out of his sight; why did not Byron come to Fonthill to peruse the work in the shadowy and exotic setting which had given it birth?[1] Subsequently he reflected on the meeting that could never be. 'To what good would it have led? We should have both met in full drill — both endeavoured to have been delighted — a correspondence would have been established, the most laborious that can be imagined, because the most artificial. Oh gracious goodness, I have the opportunity of enjoying the best qualities of his mind in his works, what more do I require?'

Now Hobhouse and Byron pottered about the last of Beckford's *quintas*, not Ramalhão but Monserrate, which he had leased in the autumn of 1794; the villa, still standing, is a Moorish structure, rather ugly on the outside but with a romantically lacy interior in pale stucco, which hangs on a platform far below the mountain road and commands on all sides the most delicious prospects of palms, pines and auracarias, with magnolias, camellias and tree-ferns fringing a meadow-lawn tumbling down to a lake, and everywhere amongst the rocks and shrubberies the sound of water. The two also climbed to the convent of Nossa Senhora de Pena. The atmosphere was suitably Beckfordian, 'the torrid crags, by toppling convent crowned' and 'the variegated maze of mount and glen', although as a moralist the youthful poet had to comment on the transience of earthly things.

> There thou too, Vathek! England's wealthiest son,
> Once formed thy Paradise, as not aware
> When wanton Wealth her mightiest deeds hath done,
> Meek Peace voluptuous lures was ever wont to shun.

Such references annoyed Beckford when he read them. 'One seems to see the portentous Byron (a 'Fanfaron des crimes' as Louis XIV called the regent Orléans) running a furious muck with Serpents (which turned out to be stuffed eels) and pretending to whip himself into madness.' Beckford would certainly have been riled had he learned that, at a party given by Germaine de Staël at Coppet in 1816, his sister

---

[1] A different building; 'Splendens' had given way to the abbey.

Mrs Hervey, then sixty-five, was so impressed by Byron's daemonic appearance and reputation that she swooned away.

From Portugal the two travellers rode through Spain to Seville and Cadiz, 'a gentle gallop of four hundred miles', with the servants left behind to bring the luggage to Gibraltar by ship. 'The horses are excellent, we rode seventy miles a day. Eggs and wine, and hard beds, are all the accommodation we found, in such torrid weather, quite enough. My health is better than in England.' (Boswellian sentiments these.) 'Seville is a fine town, and the Sierra Morena, part of which we crossed, a very sufficient mountain; but damn description, it is always disgusting.' At Seville, the birthplace of Don Juan, they left cards with the British Ambassador, none other than the John Hookham Frere whose burlesque poem, *Whistlecraft*, was one day to give the inspiration for Byron's own *Don Juan*. What now impressed him most was the cathedral; it remained his favourite Gothic building to the end of his life. Since description was 'disgusting', and he had little eye for works of architecture and art—even in Athens the Parthenon was to strike him as 'very like the Mansion House'—he does not mention the strong but delicate Giralda tower, a masterpiece of Moorish workmanship rising beside the *patio de las naranjas*, and echoed in one of the stained glass windows within the cathedral next door, whose subject is the occasion when the tower was threatened by an earthquake and two early Christian ladies, virgins and martyrs, returned to stand beside it and very gracefully to prop it up. Nor does he seem to have been able to visit the Alcázar.

The two travellers went on to Cadiz, a city which Byron liked. Compared to its noble Atlantic rivals, Vigo and Lisbon, which are both situated on estuaries, Cadiz shakes itself free of the land across a long causeway over salt-marshes and lagoons, dropping the township of San Fernando as it goes, so that when you eventually get to it you find it bright and braced to face the true ocean swells, with the sultry plains of Andalucia sunk in the distance, and itself rising in a world of its own, an island shaped like a pearl or a great water-drop, brimming up from a perimeter of sea-walls and gardened esplanades above fangs of rock, its network of always busy and often squalid streets opening to squares of glittering whiteness dotted with palm trees. Such trees stand to each side of the baroque cathedral, a curious building of white and bee-coloured stone, at once pompous and wandering, for the twisted and bulbous flanking towers seem too big for the portal and dome, and the effect is that the building has been pressed apart by the wind from the sea, or that, divested of heart and vital core, it has the elaborate vacancy of a sun-bleached shell lying upon the beach.

Arrived at Cadiz, Byron and Hobhouse attended a bullfight across the bay at Puerta Santa Maria. Both disliked the brutal treatment of the horses. As Hobhouse was to put it later, 'an Englishman who can be much pleased with seeing two men beat themselves to pieces, cannot bear to look at a horse galloping round an arena with his bowels trailing on the ground, and turns from the spectacle and the spectators with horror and disgust.' Yet the *corrida* occupies several stanzas of *Childe Harold* where the description of the progress of the fight, with the bull wounded by numerous 'darts' and 'lances' (in that order) and no mention made of the climactic *faena*, suggests either that Byron had been too shocked to look clearly or that things were done differently in those days. The conclusion, though, is accurate and implies a neater kill than many seen of recent years, even when it was Dominguin's or Ordonez's moment of truth.

> Where his vast neck mingles with the spine,
> Sheathed in his form the deadly weapon lies.
> He stops — he starts — disdaining to decline:
> Slowly he falls, amidst triumphant cries,
> Without a groan, without a struggle dies.
> The decorated car appears — on high
> The corse is piled — sweet sight for vulgar eyes —
> Four steeds that spurn the rein, as swift as shy,
> Hurl the dark bulk along, scarce seen in dashing by.
>   (*Childe Harold*, Canto I, lxxix)

At Cadiz Byron flirted on his last night ashore with the daughter of a Spanish admiral. But his delight in Spanish beauty, and his character-istic traveller's comparison of fiery foreign girls with prim English ones, did not destroy his critical sense. 'The Spanish women are all alike, their education the same...Certainly they are fascinating; but their minds have only one idea, and the business of their lives is intrigue.' The next morning Byron and Hobhouse sailed in *Hyperion* for Gibraltar, where servants and baggage had not yet arrived. To my mind the Rock today has few attractions, except for something of a Regency air to ramparts and watergates, a sort of congealed English-ness of the Gentleman's Relish, Oxford Marmalade variety under its umbrella of cloud, except that the helmeted bobbies have brown emotional eyes. Byron certainly disliked it on sight. 'Cadiz is the

prettiest town in Europe, Seville a large and fine city, Gibraltar the
dirtiest and most detestable spot.'

He was somewhat consoled, however, by the garrison library — it
was here that another traveller, the perceptive and critical John Galt,
saw him for the first time — and he used to ascend the cliffs at sunset in
order to look across the sea to Africa which he hoped to visit although,
the winds being contrary, he had to make do with Algeciras instead.

> Mauritania's giant-shadows frown,
> From mountain-cliff to coast descending sombre down

and one can only add that this is indeed the greatest sight of the region,
preferably seen not from the Rock but from a more oblique and hence
slowly unfolding vantage point, such as the road to Faro de Punta
Carnero beyond the ugly but cheap and hospitable town of Algeciras
or, better still, not sought for but come across by accident as in the
course of exploring the white alleys of Tarifa, or swimming out past
some rock in the bay of Estepona far to the north-east; huge mountains
like petrified cloud that seem all precipice and sharply plunging line,
shadowy and sterile and portentous in the haze, so that the traveller
may at first sight get his directions wrong and think the veiled prodigy
ahead Gibraltar, for nothing could seem more near, until, the line
continuing, it is obviously Africa and the Rif which have made him
speechless. But to all this Byron, in fact, added moonlight.

> Through Calpe's straits survey the steepy shore;
> Europe and Afric on each other gaze!
> Lands of the dark-eyed Maid and dusky Moor
> Alike beheld beneath pale Hecate's blaze...

It was in Gibraltar that Byron bought from a local tailor for fifty
guineas a 'superb' uniform to serve as court-dress. And finally the
servants appeared. On 16th August, having sent Murray home because
he was too old, and the 'little page' Robert Rushton also because he was
of tender age ('Turkey is in too dangerous a state for boys to enter'),
Byron, Hobhouse and Fletcher departed for Malta. Galt was also on
board and taking notice: 'his lordship affected, as it seemed to me, more
aristocracy than befitted his years, or the occasion...' At Malta Byron,
after a brief sulk because there was no salute from the batteries in
honour of his arrival, entered into the life of the place to the extent of
falling quite seriously in love with a certain Mrs Spencer Smith and

challenging the aide-de-camp of the general at Valetta to a duel which was only averted at the last moment. As to the lady, Byron later told Lady Melbourne, 'I was seized with an *ever lasting* passion', in fact signalised by a promise to meet in a year's time; as to the duel, Hobhouse was to tell Tom Moore that his friend had behaved with 'cool and manly courage'.

Thus it was that Byron came to Greece, in the naval ship, *Spider*, escorting a convoy of British merchantmen to Patras and Preveza. At Patras they briefly disembarked and went pistol shooting amongst some currant bushes. Then they turned north to Preveza. To Byron this was Turkey as much as Greece; in a day or two it would also be Albania.

No Alps, then, on this trip. Byron was to have his Swiss period during those first months of his exile in 1816 when he lived at the beautifully situated Villa Diodati on the shores of Lake Leman, saw much of Percy and Mary Shelley whose house was only ten minutes' walk away, and otherwise licked his wounds, coped with the vain and ultra-sensitive Dr Polidori (of his party) and the too demanding, too passionate Claire Clairmont (accompanying the Shelleys) and started one of those drastic slimming diets of his. From his balcony he would gaze across the lake at the distant Jura or take his boat and row out.

> It is the hush of night, and all between
> Thy margin and the mountains, dusk, yet clear,
> Mellowed and mingling, yet distinctly seen,
> Save darkened Jura, whose capt heights appear
> Precipitously steep; and drawing near,
> There breathes a living fragrance from the shore,
> Of flowers yet fresh with childhood; on the ear
> Drops the light drip of the suspended oar,
> Or chirps the grasshopper one good-night carol more.

> (*Childe Harold*, Canto III, lxxxvi)

Indeed in late June the two poets sailed round the lake in order to see the places immortalised by Rousseau, whose *Nouvelle Héloïse* Byron knew almost by heart. They visited Meillerie, the castle of Chillon, Clarens where they walked amongst the hay-makers in *le bosquet de Julie* and Vevey where Rousseau had planned the novel and where Byron now wrote *The Prisoner of Chillon*. In this lake haunt of international

Athens, early 19th century

Byron by Thomas Phillips

sensibilities and of minds in exile, place of Boswell's encounter with
his heroes and of the seventeen-year-old Beckford's solitary ascents of
Mont Salève—the first mountain whose climbing had been celebrated
in modern times, by Petrarch himself—they thought also of the more
tough-minded geniuses of the preceding age. On 27th June, the anni-
versary of the day Edward Gibbon completed his *History*, they paid a
visit to the famous summerhouse, and Byron picked a sprig of acacia
to send home to his publisher, John Murray. They were remembering
famous words which Byron, a life-time admirer of Pope, could respect
for a classical control he himself found difficult to achieve: 'The air
was temperate, the sky was serene, the silver orb of the moon was
reflected in the waters, and all Nature was silent. I will not dissemble
the first emotions of joy on the recovery of my freedom, and perhaps
the establishment of my fame. But my pride was soon humbled, and a
sober melancholy was spread over my mind by the idea that I had taken
an everlasting leave of an old and agreeable companion...'

Distant Alps were followed by Alps close at hand. With the end of
August the Shelleys and the now pregnant Claire Clairmont left and,
Byron's friends Hobhouse and Scrope Davies having arrived, there
was an expedition to Chamonix and its great view of Mont Blanc.
More important, this was followed in the middle of September by a
tour of the Bernese Oberland undertaken by Byron and Hobhouse
alone. Byron kept a short journal of this trip for his half-sister Augusta;
its pages make an indispensible contribution to our theme of Over
the Alps. The Alpine passages in *Childe Harold* are vague, noble and
pantheistic; Shelley had been feeding Byron too much Wordsworth
too fast; the romantic doctrine is there all right but to my mind its
gestures are too rhetorical to carry full conviction, besides which there
are few concrete particulars—certainly nothing up to the Master's
'stationary blasts of waterfalls'—while the tone is heavily solemn.
The mountains are 'the Palaces of Nature'; the presence of Man is
oppressive and infective and should be renounced for creative solitude
—'To fly from, need not be to hate, mankind'; such solitude establishes
the sense of a universal link—'I live not in myself, but I become /
Portion of that around me'—and ultimately an entry into something
like the Platonic Absolutes—'The bodiless thought? the spirit of each
spot? / Of which, even now, I share at times the immortal lot?' All of
which is followed by a long apostrophe to Rousseau, and later a comparison of Rousseau and Voltaire, interspersed with a description of
the nocturnal lake and of a thunderstorm over it which crystallises the

6

shamanistic desires of the poet, who wishes for the one perfect word to strike like lightning.

Very different is the journal. Here we have the country carriage, described as a *Charaban*; the damp sheets at the inn at Ouchy ('swore and stripped them off and flung them—Heaven knows where'); the careful deciphering of churchyard epitaphs and the quick glance at the titles of volumes lying on château tables; the amusement at the ways of English tourists (a woman asleep in her carriage near the Castle of Chillon, 'fast asleep in the most anti-narcotic spot in the world'); the guide who reveals the common fault of the half-literate when, confusing author with book, he talks of St Preux as though he were Rousseau; the bull that nearly leaps into the *charaban* and the kid which Byron helps over a fence; the pretty girl whose pears must be bought and whose cheek patted; Hobhouse knocking his head on the door of the next room and cursing; Hobhouse going off to fish and catching one and then going off again and catching nothing; falling off a mountain and cutting your finger; getting yourself and your horse stuck in river mud; and then the avalanches crashing down 'every five minutes nearly', the shepherds piping from crag to crag, the cow-bells ringing, the girls singing, the life truly Arcadian ('solitary, savage, and pastoral') and the peasants to be watched at their waltzes, 'the English can't Waltz, never could, nor ever will.' Beauty is everywhere and there is not a cuckoo-clock in sight. The scenery is 'worthy of I know not whom', 'the whole day's journey Alpine and proud', and as they go up to the Dent Jamant the route is 'beautiful as a Dream'. From the summit of the Wengern Byron sees the glaciers of the Jungfrau, the Dent d'Argent 'shining like truth', the two Eigers and the Wetterhorn. Below him on the opposite side is 'a boiling sea of cloud...the clouds rose from the opposite valley, curling up perpendicular precipices like the foam of the Ocean of Hell, during a Spring tide—it was white, and sulphury, and immeasurably deep in appearance.' He made a snowball and 'pelted' Hobhouse.

Here, rather than in the poem, are the bright sharp images, reminiscent of those of Coleridge and Dorothy Wordsworth, predecessors to the word-painting of Gerard Manley Hopkins and Ruskin. At Grindenwald the glacier is 'like a frozen hurricane'. A waterfall resembles 'the tail of a white horse streaming in the wind' and, seen again early next morning, it becomes 'a rainbow of the lower part of all colours, but principally purple and gold; the bow moving as you move; I never saw anything like this; it is only in the Sunshine.' At the Dent Jamant

he found a lake 'in the very nipple of the bosom of the Mountain' and
then 'came to some snow in patches, upon which my forehead's
perspiration fell like rain, making the same dints as a sieve...' Yet his
boyish pleasure (could this be the monster of the London scandal?)
was tinged with sadness: '...in all this – the recollections of bitterness,
and more especially of recent and more home desolation, which must
accompany me through life, have preyed upon me here; and neither
the music of the Shepherd, the crashing of the Avalanche, nor the
torrent, the mountain, the Glacier, the Forest, nor the Cloud, have for
one moment lightened the weight upon my heart, nor enabled me to
lose my own wretched identity in the majesty, and the power, and the
Glory, around, above, and beneath me.' It was, however, a creative
unhappiness. The lines of *Manfred* were forming themselves within his
brain.

Accompanied by Hobhouse, Byron crossed the Simplon at the
beginning of October and so began his final and of course longest
sojourn in the south. After some weeks in Milan he travelled along the
shores of the Lago di Garda to Verona, where he had a good word to
say for the Scaliger tombs and found the amphitheatre 'wonderful –
beats even Greece', which was high praise from him. He then settled
in or near Venice. 'It is a place which I like, and which I long anticipated I should like.' But if his stay there began by being tranquil and
relaxing, under the 'great black eastern eyes' of his first mistress,
Marianna Segati, it was to develop into the wild and persistent
debauchery of the Palazzo Mocenigo, with its menagerie of animals,
its floating population of prostitutes and pimping gondoliers, and La
Fornarina herself, wittily proletarian, superbly animal, tigerishly
possessive as when she awaited the return of his gondola in a storm: 'I
found her on the open steps...with her great black eyes flashing through
her tears, and the long dark hair, which was streaming, drenched with
rain, over her brows and breast.' Venice appealed to Byron because it
was still an eastern city, a gateway to the Levant. He enjoyed, too, its
atmosphere of decay: 'I have been familiar with ruins too long to
dislike desolation.' The ambiguity consequent upon its mingling of
land and sea, where ceremonious palaces echoed all day to the lilting
gossip and deft insinuations of water, and the chequered dimpling *rio*
winked behind the back of the ornate façade, intrigued him as much
as it was to intrigue Baron Corvo or John Addington Symonds. Venice
was the Sea-Sodom and Byron, even more eager than Beckford had
been to show himself in a bad light, could there disgust and then

frighten his high-minded friend, Shelley. The latter, having declared of one part of Byron's entourage that 'countesses smell so strongly of garlic, that an ordinary Englishman cannot approach them', went on to speak of another, of 'wretches who seem almost to have lost the gait and physiognomy of men, and who do not scruple to avow practices, which are not only not condoned, but I believe even conceived in England.' By the end of his second year in Venice Byron was visibly ageing. But if the noble and melancholy Alps, still visible on the horizon, had produced *Manfred*, this bohemian period prepared the way for his masterpiece, *Don Juan*.

And now we must return to those Alps and look back through them, as through an arch of fire and snow, upon the younger, happier man about to encounter the mountains of Epirus.

Preveza was rather disappointing; it has nowadays a bad reputation among Greek towns, the poet Katiotakis having committed suicide there after writing a poem of detestation about its 'dirty, insignificant streets / With their pompous, brilliant names.' Personally I found it atmospheric in a way half sordid, half sultry; I recall walking amongst market-gardens and vineyards, breaking through tall reeds to find a hotly thatched café on the limpid Ambracian Gulf and then negotiating a shoreline of matted and soggy ribbon-weed. At night the silence, as profound as at early-to-bed places like Corinth or Tripolis, suddenly shattered to the sound of bouzoukia clarinets from a pair of ramshackle brothels where brandy came by the carafe. It was here that Byron made a mistake about *to meros* (the place, i.e. the lavatory). The British Consul's house had a mere triangular hole in the ground, with a bench above it; misunderstanding the nature of the required manoeuvre, Byron ignored the bench and sat down on the hole, with his knees up to his chin. I cannot resist finding a parallel to this in a mistake I once made at the Rest House in Malacca where, finding a large earthenware pot more than half full of water on the verandah devoted to ablutions, I gingerly inserted myself into this claustrophobic and slightly slimy jar, with a terrible gulp of suction followed by a considerable slop of overflow, when all I was meant to do was to insert a can and splash myself.

From Preveza, after a ride out to the ruins of Octavian's city of Nicopolis, the site of his camp before the battle of Actium, Byron and Hobhouse began their journey to visit the notorious Ali Pasha, the semi-independent despot of the whole area. It should be remembered

that there was at this time great interest in 'the East' — an interest
already seen in William Beckford but also to be found in such works as
Tom Moore's *Lalla Rookh* and Robert Southey's *Curse of Kehama* — and
that Byron regarded his Grecian wanderings as no more than the
prelude to visits to Arabia, Persia and even India. At the moment Turks
(and Albanians) were quite as important to him as Greeks, despite his
saturation in classical literature. The hazardous journey to Ali Pasha
is the story of a love-affair with wild, gorgeously dressed soldiers and
banditti, proud but courteous Turkish officials and a mountainous
landscape of supreme savage beauty. It was the more exciting because
Byron knew that the country was almost unexplored by Englishmen.
As *Childe Harold* puts it, 'The scene was savage, but the scene was new'.
It provoked in him his feudal delight in rank and that aristocratic
freedom of manners, so unlike poor Boswell's, which had already made
him the friend of jockeys and prize-fighters. Having sailed to Salaora
on the same Ambracian Gulf, he was already enjoying the company of
the Pasha's Albanian soldiers in the barracks there, drinking coffee
with them, smoking the *narghile* and listening to their acrid singing
and their unmannerly belches.

On 3rd October they set off with ten horses, four for the baggage,
two servants (Fletcher and a Greek hired at Patras) and two of the
soldiers. They went by Arta, that town of hawks and Byzantine
churches where the bridge enshrines a tragic legend, and on the 5th
reached Ali's lakeside capital of Ioannina. The Pasha was not there but
he knew of their approach and had made the most hospitable provision
for them. They were taken over the palace of Mouctar Pasha, Ali's
eldest son, by a charming ten-year-old, Mahmout, who was Ali's
grandson. They met the only Englishman in the region, the British
Resident, Captain Leake. They saw a Greek wedding-procession and
ventured into a Turkish bath. Only the sight of a human arm dangling
from a tree reminded them of the other side of Turkish domination.

They had then to ride in very bad weather seventy miles over the
mountains to Tebeleni, where Ali was finishing 'a little war'. Caught
for nine hours in a thunderstorm, Byron composed a poem to Mrs
Spencer Smith and only arrived at Zitza at three in the morning. He
thought the monastery there, on its oak-clad hill, the finest for situation
of any place he had seen except Cintra. He would declare it in fact 'the
finest in Greece', with Delphi and Parnassus, for all his pleasure in
them, 'very inferior'. Several stanzas of *Childe Harold* describe place
and view.

Monastic Zitza! from thy shady brow,
Thou small, but favoured spot of holy ground!
Where'er we gaze—around—above—below—
What rainbow tints, what magic charms are found!
Rock, river, forest, mountain, all abound,
And bluest skies that harmonise the whole...

It was the approach to Tebeleni, however, which now gave Byron
the greatest thrill. Here, indeed, was the exotic East. He described it
all in a letter to his mother. 'I shall never forget the singular scene on
entering Tepaleen at five in the afternoon, as the sun was going down.
The Albanians, in their dresses (the most magnificent in the world,
consisting of a long *white kilt*, gold-worked cloak, crimson velvet gold-
laced jacket and waistcoat, silver-mounted pistols and daggers), the
Tartars with their high caps, the Turks in their vast pelisses and
turbans, the soldiers and black slaves with the horses...two hundred
steeds ready caparisoned to move in a moment, couriers entering or
passing out with the despatches, the kettle-drums beating, boys calling
the hour from the minaret of the mosque...' Furthermore, Byron was
received with kindly suavity (and a hint of underlying eroticism) by
the terrible Turk. In a hall paved with marble, a fountain tinkling in
its centre and against the walls ottomans no less scarlet than Milord's
splendid dress-uniform, the portly blue-eyed Pasha received him
standing ('a wonderful compliment'), bade him sit at his right hand
and almost immediately sent his respects to his visitor's mother. 'He
said he was certain I was a man of birth, because I had small ears,
curling hair, and little white hands, and expressed himself pleased with
my appearance and garb. He told me to consider him as a father while
I was in Turkey, and said he looked on me as a son. Indeed, he treated
me like a child, sending me almonds and sugared sherbert, fruit and
sweetmeats, twenty times a day.' And thus, after coffee and pipes, the
first of several meetings came to an end. Byron was delighted by the
reference to his personal beauty as a sign of high birth—he lectured
Hobhouse on the subject the same evening—nor was he unduly
suspicious of the undercurrent of affection, which he was to meet with
again in the more demonstrative attentions of Ali's second son, Vely,
the Pasha of the Morea. Of course he knew Ali was a rogue: the prototype, perhaps, of the pirate Lambro in *Don Juan* and of Giaffir in *The
Bride of Abydos*. Tales of the Pasha's ruthlessness and cruelty were manifold. On the complaint of a favourite daughter-in-law that her husband

was neglecting her for other women, had not Ali demanded the names of any possible rivals and when the distracted lady mentioned, more or less at random, fifteen beautiful Greeks and Turks, ordered them to be arrested, sewn into sacks and dropped into the lake of Ioannina?

The return journey to the capital took only four days. Once more 'a sprightly pretty boy' met them in a palace (now it was Vely's son); 'they are totally unlike our lads, have painted complexions like rouged dowagers, large black eyes, and features perfectly regular. They are the prettiest little animals I ever saw, and are broken into the court ceremonies already.' Once more they rode the Vizier's horses, this time to the great amphitheatre not yet known to be Dodona. And it was here at Ioannina that Byron, stirred by some stanzas of Spencer's *Faerie Queene* in an anthology, *Elegant Selections*, which he had with him, began on the last day of October to write *Childe Harold*.

This work almost amounted to instant poetry. In the midst of encountering new scenes and places, Byron was busy with his experiences of only a few weeks before in Portugal and Spain. He was so excited by his first view of Parnassus that he interpolated some stanzas about Delphi and the sacred mountain in an account of the ladies of Seville. And when a rainy day at Thebes gave him the leisure to describe the differences between a Spanish and an English Sunday, a mysterious reference to 'Boeotian Shades' hints at the verses' place of origin. But it is Canto II, concluded at Smyrna in March of the following year, which covers the first months in Greece. Framed in awe at past greatness ('Where'er we tread 'tis haunted, holy ground'), regret at present conditions ('Fair Greece! sad relic of departed Worth!') and pleasure in the beauty of the climate and the landscape ('Yet are thy skies as blue, thy crags as wild' or 'Apollo still thy long, long summer gilds'), the poem records with enormous gusto a great many of the experiences of the real-life Byron. These range from pleasure in travelling in a trim naval vessel ('White is the glassy deck, without a stain') to cynical reflections on the art of seduction ('Brisk Confidence still best with woman copes'). The journey is comprehensively sketched in and Byron's particular enthusiasms are emphasised: 'Dark Suli's rocks, and Pindus' inland peak'; Ali Pasha as 'a man of war and woes' and ferocious enough for all his apparent gentleness to be marked 'with a tiger's tooth'; the descent into Tebeleni and the barbaric splendour of the scene he was shortly to find at Utraikee, as the flames gleamed along the faces of the 'kirtled clan'. After Albania, the Canto offers little that is specific beyond the general sense of ruin and ruins. There is the bitter

attack on the Earl of Elgin, of which more later. And where so much
is declamatory or reflective Byron has to remind himself that he has a
hero to his story. It is towards the beginning of the Canto that we have:

> But where is Harold? shall I then forget
> To urge the gloomy Wanderer o'er the wave?

Thus *Childe Harold* now accompanied Byron back to Preveza and
then to a near shipwreck in one of the Pasha's armed galleys, for the
Turks were hopeless sailors, and thence, further sea voyages being
abandoned, across the wilds of Acarnania to Messalonghi and Patras.
Yet the professional writer at the time was not Byron but Hobhouse.
It was the latter who kept taking notes for his projected travel book.

'I like the Albanians much,' Byron wrote from Preveza again on
12th November 1809. Two of them, in fact, became his servants and
he had already bought more than one of their splendid costumes. He
had been impressed by the way a village chieftain had refused to accept
money for helping them after the boat had got into difficulties and they
had landed on the Suli coast: 'I wish you to love me, not to pay me.'
A few days later, at Utraikee, they spent a night in a place recently
marauded by robbers, their companions soldiers who were scarcely
more law-abiding. A goat was roasted and there was dancing, 'bound-
ing hand in hand, man linked to man' while a song was shouted,
Robbers all at Parga. This was the essence of picturesqueness, in some
ways the climax of the whole tour. To Philhellenes today it will recall
the rock of Zalongo, where a band of women Souliotes committed
suicide by leaping one at a time over the cliff when waylaid on the road
to Parga by Ali's troops, although he had himself ordered the freedom-
fighters to repair to that small but lovely port; it will bring to mind the
precipitous fringes of the Suli coast and the desolate plateau behind it
where flows the river Acheron and where Charon waits amongst the
reeds and choking water-lilies of Acheroussia until the corpse arrives
with the *obol* fare held in its teeth; and it will suggest, too, the clear
statements of Philhellenism to which Byron himself would come.

> Fill high the bowl with Samian wine!
>   On Suli's rock, and Parga's shore,
> Exists the remnants of a line
>   Such as the Doric mothers bore;
> And there, perhaps, some seed is sown,
> The Heracleidan blood might own.
>   (*Don Juan*, Canto III.)

Now Byron travelled through Delphi and Livadhia to Athens.
Behind him we feel Greece: the valleys of olives floating down to Itea,
as crisply woolly as a negro's head; the Phaedriades, the Shining Rocks
of Delphi, which for all their majestic beauty bear colours that remind
one of the grey and pink of tinned salmon; Aráchova on its height,
source of one of the best red wines, and the dark puzzle of interfolding
hills and wiry scrub where Oedipus slew his father; so to Livadhia, site
of the suffocating subterranean constrictions through which you
dropped and crawled and were sucked to find the Oracle of Trophonius,
home too of the springs of Memory and Forgetfulness flowing down to
form the municipal water-supply; up there Chaeronea, a monumental
lion against the pines and the hillside, and out across the marsh
Orchomenos, where there is a beehive tomb from Minyan days; the
cliffs of Parnes and Cithaeron with their ancient battlements; soft pine-
brushed Daphni, Apollo's temple long since a church; and then beyond
Athens, the violet-crowned, the promontories and bays of a maritime
power, establishing themselves in a kind of absolute geography, burning with the passion of a philosophic truth; and farther still the islands,
first a calligraphy of blue and cinnamon and rose, suave hieroglyphs of
rolling dolphin and skimming gull, and then aromatic hillsides set in a
sea of sticky indigo like wet paint, a huddle of white houses and the sun
riding the whitewash bareback, digging molten spurs and whistling a
lassoo of golden wire and pigeons and wasps. From such islands
Byron's supreme tribute to Greece, the Haidée episode in *Don Juan*,
would one day be made.

Byron reached Athens on Christmas Day, 1809; from a point near
Fort Phyle, on the borders of Boetia and Attica, 'Athens, Pentelicus,
Hymettus, the Aegean, and the Acropolis, burst upon the eye at once'.
He stayed there until the following March, renting half a house on
Aghias Theclas Street from Mrs Tarsia Macri, the widow of a Cephal-
lonian doctor who had been British Vice-Consul, and thus coming into
close contact with her daughter, Teresa, the thirteen-year-old 'Maid
of Athens', together with her two sisters. The family was in reduced
circumstances but, to judge from Hobhouse, the accommodation was
pleasant enough. 'Our lodging consisted of a sitting-room and two
bedrooms, opening into a courtyard, where there were five or six lemon
trees, from which during our residence in the place was plucked the
fruit that seasoned the pilaf and other national dishes served up at our
frugal meals.' The girls sound charming. Not long afterwards another
English tourist described them as follows: 'Their apartment is

6*

immediately opposite to ours, and if you could see them, as we do now, through the gently waving aromatic plants before our window, you would leave your heart in Athens...Their persons are elegant, and their manners pleasing and ladylike, such as would be fascinating in any country. They possess very considerable powers of conversation, and their minds seem to be more instructed than those of the Greek women in general.' It is not surprising that Byron soon had a door opened between the two parts of the house.

During the next two months he thoroughly enjoyed himself. Athens was then a small city of something over a thousand houses or hovels and with a population of about ten thousand; it was crowded against the northern and eastern sides of the Acropolis and was encircled by a wall round which Hobhouse was able to walk in forty-seven minutes. In importance it ranked as only the forty-third city of the Turkish Empire. The Acropolis was a supposedly military installation to which admission was somewhat difficult; it was dominated by a Florentine watch-tower, eighty-five feet high, while the Parthenon contained a small mosque and lay next to a Turkish barracks. A few years before Byron, Châteaubriand had reached the city in a cloud of romantic prose. Approaching Daphni along the Sacred Way he declared: 'I am certain that the most devout initiate of Demeter never felt a livelier happiness than mine.' Yet Athens itself was not so much beautiful as picturesque. 'At the foot of the Acropolis, Athens revealed herself to me: her flat roofs mingled with minarets, her cypresses, ruins, isolated columns, the domes of mosques crowned with big stork-nests, made a pleasant effect in the rays of the sun. But if one still recognised Athens in this debris, one saw also, in the mixture of her buildings and the general character of her monuments, that the city of Minerva was no longer inhabited by her people.' This suggestion of the unworthiness of the modern Greek was no doubt fostered by the French Consul, Louis-François-Sébastien Fauvel, with whom Châteaubriand stayed and whom Byron in his turn was to know and like. (Most Franks in Athens had a low opinion of the natives.) It was at Fauvel's that Châteaubriand first tasted retsina and reflected mournfully, for he couldn't stomach the wine, that the pine-cone was sacred to Bacchus.

The two principal antiquarians in Athens were Fauvel, who had been the agent for the Comte de Choiseul-Gouffier, and Lusieri, Lord Elgin's agent, whom we shall meet again shortly. Both were concerned with the pillaging—or from another point of view the rescue—of classical artefacts in a really big way; Fauvel's original instructions had been explicit: 'Enlevez tout ce que vous pourrez. Ne négligez aucune occasion de piller dans Athènes tout ce qu'il y a de pillable. N'épargnez ni les morts ni les vivants'. The effect of such seriously predatory antiquarianism was beneficial to the extent that it largely put a stop to the Turks' habit of chipping off small, pocketable pieces which could be quickly sold to passing tourists. Both Fauvel and Lusieri had their collections, their casts and drawings, and also their contacts and their scale of bribes. Both were terrified when a French or English frigate anchored in the Piraeus because they knew that the young midshipmen would swarm ashore determined on acquiring artistic souvenirs. As one observer remarked of a period when the Acropolis was unusually accessible: 'The last time I visited the citadel...I was much displeased at seeing an English traveller, an officer of the navy (for such his uniform bespoke him to be) standing upon the base of one of the caryatids...endeavouring to knock off the only remaining nose of those six beautifully sculptured statues. I exerted my eloquence in vain to preserve this monument of art' (P. E. Laurent, Reflections of a Classical Tour, 1821). Both Fauvel and Lusieri, in the midst of fighting out their private Napoleonic war, acted as guides to the sights. Byron used them both.

So it was now that he saw the ruins, which certainly looked more solid than most of the shanties surrounding them, although several large and important monuments had disappeared entirely in the last hundred years; as Christopher Wordsworth was to remark after the revolution, 'there is now scarcely any building at Athens in so perfect a state as the Temple of Theseus. The least ruined objects here are some of the ruins themselves' (Athens and Attica, 1837). While peasants ploughed the ancient agora, he visited this much admired but curiously dull temple, now known to have been the Hephaesteion. He sat on a fallen column of the Temple of Olympian Zeus, as he explains in Childe Harold, and doubtless looked from that vantage point through Hadrian's Arch up the Street of the Tripods. He climbed the Acropolis and compared the Doric masculinity of the Parthenon with the delicate grace of the even holier Erechtheum, one time shrine of the olive-wood cult statue of Athena Polias. He rode often to Piraeus and the Bay of Phaleron, where he used to swim. Further off, he visited Eleusis and the Temple of Poseidon at Cape Sounion; he is said to have followed the usual practice and carved his name on one of its columns, although the inscription now shown may be a fake. He explored Mount Hymettus and inspected the marble quarries of Mount Pentelikon. But he was just as absorbed by the social life of the Athens Carnival and when,

early in March of 1810 a 'lift' to Turkey on a British ship presented
itself, he and Hobhouse so hated leaving that, as the latter said, they
rushed down to the port, 'galloping at a quick pace in order to rid themselves, by the hurry, of the pain of parting'. Châteaubriand, incidentally,
had much the same feeling: *'J'étois bien aisé de quitter Athènes de nuit;
j'aurois en trop de regret de m'éloigner de ses ruines á la lumière du soleil...'*

Byron went to Smyrna, the Dardanelles and finally Constantinople
where he attended (to his annoyance, inconspicuously) an audience
held by Sultan Mahmoud II. His own favourite adventure was his
swimming of the Hellespont from Abydos to Sestos (the wrong way
round from Leander's exploit and with no return journey) in an hour
and ten minutes and only on the second attempt. At the end of this
expedition to Turkey proper Byron parted from Hobhouse, their
token of farewell the two halves of a posy; he returned to Athens and
'tranquillity under the blue skies of Greece' on 18th July, 1810. He
now moved from the Macri household to the Capuchin convent whose
buildings included the choregic monument of Lysicrates and which was
part school, part guest-house. This seems to have been a period of
livelier social activity and of greater emotional experimentation than
the cautious and conservative Hobhouse would have approved. 'I am
most auspiciously settled in the Convent, which is more commodious
than any tenement I have yet occupied, with room for my *suite*,' he
wrote his friend in August. 'It is by no means solitary, seeing there is
not only "il Padre Abbate" but his "schuola" consisting of six "Rag-
azzi", all my most particular allies. These gentlemen, being almost
(saving Fauvel and Lusieri) my only associates, it is but proper their
character, religion and morals should be described...Their names are
Barthelemi, Giuseppe, Nicolo, Zani, and two anonymous, at least in
my memory...We have nothing but riot from noon to night. The first
time I mingled with these sylphs, after about two minutes' recon-
noitring, the amiable Signor Barthelemi, without any previous notice,
seated himself by me, and after observing by way of compliment that
my "Signoria" was the "piu bello" of his English acquaintance,
saluted me on the left cheek, for which freedom being reproved by
Giuseppe, who very properly informed him that I was μεγαλος, he
told me I was his φιλος and "by his beard" he would do so again...
But my friend, as you may easily imagine, is Nicolo, who by the way
is my Italian master, and we are already very philosophical. I am his
"Padrone" and his "amico" and the Lord knows what besides...he
concluded by telling me it was proper for us not only to live, but

"morire insieme". The latter I hope to avoid—as much of the former as he pleases.' This sounds like Harrow revived but is also, although only three of the boys were Greeks, typically Athenian.

It was now that Byron made two trips to the Peloponese. The highlight of the first (Corinth, Patras and round by Tripolis to Argos) was his meeting with Vely Pasha, the son of the Despot of Epirus, who honoured him with 'a number of squeezes and speeches' and gave him a fine stallion. Vely was clearly taken with Byron and wanted more of his company: 'I will send to Athens, and you shall join me,' he assured Byron at Tripolis. 'We will eat and drink and go a-hunting.' In his letter to Hobhouse Byron added: 'He honoured me with the appellation of his *friend* and *brother*, and hoped that we should be on good terms, not for a few days but for life. The first time I saw him he received me *standing*, and accompanied me at my departure to the door of the audience chamber, and told me I was a παλικαρι and ευμορφω παιδι.'[1]

On this expedition Byron had travelled with the Marquis of Sligo's party for some of the way and had met it again at Argos; the second journey was undertaken with only one companion, Mrs Lusieri's sixteen-year-old brother, Nicolo Giraud. Byron fell seriously ill of a fever at Patras. He must have been alarmed, for his letters are full of other foreigners dying in Greece, but he joked about his illness with even more than his customary sprightliness and charm. 'I am at present in a very ridiculous situation, under the hands of Dr Romanelli, and a fever which has confined me to my bed for three days past, but by the blessing of God and two glysters, I am now able to sit up, but much debilitated (Patras, 25th September, 1810, to Hobhouse). He continued with a parody of Pope's lines on the Duke of Buckingham:

> On a cold room's cold floor, within a bed
> Of iron, with three coverlids like lead,
> A coat and breeches dangling o'er a nook,
> Where sits a doctor and prescribes a puke,
> Poor B--r--n sweats, alas! how changed from him,
> So plump in feature, and so round in limb,
> The scene of profanation, and champagne,
> Or just as gay with scribblers in a ring
> Of twenty hungry authors banqueting.
> Here victim of a fever, and its friends,
> Physicians and their art, his lordship *mends*.

[1] A good fellow and a handsome boy.

It was on this tour that Byron visited one of the great classical sites ('The other day I went to Olympia') but neither on this nor on other similar occasions did he leave any detailed description. As he explained when Hobhouse requested it, he kept no journal.

He left for England on the 22nd of April, 1811, in the *Hydra* which, ironically, carried the last shipment of the marbles Lord Elgin had acquired. A strange thing happened at the very moment of his departure. A young English architectural student, Charles Robert Cockerell, was setting sail with two German friends for the nearby island of Aegina when he spotted the *Hydra*, drew alongside and attracted Byron's attention by singing one of his favourite songs. Byron immediately invited him and his party on board for drinks. Little did the most famous of all opponents of archaeological plundering know that this same Charles Cockerell would in the course of the next few days unearth and purloin the entire sculptural decoration to the Temple of Aphaia at Aegina (to be sold to Ludwig of Bavaria's grandfather and thus to become the chief glory of the Glyptothek in Munich), after which he went on to do precisely the same thing with the sculptures at Bassae.

Byron was not happy to leave Greece. The winter had been 'most social and fantastical…we had balls, dinners, and amours without number.' And the position of the city was beautiful: 'Setting aside the magic of the same…the very situation of Athens would render it the favourite of all who have eyes for art and nature. The climate, to me at least, appeared a perpetual spring; during the eight months I have never passed a day without being as many hours on horseback; rain is extraordinarily rare, snow never lies on the plains, and a cloudy day is an agreeable variety.'

There are certain features of Byron's travelling which may be of interest to modern tourists, even if they are not Philhellenes exploring Greece. Obviously we cannot expect to undergo experiences similar to some of his. We shall not be in real danger from pirates when we visit Cape Sounion, or any other temple on the Mediterranean coast. Nor are we likely to draw our pistols and save a young Turkish girl sewn up in a sack and about to be drowned in the Bay of Phaleron because of an act of illicit love perhaps with our servant, perhaps with ourself—a girl we know well anyway, and whose story years later will be 'icy in recollection'—as happened to Byron in September, 1810. But for the rest, the constant swimming, the enjoyment of the climate, the pleasure in food (woodcock, red mullet, 'sweet cakes made of sugar and almonds'), the experimentation with the language, the solitary musing which appropriated landscape, ruins and history into a personal vision (gazing, as Leake had said, 'with an air distrait and dreaming upon distant mountains'), the endless involvement with people (Greeks, Turks, Franks) and the taking up of a passionately controversial position over the depredations of Lord Elgin together with a deeply interested and comparatively optimistic attitude towards the Greeks themselves, all this, I think, represents the kind of travelling most of us would like to undertake. Let me add that, although not so often admitted, sexual or at least emotional encounters form part of a traveller's *raison d'être*. Here we, too, can meet a Maid of Athens and share in the amusements of the boyish 'sylphs' at the Capuchin convent. Not, I imagine, that Byron's erotic athleticism is likely to invite many rivals. On 4th October, 1810, he wrote to Hobhouse about his experiences in Attica: 'I have obtained above two hundred pl- & optCs (e.g. plenum et optabile coitum) and am almost tired of them...' *Almost*, but after all he was recovering from a fever.

Byron's attitude to his travelling may be first seen in his amused irritation with the faithful William Fletcher, his valet, 'an honest-looking, though not remarkably elastic Northumbrian' as he was to be described fifteen years later when, having accompanied Byron throughout his Italian sojourn, he followed him to Messalonghi. There are constant references to this insular representative of the British working-class in the letters Byron sent home. Fletcher abroad was a 'nincompoup', a 'timberhead'. Fletcher constantly harped on their distance from home: 'three thousand miles (according to Fletcher's invariable calculation from the moment he *cleared the channel*)'. Fletcher 'yelled for his wife' and moaned of 'a watery grave' when the sea grew rough off the Suli coast; while, during a thunderstorm in the mountains, he feared 'famine and bandits' and the lightning hurt his eyes, or did he actually cry? He had been anxious to come, he had his uses — Hobhouse describes him at Tebeleni 'lousing all day with great success especially in my lord's shirt' — but things quickly got too much for him, not always surprisingly: 'we have several Albanian women washing in the "giardino", whose hours of relaxation are spent in running pins into Fletcher's backside.' He became 'refractory' at Constantinople when his master planned a long overland journey, soon abandoned. On their return to Athens he seems to have momentarily improved. 'Fletcher, after having been toasted and roasted, and baked, and grilled, and eaten by all sorts of creeping things, begins to philosophise, is grown a refined as well as a resigned character...and wonders (though I do not) that his ill-written and worse spelt letters home never come to hand' (25th July, 1810, to Mrs Byron). But he grew more and more accident-prone: 'Fletcher, too, with his usual acuteness, contrived at Megara to run his damned clumsy foot into a boiling tea-kettle.' And he was shocked to the core by a member of the party during Byron's first 'gyration of the Morea', a boy named Eustathios Georgiou who was vain, temperamental and subject to fits: 'I found the dear soul upon horseback,' Byron wrote, 'clothed very sparsely in Grecian garments, and with those ambrosial curls hanging down his amiable back, and to my utter astonishment, and the great abomination of Fletcher, a parasol in his hand to save his complexion from the heat...'

It is difficult not to see in Fletcher a prototype of that kind of tourist we all know, who wouldn't dream of being without his Nescafé and Enterovioform and whose days are punctuated by wincing evasions of fried squid, sheep's milk cheese and resinated wine, and an almost self-righteous search for bacon and eggs and beef and chips. It is only fair to add, though, that Hobhouse was also a great complainer. 'I do love thee, Hobby, thou hast so many good qualities, and so many bad ones, it is impossible to live with or without thee,' Byron wrote to his friend after he had left, but elsewhere he made it quite clear that he was glad to be alone. In the end Byron decided to send Fletcher home although his customary kindness made a point of ensuring that there would be a cottage for him at Newstead. '...the perpetual lamentations after beef and beer,' Byron wrote to his mother, 'the stupid, bigoted contempt for everything foreign, and insurmountable incapacity of acquiring even a few words of any language, rendered him, like all other servants, an encumbrance. I do assure you, the plague of speaking for him, the comforts he required (more than myself by far), the pilaws (a Turkish dish of rice and meat) which he could not eat, the wines he could not drink, the beds where he could not sleep, and the long list of calamities, such as stumbling horses, want of tea!!! etc, which assailed him, would have made a lasting source of laughter to a spectator, and inconvenience to a master.'

Byron himself was prepared to live rough, another point which may recommend him to those who really want to find out about a country. Hobhouse complained, he says, 'that I had no notion of comfort, because I could sleep where none but a *brute* could, and certainly *brutes did*; for often have the cows, turned out of their apartment, *butted* at the door all night, extraordinarily discomposed with their unaccountable ejectment'. This is the mood of the prelude to *The Siege of Corinth* where the poet looks back to the 'gallant company' of 1810:

> We forded the river, and clomb the high hill,
> Never our steeds for a day stood still;
> Whether we lay in the cave or the shed,
> Our sleep fell soft on the hardest bed;
> Whether we couch'd in our rough capote,
> On the rougher plank of our gliding boat,
> Or stretch'd on the beach, or our saddles spread
> As a pillow beneath the resting head,
> Fresh we woke upon the morrow:
> All our thoughts and words had scope,
> We had health, and we had hope,
> Toil and travel, but no sorrow.

It should be remembered that, for all the rough living, it was inconceivable for a Regency aristocrat, especially of Byron's character, actually to travel light. Although that predecessor of the modern motor-caravan, the huge green coach copied from one of Napoleon's with its library, *lit de repos*, plate-chest and dining facilities, was not acquired until 1816, Byron had with him in Albania seven trunks, the largest weighing eighty pounds, a canteen, several beds, with bedding, and four saddles and bridles.

A parallel attitude was his distrust of mere archaeological inquisitiveness. He quickly grew bored with classical sites, in those days often faint if not conjectural, although he in fact saw a great many; not only the 'musts', so to speak, but Nicopolis and Orchomenus, Phyle and Brauron, the barrows of pre-Schliemann Troy, and in the Peloponnese Mantinea and Tegea. When they were both living in Athens, it was Hobhouse who rode in the mornings about Attica; Byron stayed at home working on *Childe Harold*, and only followed in his friend's tracks in the afternoon. 'Travelling in Greece Hobhouse and I wrangled every day...He would potter with map and compass at the foot of Pindus, Parnes and Parnassus, to ascertain the site of some ancient temple or city. I rode my mule up them. They had haunted my dreams from boyhood...John Cam's dogged perseverance in pursuit of his hobby is to be envied; I have no hobby and no perseverance. I gazed at the stars and ruminated; took no notes, asked no questions.' It was thus characteristic of him to write of the plains of Troy: 'The Troad is a fine field for conjecture and snipe-shooting, and a good sportsman and an ingenious scholar may exercise their feet and faculties to great advantage upon the spot...' Byron, in fact, was no snipe-shooter; the eagle he had wounded at Patras had determined him never to kill another bird. One of his Trojan amusements was to dive for tortoises. Riding formed a great part of his sight-seeing. At Constantinople he liked best to ride around the semi-circle of land walls from the Golden Horn to the Sea of Marmara. 'Imagine four miles of immense triple battlements, covered with ivy, surmounted with 218 towers and, on the other side of the road, Turkish burying-grounds (the loveliest spots on earth)...' The note is of his own adventure, expressed in his own terms.

For, as he says, he 'ruminated'. His friend Tom Moore described how 'one of his chief delights...was, when bathing in some retired spot, to seat himself on a high rock above the sea, and there remain for hours, gazing upon the sky and the waters, and lost in that sort of vague reverie, which, however formless and indistinct at the moment, settled afterwards, on his pages, into those clear, bright, pictures, which will endure for ever...' This was the 'raptness' which John Galt had observed on board the ship from Gibraltar, after a flurry of rank-consciousness, 'In the little bustle and process of embarking their luggage his lordship affected, as it seemed to me, more aristocracy than befitted his years, or the occasion...[but soon] held himself aloof, and sat on the rail, leaning on the mizzen shrouds, inhaling, as it were, poetical sympathy from the gloomy rock, then dark and stern in the twilight.' If a scowl of abstraction did from time to time cross Byron's face, perhaps all the more noticably because his face was so remarkably smooth-skinned, there is no reason to follow Lady Hester Stanhope's Athenian snapshot: 'He had a great deal of vice in his looks—his eyes set close together, and a contracted brow.' As for those 'clear bright pictures' Moore mentions, Byron's description of sunset from the Acropolis may be taken as an example; he was evidently pleased with it for he lifted it out of his *Curse of Minerva*, a far from expert satire on Lord Elgin's depredations, to feature in *The Corsair* although he confesses, in a note, that he isn't sure it belongs there.

> Slow sinks, more lovely ere his race be run,
> Along Morea's hills the setting sun;
> Not, as in Northern climes, obscurely bright,
> But one unclouded blaze of living light!

O'er the hushed deep the yellow beam he throws,
Gilds the green wave, that trembles as it glows.
On old Ægina's rock and Idra's isle
The god of gladness sheds his parting smile;
O'er his own regions lingering loves to shine,
Though there his altars are no more divine.
Descending fast, the mountain shadows kiss
Thy glorious gulf, unconquered Salamis!
There azure arches through the long expanse
More deeply purpled meet his mellowing glance,
And tenderest tints, along their summits driven,
Mark his gay course, and own the hues of Heaven;
Till, darkly shaded from the land and deep,
Behind his Delphian rock he sinks to sleep.

For all his love of pleasure, Byron worked hard while abroad. In January, 1810, he let Hobhouse visit Negroponte (Euboea) on his own because he was busy with *Childe Harold*. He was also, of course, gathering material for a whole series of oriental tales: *The Giaour* and *The Bride of Abydos* to be published in 1813, *The Corsair* which followed in the next year (and sold 10,000 copies on its first day) and *The Siege of Corinth* which appeared early in 1815. Towards the end of his stay he was writing his *Hints from Horace*, a work he thought at the time considerably superior to the long poem embodying his experiences. It is significant that he supplemented the imaginative poetry with careful explanatory notes of a factual travel-book nature, explaining foreign words, customs and peculiarities: that Turks' beards curl when they are angry and that when they are very angry they pluck them out, or that their scimitars are engraved with a verse from the Koran (and sometimes the name of the maker), or that dervishes are divided into colleges, or that Muslims must *skate* into Paradise over a bridge 'by breadth less than the thread of a famished spider'. All this is in something of a Hobhouse strain. Thus Cape Sounion rates thirty-five or so lines of explanatory prose, beginning with: 'To the antiquary and artist, sixteen columns are an inexhaustible source of observation and design' etc, continuing with a reference to Falconer's shipwreck and then describing Byron's own adventure with the pirates. Such documentation reminds us that much of Byron's popularity with the reading public must have been due to his travelogue aspect; he was telling people about places in which they were interested but of which they knew little. It also suggests a substratum of solid fact-mongering in himself. The tales themselves are all passion and action, predominantly Turkish and exotic in their setting, and reinforced by references to such things as the 'simoon' and the bulbul and the blue-winged Kashmir butterfly and Persian attar of roses and the suicide of scorpions and the giving of bread and salt, together with any number of details as to weapons and costumes; it is not so easy to find detailed description that is particularly relevant to Greece today. There is the grotto, the defile, the mountainside alongside harem, mosque and encampment, and there is often the sea. There is the cypress: 'Dark tree, still sad when other's grief is fled, / The only constant mourner o'er the dead!' And the dried-up stream, 'where the winds and the desolate dust are spread':

> 'Twas sweet of yore to see it play,
> And chase the sultriness of day.
> As springing high the silver dew
> In whirls fantastically flew,
> And flung luxurious coolness round
> The air and verdure o'er the ground.
> 'Twas sweet, when cloudless stars were bright,
> To view the wave of watery light,
> And hear its melody by night.

Byron, like Boswell, was a socially adaptable traveller; despite its utter lack of hotels, Athens was a popular centre of tourism then as now; and Byron appreciated the stimulus of other visitors, although he liked to discriminate between them. In the autumn of 1810 he told Francis Hodgson that he was 'on good terms with five Teutones and Cimbri, Danes and Germans, who are travelling for an Academy'. This was a group led by two Danish archaeologists with one of whom, Dr Peter Oluf Bronsted, Byron contracted a particular alliance for he was 'as pretty a philosopher as you'd wish to see'; it also contained a Bavarian painter whom he commissioned to provide him with land-scapes. All were intelligent people and it is likely that they directed him to some understanding of what was going on in Greek literary circles. He had already talked with the patriot schoolmaster, Psalidis, at Ioannina and now Bronsted and his own Greek language tutor, Mar-marotouri, told him of the important role played by the language in the stirrings of Greek nationalism and showed him the work of modern poets. Strangely, though, he seems to have had little interest in the

Orthodox Church, preserver of the language over the centuries and instigator of the 'secret schools'. He himself liked to speak Romaic. As he wrote long afterwards, 'when I left Greece in 1811, I could garble Romaic pretty fluently'—indeed Lady Hester Stanhope used to make fun of him by imitating the grave way he gave orders to his servant in that language. He used a Greek refrain for his Maid of Athens poem (Ζωη μου, σας αγαπω), made his own version of a song very popular amongst the girls of Athens in the winter of 1810–11 ('I enter thy Garden of Roses / Beloved and fair Haidée') and translated the Marseillaise-like anthem written by the revolutionary martyr, Righa, twenty years before. (Δευτε παιδες των Ελληνων, 'Sons of the Greeks, arise.')

His attitude to the Greeks wavered but it was certainly more optimistic than that prevalent amongst the Frankish inhabitants of Athens, although it had none of the sentimental idealisation to be found in some Philhellenic circles, notably with reference to the 'Spartan' virtues of the inhabitants of the Mani. To Byron the Greeks were people. 'I like the Greeks, who are plausible rascals, with all the Turkish vices, without their courage. However, some are brave, and all are beautiful, very much resembling the busts of Alcibiades, the women not quite so handsome.' (In Albania, too, he had found the women rather less attractive than the men.) In one of the notes to *Childe Harold* he sprang quite passionately to their defence. 'They are so unused to kindness that when they occasionally meet with it they look upon it with suspicion, as a dog often beaten snaps at your fingers if you attempt to caress him. "They are ungrateful, notoriously, abominably ungrateful!"—this is the general cry. Now, in the name of Nemesis! for what are they to be grateful? Where is the human being that ever conferred a benefit on Greek or Greeks? They are to be grateful to the Turks for their fetters, and the Franks for their broken promises and lying councils. They are to be grateful to the artist who engraves their ruins and to the antiquary who carries them away.'

This is nobly said. But in January, 1811, Byron also declared that 'the interposition of foreigners alone can emancipate the Greeks, who, otherwise, appear to have as small a chance of redemption from the Turks as the Jews from mankind in general.' This accords with the low opinion expressed in the opening of *The Giaour*, where we have, after a striking image of Greece as a beautiful dead body which is reminiscent of Paoli's description of giving the 'kiss of life' to Corsica, the story of its decline:

> Such is the aspect of this shore;
> 'Tis Greece, but living Greece no more!
> So coldly sweet, so deadly fair,
> We start, for soul is wanting there.
>
> 'Twere long to tell, and sad to trace,
> Each step from splendour to disgrace;
> Enough—no foreign foe could quell
> Thy soul, till from itself it fell;
> Yes! Self-abasement paved the way
> To villain-bonds and despot sway.

This is shortly followed by a portrait of the modern Greek which in fact goes right back to Juvenal's cutting phrase about the Greek's insinuating cleverness, *Omnia novit Graeculus esuriens*, and so to Roman (and later Western European) pride in our supposed Trojan origin which led to the view of the Renaissance, including Shakespeare, that Greeks were either frivolous and licentious or unscrupulous and conniving.

> Still to the neighbouring ports they waft
> Proverbial wiles, and ancient craft;
> In this the subtle Greek is found,
> For this, and this alone, renowned.

Byron had been disgusted to find that the Governor of Athens was appointed by the Kislar-Aghasi, the slave in charge of the Seraglio— 'A pander and eunuch...now *governs* the governor of Athens!'; he had been delighted when, at Vostitza on the Gulf of Corinth, a rich Greek who acted as Cogia Pasha (a sort of Prime Minister to the Turks) had burst into passionate denunciation of his country's plight. *The Giaour* in fact contradicts what Byron had said earlier in *Childe Harold*: 'Who would be free *themselves* must strike the blow', as well as the later 'Isles of Greece' passage in *Don Juan*: 'Trust not for freedom to the Franks' and the belief expressed in *The Age of Bronze*: 'Greeks only should free Greece'. In a mood of depression shortly before sailing home he had included amongst 'four or five reasons in favour of a Change' the fact that 'I have seen mankind in various Countries and find them equally despicable, if anything the Balance is rather in favour of the Turks', a remark certainly likely to affront modern Philhellenes.

In any case it was the middle-class and the urban population whose apathy distressed Byron; for Albanians, Souliotes and Corsairs he

always had the greatest regard, and he was not displeased when people
in England assumed that he himself had been a corsair during part of
his sojourn. Concern about the Greeks was unavoidable at the time;
Hobhouse, too, had many interesting things to say on the subject in
his book, including: 'The Greeks are devotedly attached to their
country and nation, and, even to a degree which may appear foolish
and incautious, continually express their hatred of their masters, and
their confidence in themselves' but I would argue further that some
degree of speculation, anxiety and criticism on this score is the price of
involvement even to this day. The Greek experience, perhaps love-
affair would be a better word, is a complex one: a world of distant
heroes and artists, peculiarly our own because we are its spiritual
descendants, reawakes into glimmering, hallucinatory life under the
power of intense heat and a ferociously beautiful landscape, and is
invaded by the vivid, noisy Levantine present. Hellas and Romiosyne,
garlic and marble, *bouzoukia* music and tinkling cicada-murmurous
pastoral isolation, motor-cars and donkeys, friendliness and egotism—
such things are difficult to hold in equilibrium.

If Byron was uncertain about the people, he was in no doubt over the
question of the Acropolis sculptures. With the arch-plunderer, Lord
Elgin, he had already taken issue before he left for Constantinople.
Byron had seen some of the Elgin marbles when they were first put on
display in Park Lane in 1807 and at that time he had shared the common
opinion that, apart from moral considerations as to their provenance,
they were mediocre works of art: in his early satire *English Bards and
Scotch Reviewers* he had laughed at 'mutilated blocks of art' and 'misshapen monuments and maim'd antiques'. But in Athens, as we have
seen, he became friendly with Giovanni Battista Lusieri (whose young
brother-in-law was that Niccolo Giraud who taught him Italian and
was his sole companion on the second Peloponnesian tour); Lusieri
had first been employed by Lord Elgin to make drawings of the
Acropolis and was now superintending the shipments to England and,
in the course of expeditions they made together—they first visited the
Acropolis after many formalities on 8th January 1810—Byron became
more and more involved in a controversy which, as Hobhouse said,
'enlisted all the Frank settlers and the principal Greeks on one or the
other side'. One of Byron's first positive acts as a Philhellene was to
denounce Elgin and other predators in the prologue to Canto II of
Childe Harold, taking up a position which may have been unfair but
was certainly effective, especially as the rest of the poem was far from

being a satire. To quote Elgin's most recent biographer, 'the young lord who had used Elgin's painter as his guide to Athens and had sailed in Elgin's ship from Greece to Malta was destined to do him more damage than Payne Knight (the London connoisseur who first doubted the value of the marbles) or even Napoleon Bonaparte.'[1]

> But most the modern Pict's ignoble boast,
> To rive what Goth, and Turk, and Time hath spared:
> Cold as the crags upon his native coast,
> His mind as barren and his heart as hard,
> Is he whose head conceived, whose hand prepared,
> Aught to displace Athena's poor remains:
> Her sons too weak the sacred shrine to guard,
> Yet felt some portion of their mother's pains,
> And never knew, till then, the weight of Despot's chains.
>
> (*Childe Harold*, Canto II.)

On his return from Constantinople he continued the assault in *The Curse of Minerva*, a poem privately printed, then suppressed but inevitably pirated. After a reference to more venial despoilers Byron continues:

> So when the Lion quits his full repast,
> Next prowls the Wolf, the filthy Jackal last:
> Flesh, limb, and blood the former make their own,
> The last poor brute securely gnaws the bone.

He then describes the scene when the sculptures are displayed in London:

> Round the thronged gate shall sauntering coxcombs creep,
> To lounge and lucubrate, to prate and peep;
> While many a languid maid, with longing sigh,
> On giant statues casts the curious eye;
> The room with transient glance appears to skim,
> Yet marks the mighty back and length of limb;
> Mourns o'er the difference of *now* and *then*;
> Exclaims, 'These Greeks indeed were proper men!'

Shortly before he left for home Byron was still thinking of further adventures: 'I am off in spring for Mount Sion, Damascus, Tyre and

[1] *Lord Elgin and the Marbles*, William St. Clair, Oxford, 1967.

Sidon, Cairo, and Thebes' he wrote to Hobhouse. By now he considered himself a practised and philosophic traveller. As he had written to his mother in January, 'I am so convinced of the advantages of looking at mankind instead of reading about them and the bitter effects of staying at home with all the narrow prejudice of an islander, that I think there should be a law amongst us, to set our young men abroad, for a term, among the few allies war has left us.' This can be the epitaph to his tour. He had been often happy—'I am vastly happy and childish' he had announced from the Capuchin convent—although his financial difficulties in England had been a worry and latterly his health had been far from perfect: 'I have been fat, and thin (as I am at present) and had a cough and a catarrh and the piles and be damned to them, and I have had pains in my side and left off animal food...' (to Hobhouse, March 5th). He had met all sorts of people: 'The day before yesterday the Wayvode (or Governor of Athens) with the Mufti of Thebes (a sort of Mussulman bishop) supped here and made themselves beastly with raw rum, and the Padre of the convent being as drunk as *we*, my *Attic* feast went off with great *éclat*' (November 14th, 1810).

And now he took his leave. The Maid of Athens might have come with him: 'I was near bringing away Maria Theresa, but the mother asked 30,000 piastres!' His Albanian servants wept and one of them dashed the money due to him to the ground. His particular young friend, Nicolo Giraud, accompanied him to Malta; left £7,000 in Byron's will until, alas, it was altered, he wrote in 1815 one of those letters which expose the faithlessness of exotic friendships in far-off places (lucky the man who has not received one): 'It is now almost three years that I am at Athens, and I have sent to you many letters, but I have not received any answer...pray your excellency to not forget your humble servant which so dearly and faithfully loves you.' For the rest he took with him an interesting collection of tourist's booty: 'four ancient Athenian skulls, dug out of sarcophagi—a phial of Attic hemlock—four live tortoises—a greyhound (died on the passage)—two live Greek servants, one an Athenian, t'other a Yaniote, who can speak nothing but Romaic and Italian—and myself...' His mind was well stored, his sensibility had been truly touched, and his evocation of Levantine scenes was soon to make him famous.

The Ever Recurring Journey to the Palace of Queluz

A Personal Travel Diary

PORTUGAL IS WHITE, sparkling and gay; Spain is tawny-brown, distance-haunted and sombre. Portugal is an Atlantic rock-garden, moist and often lush; Spain is a slab of Africa, dry and frequently sterile. Portugal charms with the stone fantasies of its mariners and the grace of the Rococo; Spain impresses and awes with Gothic or Baroque façades and darkly elaborate interiors. Portugal feeds one sardines and cod, with which one drinks a wine that is white or green; Spain dispenses prawns and paella, with which one drinks a wine that is red or amber. Generalisations such as these are invariably inaccurate but somehow remain indispensable to the traveller. It is always with a touch of exhilaration, a bubbling-up anticipatory of the first glass of *vinho verde*, that I cross the frontier into Portugal...

This is journalism, and sounds like it. Although I don't do journalism very well, I get a kick out of seeming so worldly and knowledgeable, and compressing a number of ideas into a very short space. Actually, although I know a good deal about Spain, I have only been to Portugal twice. Since I have stressed the personal note in travel-writing throughout this book, I propose to conclude it with extracts from the journal I kept during the first, and therefore freshest visit in April 1966, when I was on the track of William Beckford, Travelling with an old friend, I drove a mini down through France, and then by way of the Pyrenees and the *meseta* to the Portuguese border at Fuentes de Onoro. For several days I felt exceedingly cold...

Irun. What a place to stay; dark green mountains occasionally gleaming through ragged sponges of cloud, hoardings in the form of black bulls and cloaked hidalgos perched over the road to the south, railway lines fraying into marshalling-yards on the banks of the Bidassoa, a dingy street full of shops for tourists. Cut-rate bottles of Pernod and Chartreuse; picture postcards of El Cordobes (the Beatle Matador) and of señoritas with three-dimensional satin flounces to their skirts; miniature wine-skins, paper-knives of Toledo steel.

Why do we come here? And ask for our usual room at the Hotel

Norte y Francia, opposite the ugly domed church, in the narrow street leading to the station? And then have to put up with Room Number Nine which faces a row of tenements, their balconies occupied by larders made out of biscuit tins but also hung with washing and piled with junk, with the brilliant orange of a cylinder of Butane gas only a couple of yards from our curtains?

Dirty brown town. Treacherous weather. Nowhere to sit in the hotel supposing one wanted to. Chill dining-room with damp table linen and one irregular wall almost all window, past which buses throb and rattle, and sad, squat figures in black trudge towards the station, cardboard suitcases tied with string in their hands. We stay out of conservatism, I suppose—a safe place we know, where the people have always been friendly; and because the hotel is cheap, 'our sort of place', the discovery and adventure of poorer years; and because once or twice, how long ago now? we were served an excellent flat-fish here which we have managed to turn into a legend.

There is also Fuenterrabia. Two miles away. I called it Almaseda in one of my books. The picturesque gloomy huddle of narrow streets and deeply eaved houses about the church and castle on the hill; one good restaurant and several lively bars in the lower town; and then the port (tunny fishing), the esplanade, a dreary municipal expansiveness flanked by villas of the Tudor-chalet variety, with a vast, usually sea-less inlet of a beach. And far out there, past the second harbour and the tiny castle of St Elmo, if you squeeze along a gorse-bounded ditch, you come upon a headland or two and a small grim cove. This also has become a legend.

My first experience of southern spring was in this place; asphodels, scillas, lithospermum intensely blue, some orchids and irises. They are still there but today the sea rages, rain-clouds march in from the Atlantic, France is blotted out. My first view of Spain was Irun and Fuenterrabia; my first room in an establishment above a bar in the latter place, soon closed by the police as a brothel. I remember walking late at night between the heavily timbered houses, whose beams and balconies and shutters are painted the same monotonous red, blue and green as the fishing-boats, and catching the smell of garlic sizzling and smoking in an iron pan—it was Singapore again, after three years during which I had travelled nowhere. Years of hiatus and, largely, of failure. In the upper town I was introduced to *anis* in bars where it was always twilight and on the walls brown birds perched in brown cages. In the early morning I heard the cry of Maria Ganiz, the fish wife, an unforgettable falsetto shriek and ululation on the final word, 'fresca', a real enormity of sound, a sort of controlled, projectile hysteria, which announced the basket of sardines and bedraggled sea-gulls on the cobbles at her feet. One evening the steep Calle Major was full of couples dancing, in plastic raincoats and with raised umbrellas, for the weather was as bad as usual and their gaiety had the damp gleam of frogspawn. On my third visit I stayed on for the *fiesta*. At noon rockets whizzed from the battlements of the castle. At six a band began to play on the roof of the public lavatory.

Now, with a car, we can go farther afield. Up adjacent Mount Jaixquibel to the church and convent of Nuestra Señora de Guadalupe, where a notice in the porch proclaims, 180,000 *Personas van a morir en todo el mundo!* followed by the exhortation, *Rogar por los agonizantes de cada dia. Rogaran por vosalvos cuando esteis en la agonia.*[1] And then along the burnt pine-forests of the huge, sullenly swollen headlands to the rocks and gorse below the Hostal Provincial, with a view across the valley of the Bidassoa to the Pyrenees. Over there we drive to Oyarzun and across the pass into Navarre. Spring flushes the mountains. The scrub hazes to mauve and yellow. In the church at Lesaca we read, from enamelled plates on the pews, the weird Basque names: the Family Txatxikoenea...Señora B. Irazogui...the Family of José Echepetelecu. Children are carrying branches of bay in honour of Palm Sunday.

Since it is too cold and wet to go often to Fuenterrabia I spend much of the time sitting in the Algorta Bar across the road from the hotel. Absolutely no evidence of tourism here. Institutional grey-green walls, sawdust on a floor of liver-coloured tiles, bar of smoky marble embellished with black grooved pilasters and a stout brass rail, and a dense crowd of Basques in black berets and dark-blue rompers: surely the Basques are the greatest pub-crawlers in the world? I crouch on my Aerated Bread Company chair, with my back to some card-players, my left foot wedged by a temporarily abandoned suitcase, my right cheek pierced by the draught from a small window, and most of my attention nagged by the spasms of a pin-ball machine, *Gran Casino*, whose somehow disappointingly astronomical numbers flash through the bare midriff of a blonde in a top-hat. Nevertheless one can sit about, and merely look, too much. How often on a café terrace in Greece I have watched the cats, then the frilly children, then the *volta*, and finally the

[1] 'In the whole world today 180,000 people will die. Pray for those in each day's death-agony. Pray for yourselves when you shall be dying.'

bourgeois ladies positioning themselves for a pre-dinner drink. In Morocco my incessant sitting taught me all about pin-ball machines; in Germany it was one-arm bandits; in Italy the apparatus for making espresso coffee; in Yugoslavia the dilapidated bicycles used by the workers on their way home. I am not a voyeur. I should get to know these people. I feel ashamed to dissolve myself into an eye spread sensitive but shallow, naked hunger, naked vulnerability, where these barrel-chested toughs in their baby rompers trample and spit. I feel depleted. I must get myself another drink — a big *El Leon* this time, for these tubsical little bottles are ridiculous. In a moment of depression I tell myself that I am a lousy traveller: afraid of rough seas, not because I get sea-sick (which I don't) but because I think the ship will capsize; afraid of heights, especially when they involve lifts; afraid of hotels catching fire; cautious about drinking the water and eating the salad; shivering now in expectation of a cold.

What would Byron do? He would take to his horse and explore Wellington's battle-fields. He would go in search of Roland at Roncesvalles and fall in with smugglers on the way. And Boswell? Having met some jolly British officers at the port he would repair to the brothel near the Plaza de España, where he would be deeply shocked to find that the girls were dressed as nuns.

To Burgos, which I know well, and then to Salamanca for the first time. In this cold April weather the central plateau of Spain is not encouraging. (Winter for eight months, they say, and hell for four.) Beyond Alsasua the sun breaks through the cloud and there is an icy sparkle: brown clustered villages with a church flanged by buttresses and lifting a sturdy, near-golden tower; distant blue lines of mountain bearing glints of snow; sometimes cherries or blackthorn in white bloom. At Vitoria you notice the tiers of glassed-in balconies, framed in wood the colour of clay or dried blood; you walk in dappled sunlight under planes so cruelly pollarded that they dig arthritic fingers with needle-sharp finger-nails into each other's flesh. Magpies are the dandies of this landscape. Hawks are its guardians.

The Eye Earthy dwindles soon after the savage but thrilling desolation of the village of Pancorbo, a place stabbed by successive ridges of fantastically withered rock. There is nothing more to hold it in the slow lift and fall of the empty downs of the Meseta. (It will recover, rather sluggishly, when it encounters my old friend, the stuffed and now very dusty eagle-owl in the parlour of the Hotel Avila at Burgos.)

But Castile, like all of Spain, has much to offer the Eye Extravagant. From its classical past this dour, proud country has retained only some ruins and the Roman *gravitas*. Yet at the time of Isabella and the discovery of the New World, and again in the eighteenth century, it poured its wealth into buildings and decorations which would astonish, entrance and even bludgeon the beholder into an awed recognition of the supremacy of a militant faith. First there were the Moors to contend with, then the Protestant heresy. The result was that the prevalent Gothic grew flamboyant, profusely decorated or overlaid with the Churrigueresque, a version of the native Baroque, itself a style that quickly overwhelmed any tendency to a purer classicism. The sweetness and graciousness of the Renaissance (Bramante's Tempietto, for example), the urbanity and welcoming voluptuousness of the Rome of Bernini and Borromini, have neither of them any place in austerely Catholic Spain. Only the Moors were able to relax. It is a country with few palaces that are not castles or monasteries, and fewer villas. It is significant that an apparent exception to this, the town house of the Marques de Dos Aguas at Valencia, balances a marvellously elaborate façade with the greatest simplicity within.

The overwhelming façade, such as that of the cathedral at Santiago de Compostella, the vertically conceived and self-contained work of art, such as the Transparente at Toledo, are the features that command attention. Both are reminiscent of the brocaded stiffness, containing the graceful but ritually limited gestures, of a matador in his suit of lights, or of a male dancer. Although the details may be charming or fantastic, there is always an air of reserve about Spanish buildings. Inside, the huge churches with their enclosed choirs and their many grilles unfold layers of darkness. The beating fans of women penitents suggest the fluttering of birds in a cage far too large to bother about any individual imprisonment. And the public places too (one thinks of the Plaza Major in Madrid) have a grim solemnity. At Salamanca I find myself longing for statues and fountains, or even a greater profusion of trees.

Nevertheless the eye is delighted. My first surprise was during a brief stop at the city of Valladolid. The 'fronts' or façades of San Pablo and San Gregorio are wonderfully intricate; they could be carved ivory or bookbindings of embossed leather. That of San Gregorio represents a naturalistic fantasy together with effigies and armorial embellishments; within its vertically arranged compartments everything buds, sprouts, twists and uncurls until the whole composition seems to

7

crackle, sometimes with the sound of a snapped twig, sometimes with that of an opening fern. The stonework imitates bundles of knobbed sticks or woven basketwork, against which stand hairy satyrs, while above, babies climb a vine towards a great shield. And, inside the façade, there is a cool and beautiful patio whose equally extravagant designs are controlled and held back with characteristic austerity, for the twisted pillars of the colonnade seem metallic as though turned on a lathe and the swagged arches of the upper cloister could almost be made of pastry. Nevertheless the observer feels a bit uncomfortable. The shock of such triumphantly complete work, rising on a windy hill in a rather dull town, takes his breath away. But there is no warmth, no human sweetness to which he can relate. The lack of any sympathy with the Catholic ideology and even the history of Spain means that these buildings appeal to one's remoter, colder, more purely aesthetic resources.

And now, to tell the truth, I feel rather the same in Salamanca. The effect of these cities cannot be divorced from that of the monotonous plateau surrounding them. After miles and miles of homelessness, where the red-ochre and pale green landscape lifts and tilts and flows, and the pale line of the horizon now tightens within a mile or so and then dips to expose endless cloud-haunted distances, you see from afar the small-seeming, ragged interruption that is a Castilian city. A quarry of half shaped stones, you might say, or a fleet ship-wrecked upon some hidden reef. (Avila, shrivelling within its circuit of towers, or Segovia, splendid enough on closer acquaintance, like a galleon moored to the land by its Roman aqueduct.) If the city is Salamanca, it will eventually reveal itself as large and stately but with perhaps even less life than it had in George Borrow's time. Soon after our arrival yesterday I watched the westering sun flood over façades whose normal colour is a warm red, standing first in front of the decorated entrance to the University, then before the portal of the New Cathedral and finally at the foot of the western façade of the church of San Esteban. All three share the shallow, rather tight carving which, since it reminds Spaniards of the work of silver-smiths, is called *plateresque*. I was aware that behind me spiky balustrades of stone fretwork stood silhouetted against a sky whose blue and gold was misted with crystalline specks. There were cloisters and patios, each with its air of privileged enclosure and of a secrecy that refused to yield. There was the cupola of the Catedral Antigua (the two cathedrals lie side by side) whose shape is faintly Hindu. There was also much space, some of it no more than waste ground, and into this space there crept the solitariness of the surrounding countryside so that, as on the approach to the city but now on a much grander scale, several of the buildings gave the impression of things hugely stranded, nakedly exposed, like beached ships or whales.

This morning I find myself actually trembling, not so much with excitement as anxiety, as I think of the great number of things I must see during the coming day. It is exhausting to be so nervous. The Casa de las Conchas, the convent of Las Duenas, the Jesuit Clerecia. Why this rage of sight-seeing? I decide that I am an auto-didact, for eighteen years of expensive education did not teach me the things that I really wanted (as it now appears) to know. Each new church or cloister gives me a bit more confidence, a slight increase in worthiness, for what I learn and appreciate I can share and teach (or, since human intercourse is difficult, write).

Portugal, the books say, will be different. Instead of the Isabelline, the even more fantastic Manoeline from the same period: also a warmer Baroque and plenty of Rococo. Spain was rarely if ever a humanist country. It isolates one into too much of an aesthete. Nevertheless, earth-brown and twisting, soaring gilt, Sancho Panza and Quixote, Velasquez and El Greco, it's not a country one could do without. Especially in late spring or early summer. Especially in Andalucia.

Road to Portugal. Third day of the plateau. Appearances improve, however, with the arrival of cork trees, dusty though they look, and undulations which become now and then actually pastoral: cows, and in walled fields. Also a good many pools and streams whose surface is covered with a cress in delicate white flower. More hawks than on the previous days: sinister slow confidence of floating spirals...flush of mottled red-brown...ragged edges to the wings...mapping for pulses of fur, purses of heart-beat.

Ciudad Rodrigo is Spain's last rampart. A pleasant dignified little town. I walk behind the cathedral into a bare place fired by a judas tree in bloom and two choir-boys run out as I stand there, short lace-edged surplices over tunics of the deepest scarlet, playing with a silver censer as though it were a toy. Steps lead up to the town walls; a track runs along the top; standing there you face the blue wheel of distance. At one point rises the castle, now turned into a *parador*. Astonishing to find roses blooming on the wall of a house nearby. Inside the cathedral the choir is a-drone with harsh male voices while one or two people kneel before Our Lady of Something already perched in her cart and pensively pretty above a brood of candles; going close, you can make out the small grilles through which the bearers will peer during the Easter Procession. The chanting over, first one and then another bobbing prelate emerges until the whole flock sweeps off into the windy sunshine, flouncing and gossiping.

A few miles beyond Ciudad Rodrigo we begin to think that the plain will lose its appearance of fertility once more. But, rather suddenly, it is Portugal; a sophisticated bourgeois-brisk custom house; and then, with no appreciable climbing, the landscape grows agitated and mountainous, the narrow road dipping and curving. We are driving through a kind of Dartmoor upland which is such a relief from the plateau that we do not find it bleak. The wind roars, the sun flashes from racing cloud, a rise in temperature is so necessary that at least we imagine it—even though the town towards which we are heading, Guarda, has been described as the coldest in Portugal. Tufts of broom in white blossom are everywhere and now and then there is a tree all white or pink. Saxifrage and ragged robin grow by the road: also a smoky blue flower which may be lavender or camphor. The hillsides, hazed with trees not yet in leaf, are all brown rock, great lazy fluid slabs of it and boulders piled on boulders, and all this rock is yellow with moss. We feel like shouting with joy to find such manageable scenery.

Actually, having risen almost to Guarda, we skirt the town. We drop down into a broad valley. Opposite, a precipice rises to fanged mountains, the Sierra da Estrela: will we have to cross these, is our journey to become difficult and perhaps dangerous? Floating down we pass rosemary in bloom and then lilac; noticing more and more greenness (laurel, eucalyptus) we are taken unawares by a mist of olives. Olives only twenty minutes from the top of the world! I say it's incredible: some sort of willow, surely, such as deceives one in Macedonia?...but no, the thin-leaved spume, the bossed gnarls, these are olives indeed. And those glossy little trees are oranges. And that house is buried in wistaria. It is raining now but with the sun in it, a steaming rain. In the confusion of rain and sunlight we climb out of the valley, but not by hairpin bends across the precipice wall which has fallen away behind. We are hungry. We should have stopped for food at Guarda. Why are drivers so obstinate, why do they always suppose a better place and go on?

Somewhere above the valley there is a town, perhaps only a village

—Celorico da Beira—and as we arrive in Celorico I spot a house across the road with *pensao* written on it. Just now it's pouring with rain. I nose the car on to a bit of gravel parking-place; we get out and run across the road into a small public garden ablaze with flame-coloured and deep red azaleas; beyond this we enter the *pensao*, shaking the rain from our shoulders and rather out of breath. Nothing has told us this is a restaurant but I have a feeling of absolute confidence that all will be well. We find a big wooden room where people are already eating, sit at a table under a small window and are accepted immediately by a gentle, somewhat adenoidal girl of sixteen who is the waitress. No menu, no fuss. She brings us purple wine in a huge carafe. We see through the window that the *pensao* hangs over a small pastoral ravine. We tear bread greedily, swill down the deep iron-tasting wine and notice that there are two priests amongst the guests at the next table: a family party, perhaps, and with an air of being interested in food.

The soup arrives. It is in the best peasant style, very hot, very clean-tasting: a heavy potato purée streaked with a dark green I take at first to be spinach and then decide is shredded cabbage. *Caldo verde*. Nothing could be more delicious. In fact I tried to make a soup like this the summer before last in Essex, working purely by imagination: a slow simmering of potatoes and then several pensive visits to the garden to select lettuce leaves, still fiery with dew, peas in their pods and broad beans and a radish or two; it was turning out excellently when I added, without any reason except the desire to experiment, a packet of powdered onion and so sealed adventurousness with orthodoxy. The second course is, in fact, very young peas in their pods blanketing pieces of lamb, a confirmation that this is country eating and as plentiful as anyone could wish. The third is a huge omelette braced with ham and served with potatoes. The fourth, as we notice from adjacent tables, will be fish sprinkled with lemon but here we make a stop, declaring ourselves full, which brings us nonetheless a dish of fruit. All this, for two, costs 60 escudos or about seven shillings per person. I say to my friend, 'We mustn't expect Portugal to be always like this', but in our short stay we are to have two similar meals, one even bigger, and we are to meet variations of the soup several times.

From now on the drive becomes more and more idyllic. We stop at a small lay-by; the utilitarian word gives nothing of the charm of these places in Portugal where neither wildness of scenery nor poverty of inhabitants prevents the solemnity of small cypresses by the road to-gether with, say, a curving hedge of rosemary or laurel. Here the rosemary is full of bees and variegated by bushes of cistus, the big flowers crinkly white around yellow centres, and with purple spots just revealed at the base of the petals; beyond, heath stretches amongst pines, the heather in white bloom, the lithospermum miraculously blue, the air scented and droning in the increasing heat of the sun. Cottages are whitewashed and nearly every cottage has a clump of arum lilies by its door. We are soon aware of a river twisting below us which must, whatever the map says, be the Mondego; its meadows are yellow with charlock and all about it hang the trees of this lushest of landscapes, planes of the tenderest yellow-green, huge chestnuts, eucalyptus, pines, walnuts and olives. We stop, get out to pick doroni-cums and begin to discuss which of several houses above the river we should like to have. The Portuguese, my friend decides, are pleasant to look upon: round-faced, ruddy, stocky as gnomes.

Thus to Coimbra, where we spend the night. A glittering rackety hill of a town, it is famous for its university; hideous modern faculty buildings obstruct the way to an inner court and a lovely Rococo library perched high above the Mondego. Then to Leiria with its black and tan castle (pretty but a bit dull for a stopping place) and on to the sea at Nazaré. Beckford's abbeys are now quite near. Apart from some hawk-brown Romanesque buildings (cathedrals usually), Portugal is granite and white stucco, buildings which smile, bulge, twist and swirl.

We drove through pine-woods, heath and dunes. Where the road divided at a bare place I stopped. The bare place was the summit of yellow cliffs. Looking left, under that heavy dark sky, I caught my breath. Far below there stretched an immense beach of tawny sand, remote as though in another dimension from the blurred, rain-lashed features around me, holding and breathing a colour which seemed on such a stormy day to have no right to be there: a tone, a glow, like that seen in fog when it appears on the point of lifting, but perhaps more active, more strange, like some mealy fermentation. And parallel with this stretch of sand but also mixed with it, for the beach's remoteness was partly due to a queer opacity in the atmosphere, something almost too sharp to be mist, rolled furrow upon furrow of Atlantic breakers.

The two together made a violent geometry, the wide beach of surf whose details were only glimpses to be lost in a chaotic turbulence, muddy green shattered continuously to dirty white, and the scarcely wider reach of spray-impregnated sand running out into the distance, into the slow flat turn of the coast. There was even, on closer observation, a third component to this composition of parallels, for sand-dunes rose behind the beach, frost-green and dumpish, scooped here and there into a dim fluffy glow and echoing to some degree the fermenting ocean.

To the right, higher than our present position, stood that part of Nazaré known as Sitio; a rampart village extending along the cliffs (up which a funicular climbs) and ending in a great bare plaza which flings a taut ribbon of whitewashed wall out over the Atlantic; below this, steep yellow streets would take us to boats and beach. Arrived there, we found shelter from the continuing downpour in a less than grand café off a small supernumerary square. This café was full of boys of fourteen to sixteen (the age, seemingly, of most of the boys of Nazaré) and all of these olive-skinned youngsters, whose faces were lean and hungry with puberty and whose behaviour broke from silent herding-together into raucous exclamations and clumsy, white-toothed, salival grins, wore the same costume: namely, a peaked cap (to keep them predatory and tangential), a shirt or a light jacket patterned in Scots plaid, gaberdine trousers (one in a dog-tooth check) and cheap shoes sometimes fancy enough to be two-toned. Leaning against the door stood a grizzled sailor in a black jersey and a long black stocking-cap with a pompom. Stocky, barrel-chested, with small eyes glinting deep in a wrinkled brown face, he resembled a satyr. And this was interesting because, no sooner had I opened my Sacheverell Sitwell, than I found a reference to satyrs — and then to Scots checks — and so, in the course of several enthusiastic pages which I had somehow missed so far, came an introduction to the pronounced peculiarities of Nazaré.

The rain lessening, we searched for somewhere to stay. Pineapples alternated with langoustines in the windows of the first pension on the front, if so primly English a word as 'front' can be used to describe road and waste in front of perpetual *Götterdämmerung*; the restaurant was crowded with people at luncheon; no one answered us as we waited in the cubby-hole devoted to Reception and no one answered us at the next place either. However, the town was not really crowded. A few hundred yards back we found a huge pension, the Pensao Clube, where we were welcomed as the only guests. A solemn waiter served us a solemn meal washed down with Mateus Rosé plunked in an ice-bucket. A grey siesta followed. Opening my windows I found that the Atlantic air, intermittently almost a gale, was quite warm. If I peered out to the left I could just see the ocean but right in front of me rose the cliffs of Sitio which would become a string of lights at night — usually, anyway, for several times the current failed. We had separate rooms, mine the bigger but with a small musical leak in the ceiling. I slept.

Beckford complained of wind and changeable weather at Cintra but storm-tossed Nazaré was outside his geographical range. I have found a vantage-point from which to observe these un-Beckfordian surroundings: the tavern of Senhor Alfonso Augusto Ova where I drink a pale pink port and listen to the rattle of the football-table. This Taberna de Cacao (swordfish, I think) is the third or fourth along the front from the principal square, one amongst many, in fact, and all of them are as rough and practical as the simplest tavern in Greece; there are cafés in the town but nowhere here by the sea is remotely like a Greek coffee-shop with its air of shabby decorum, its marble-topped tables occupied by worthies playing backgammon. There is very little that even pretends to be middle-class, although a long way off I have discovered a glass box of a café-restaurant, quite empty, and out there in the hinterland is also an hotel and a couple of châlets. Summer may change the focus; crowds of holiday-makers doubtless trail along the sea-road to points far beyond my exploration; distant places may sprout beach umbrellas; but, for my part, Nazaré is here on this immediately accessible shore, where sardine boats of elegant shape and gay colour are beached, and Mr Ova's sleepy brown eyes take in the peaked-cap boys, the sauntering fishermen, the old women in their cocoons of shawl, the young women in their tartan skirts and bunched petticoats edged with stiff crochet in orange and lilac and lime-green. Mr Ova is a round-faced burly man, with a little English picked up in the Merchant Navy, and his eyes tolerate, with sleepy knowingness, the ocean hurling itself at his door.

This is, we decide almost at once, our rickety, draughty home: companion to the Baby Café at Mykonos, the Café Vlahou or the Olympia at Athens, that run-down place on the old harbour at Thasos: so many, so many, one cannot remember (if one ever knew) their names. Certain bars have the right uninsinuating friendliness, the right personality-echoing dilapidation. Nothing in the way of décor or mechanical amenity or social pretentiousness dwarfs for a single moment an unshaved man in dungarees with his fly-buttons half-undone and a rent in his jacket who is singing a poem to himself in a corner of the bar. There was a hole in Singapore—the Café Nostalgie, Beda Lim and I named it—very small and friendly, really very decent, although the lattice was full of rats and pee had a way of fanning out from the lavatory door. Nowadays, in Essex, there is the tiny Smithy Inn, one room, one passage, not an improvement in sight and a back-door to sit by which gives on to flowers and sheep. Real dirt, really strong smells are only for moments of mystical drunkenness. I am not pleading for such.

Mr Alfonso Augusto Ova's tavern, to which we return from the heights of Sitio or from Alcobaça or from the gardens of Queluz, has big doors like a barn, and when the third Atlantic storm of the morning blows in (the first brought thunder and lightning, the second tore a drying sail to shreds) he watches it with just that faintly amused heightening of attention with which a man might watch a mouse on a rafter and then, at perhaps the merest flicker of a heavy eyelid or a slight pause in the motion of his towel across the bar, the peaked-cap boys, grinning, run to close the doors against rain approaching like a solid wall, and in a moment the small windows grow dark, the glass is slapped and streaked, the wood hammered, and a bristling spitting pool floods across the cement floor.

Mr Ova's bar-counter stretches right across the room with a central arch behind it leading to an inner drinking place (very dark, you can scarcely make out the battered tables and stools) and this cavernous 'saloon', since surely it is the privileged and intimate who sit there, has at one side a screened-off 'snug' for parties even more exclusive or conspiratorial; in both places people occasionally eat, gnawing their own bread or dipping into plates of fried sardines provided by Mrs Ova. The counter is wooden, blue panels framed in grey, with a composition top of chips in mosaic; the room is whitewashed, with doors, shutters and a big central pillar of that faded red resembling dried blood; the ceiling is of blue planks. The principal feature is the lopsided wooden screen behind the counter with an arch in its middle. On the top of this stand various dusty objects, a jug filled with a brown shrub, two flasks in baskets, some bottles containing a reddish liquid; along its cornice runs a series of pine-cones painted pink, orange, lime-green and blue, reminiscent of zinnias, while here and there something hangs down, a

7*

three-masted barque in partial relief mounted on sky-blue cardboard punched with a primary yellow sun, a bullfight poster advertising the Spanish cognac, *Fondador*, another advertisement for razor-blades *Nacet*, some calendars, and a card holding a display of pen-knives. The shelves of the screen are mostly filled by bottles or biscuit-tins but above the arch there is a model schooner (Mr Ova's own work) and a bunch of arum lilies now turning very brown. To the right the screen is pierced by four dried-blood barrels laid on their sides; three biggish ones in a row and a smaller one above; wines and, in the superior position, port. On the counter to the far left stands a glass case containing tins of sardines and small rounds of cheese. To the right are the current but grimy-looking bottles of brandy and anis and, beyond these, where counter joins wall, there is a sink.

Often it is Mrs Ova who sits alone behind the counter, a fine-looking woman with a face that is watchfully serene but which nevertheless seems to fill with private and perhaps scornful thought. She wears a headscarf of black touched with red, a dark green shirt with pearl buttons and a red and green apron above her voluminous bulging skirts. But it is her shawl you notice — khaki-brown, not the more usual black — because it is characteristic of the women of Nazaré to fold themselves away and this austere and autonomous gesture of the re-adjusted and ever more encompassing shawl is performed by Mrs Ova with an expert, an almost casual exclusiveness. At night she presides like a monumental shadow over the shadowy room, which a jerky electric bulb slices and swings, scarcely noting the football players, for here half the bar is not turned into a noisy alley for metal discs to be thrown at nails set in the floor, as happens up the road, and acknowledging with a faint arrogance, as one might mutely register and condemn a tourist's exiguous bikini, the beach just visible through the still open doors, the fluffy indecisive sand, puckered and drifted, the outlines of the sardine boats and out there, flashing on the fringe of vision, the slightly ridiculous frenzy of the Atlantic.

From Mr and Mrs Ova's tavern we have hardly to explore a town and people that lap about its doors. Nazaré is so distinctive that some authorities regard it as a surviving Phoenician settlement, isolated from the mainland by dunes and marshes that began to be forested as early as the thirteenth century. But would this explain the present passion for Scots plaid, bolts of which are displayed in many of the shops? Or the charming fact that many of the streets are blocked for most of the time by boys *and* girls, together with young women and even matrons of thirty, playing a mysterious but hilarious ball game which involves an up-ended fruit-crate and, for one player at least, the action of batting with the hand? (*Pelia*, Mr Ova calls this – and what a frisk of skirts and petticoats, what revelations of startlingly coloured hems it brings in its train.) But most curious of all are the cowled women, pyramids in black, who have the North African habit of squatting by walls along the street or forming groups on the sand, in the shadow of one of those high-prowed boats, where they make patterns of immobility. Obviously the picture postcards make the most of them but they do not seem in the least self-conscious. Against the glaring walls they sink in splendid isolation, darkness congealed to its essence, privacy and domesticity defined and drawn up into a kind of point (for each woman is her own tent or house) but nevertheless one will be joined by another, they will gossip together (a converse suggesting that of chessmen or small private forts) and sometimes the fringe of the enveloping shawl is drawn back to reveal a baby within, child or grandchild. Greek *ya-yas* always wear black but theirs is a normal sociability; spindle in hand they walk together or sit in some understandable comfort; they fetch kerosene tins of water from the well; under their twisted headscarfs you catch more than a glimpse of silver hair. Women in Morocco, in other ways so like these of Nazaré, will often be more smartly dressed: a garment of Gent's Worsted Suiting, navy blue with a pin-stripe, and over the mouth a flutter of green chenille. No ladies I have seen elsewhere have been quite like these outside Mr Ova's. The wives, I presume, of the satyrs.

Up above us, Sitio has its own strangeness. A bare, wide, roughly triangular plaza with four wind-lashed palm trees set in patterned pebbles, a bandstand with blue panels at its base and a rust-red roof. The whip-lash of that white wall on the precipice, looped at one place over a jutting crag, sheltering nearby a tiny chapel lined with *azulejos*. Washing dancing, clouds blowing, a house caught by the steely sun, all red-ochre and rusty balconies. Booths for souvenirs. A fine rough church on a platform, flanked by pavilions at the front, arcaded along its exterior sides where the irregular paving stones are, in their soft mauves and pinks and purples, redolent of the sea. I wonder what is the date of this church? Its interior is surprisingly all-of-a-piece, very rich, very tasteful. Grey and gold altars, transepts covered with pictures in blue tiles, marble balcony swirling in from the west above a tiled barrel-vault, high altar magnificently elaborate, and here and there Byzantine coloured-glass dropping puddles of red, yellow and blue.

From Sitio you look down on yellow, not architecturally distinguished New Nazaré (for such I imagine it is) and along the frostily-misted coast towards the less interesting S. Martinho do Pol. Or you go down past rough fields to the little lighthouse.

This divine bareness of heights and coast will not be easily forgotten.

I have been to Alcobaça!

We went this bright and windy morning as slowly and sensitively as we could, interpreting Beckford's 'jumble' as a kind of stalking process which would enable us to creep up on our quarry, enjoying the sort of things that he did on the way. In the gentle scale of Portugal it is easy to pause. First there were pine-covered hills splashed with huge yellow and magenta mesembryanthemums, the dominant flower of this region. Then we came into a small flat valley. A patch of plough was dotted with olives, a deserted house across a ditch half-hidden by canna-lilies; elsewhere vines rambled with the light sticky upon their leaves or there was a hedge of green bamboo, rustling with dry passion, like a committee of professors arguing about love. At the entrance to the small town of Alcobaça we passed a monumental mason's and an orchard of orange trees in fruit.

The town itself is pretty, overlooked by small tufted hills; the land-scape beyond, undulating and pastoral, studded with woods and plantations, with blue shadow on the ridge to the north.

A square with a public garden lies in front of the long Abbey façade, which consists of whitewashed buildings to each side, no more than two storeys high, very simple, punctuated by the stone-work of windows and pilasters and with roofs glowing a soft, deep red; in the centre the great golden church with its squat twin towers, wheel window and deep, relatively undecorated entrance arch. Here the crowd of four hundred ecclesiastics must have stood, bowing and smiling, admiring and envying, as the Grand Prior tottered from his *dormeuse*. Beckford found it all 'very imposing' and was grateful that the village and surroundings relieved the mind 'from a sense of oppression the huge domineering bulk of the conventual buildings inspire', which strikes me as being far truer of the convent-palace of Mafra, a sort of Portuguese Escorial, where the central church has higher and more imposing towers, the whole façade is of stone or dark stucco and its length is terminated by projecting wings with bulging cupolas. The truth is that Alcobaça looks almost evangelistically religious from the outside (buildings of smiling simplicity leading the eye to the church) while its interior is markedly clean, cold and high-minded. Much of this is due to the restorers, the medieval purists, who have been so fanatically active in Portugal. The quaintly sybarite life described by Beckford doesn't now accord with either the exterior charm or the interior austerity of this Cistercian building.

We didn't go in at once. We stopped by an antique shop and began bargaining for a wooden maiden with pale-blue glass eyes. We inspected picture-postcards at other shops ablaze with indifferent pottery, mostly plates and mostly blue, which made the streets as strident as Delphi's. This pause enabled us to get used to the Abbey. It had come out of a book and was really there. It was large, it didn't hide itself away, and it was beautiful. And the weather was Beckford's: 'The morn itself was most exhilarating: I never breathed in any atmosphere so pure and so elastic—it seemed to sparkle with life and light.'

When we entered all Beckford's wildness and vivacity became, as was perhaps appropriate, not part of the perceptible background but a counterpoint of dream. The church was immensely long, narrow, tall and pure. We shivered in its cold. Everything is a deathly white, the colour of naked bone, except where damp has stained it a light apple-green, a pretty shade, admittedly, but somehow shocking. For who would associate that hobbledehoy performance of the Tragedy of Dona Inez de Castro or those 'four good-looking novices, lads of fifteen or sixteen, demure even to primness' who brought the cassolettes of Goa filigree 'steaming with a fragrant vapour of Calambac'...who would associate the foot-baths, the potted lampreys, the Persian rugs, the minuets, with the remoteness of a bone disinterred from grass? The church is lit by narrow, rounded windows of clear glass set in niches high overhead; the altar is now a plain stone table set in front of an apse of open arches; the ambulatory behind has similar altars recessed in bare vaults like those of a cellar and holding palely gilded saints. It's all artistic in a puritanical English way, like some wool church of East Anglia getting by on a shoe-string, except that in England there would be prayer-books and hassocks and a sense of services being held. I thought Alcobaça more like a museum, empty and echoing: or perhaps an art-gallery, beautifully proportioned, for the contemplation of imaginary masterpieces. Once I'd grasped that all the richness, all the Baroque and Rococo extravagance had been 'restored' out of sight, I found myself strangely excited by the building. It made, so to speak, marvellous impressionist pictures of the world outside; it re-inforced, with its icy breath and the green stains on its pavement, the vitality and sensuality of the inner mind. It demanded the gayest solitude.

All the same, there is some decoration. In the transepts stand the tombs of Dom Pedro and his mistress, Dona Inez, intricately carved coffers standing on the backs of lions, for the king, but in the lady's case of stoical servitors of the bull-dog breed (they have heads and moustaches and are engaged in conversation, no doubt about their job) and surmounted by effigies so placed that, at the Last Trump, they or the persons they symbolise must face each other when they rise. Solicitously peering angels attend them; their folded wings are narrow and spiky; their hands either pat, smooth and compose the bodies for a long sleep or (as I thought, especially in view of the way they look at each other, the tensed energy of their wings and their small size, which suggests they may be apprentices) are in half a mind to push and prod their charges upright again, Last Trump or no. Very white, very well-preserved, and delicate as work in ivory, these tombs are exceedingly beautiful. Beckford visited them on his arrival, while the Priors were worshipping at the High Altar; he speaks, though, of a 'sepulchral chapel' which is hardly the case, adding that they remind him of the Beauchamp monument at Warwick, 'so rich in fretwork and imagery.'

Later he says he explored the 'most gorgeous and glistening sacristy ...adorned with furbelows of gilt bronze, flaunting over panels of jasper and porphyry', which sounds like much decoration still extant in Portugal—in the Convent of Jesus at Aveiro, for instance, or in the balcony-choir of the cathedral at Braga—but which no longer exists at Alcobaça. What we do still see is the Sacristry door in the transept behind Dom Pedro, with a similar door opposite, one of those examples of fantasy combined with naturalism which bring back the façade of San Gregorio at Valladolid and make one long to visit Batalha for its patterns of tracery or to see the swollen stone cables entwined so rhythmically to form the columns of the Church of Jesus at Setubal. These doors consist of two tree boles rising from whiskered roots through uprights studded with knots to swirl inward and eventually to cross in a fabulous ogee, sprayed to each side with massive tendrils resembling the convolutions of coral. The organic exuberance of this decoration contrasts with the Gothic carving of the tombs. I found, alas, no other example of the Manoeline, although there are some pretty terracotta angels in a side chapel much damaged by Napoleon's soldiery.

A diminutive but charming guide now appeared to take us round the Cloister of Silence; he knew at least whom I meant when I referred, in the phrasing of Franchi, the 'Portuguese Orange', to Monsieur de Beckford...Here was the immense kitchen, tiled in an oyster-grey just edged with blue; vast central chimney gaping above a hearth big enough to roast two oxen; side chimneys almost as big; two stone tables, the bigger weighing fifteen tons; a row of marble basins; a conduit fed by a canal from the Alcoa River gushing into a fishpond. Beckford was accurate enough about all this. But as we happily moved about the two-tiered cloister with its box hedges and scanty trees, past the hexagonal washing-place at one of its corners, into the bare Chapter House, the huge bare Refectory, the Room of the Kings with its swirling *azulejo* dados picturing the building of the monastery and its ledges of terracotta monarchs, I felt that the guide was committed to the solemnity and historicity of this Cistercian establishment, whose monks had been such excellent landlords, and would not wish to gossip about a 'frolicksome supper' of ortolans and quails, let alone 'certain grotto-like communications between this sacred asylum and another not less monastic, though tenanted by...the daughters of prayer and penitence'. But where were the 'fusty saloons, under still fustier canopies'? Or, better, where had been Beckford's room with its painted ceiling and tables adorned with rich velvet petticoats?

The guide left us to climb the stairs to the dormitory on our own. These steps popped up in the middle of an immense reddish pavement, no cubicles, no screens, but one side of the room was alive with sunshine and here we found a balcony brilliant with geraniums and overlooking an eighteenth century garden. At once I felt at home. Palms fanned from a lower terrace, female statues gestured languidly on its balustrade, box-edged parterres contained orange trees, and an old man sat on a bench. This, now an old peoples' home, rounded off our experience and led us back, through the huge stone room and the cloister, to the queer chaste bone-white church which, for all its damp, didn't so much moulder into age as slide stiffly across the dividing-line between life and art—or between history and timelessness—until it became a beautiful almost empty gallery awaiting, like Mallarmé's *le vide papier que la blancheur defend*, the warmth of masterpieces either of art or experience.

Batalha is different. The paradox is that where to Beckford Alcobaça was the rich, grand monastery it is Batalha which seems the more opulent today. In its general disposition it is supposed to look very English but this Englishness has come under the hands of an enchanter of the Manoeline school. It has also been made the home of the Unknown Soldier and hence a National Shrine round which people troop and gawp.

A view of crocketed spires and floreated finials, a great golden bulk streaked with black against two lines of wooded hills—this from a small charming bridge of yellow stone, decorated with obelisks and framed in four lodges of the deepest yellow ochre; but then the road sweeps on and round, becoming grand and 'national' and a sea of excavated mud, and the village it leads to is in a similar state of upheaval, mud and rubble washing at the Abbey's walls, preparatory, one suspects, to pompous parade-grounds and car-parks. Workmen's booths entangle with the stalls of a small market.

James Lees-Milne explains[1] that the basic pattern of Portuguese cathedrals is twelfth-century Romanesque embellished by Manoeline and Baroque additions, there being little native Gothic in the country. 'The two fine churches of Alcobaça and Batalha...are foreign anachronisms. The first was built to the universal Cistercian pattern, the second in the English Decorated Style—the masons even coming from England at the behest of the Plantagenet Queen Philippa of Gaunt, wife of Dom João I.' The genius here was Diego Boutaca (or Boytac) who came from Languedoc in 1490 and whose career extended throughout Dom Manoel's reign. He built the extraordinary octagonal Capelas Imperfeitas behind the main church as a mausoleum for the King's grandfather although the famous doorway was the work of Mateus Fernandes. He was responsible for the chief cloister, the Claustro Real, with its columns like the trunks of palm trees supporting traceries of foliage alternately voluptuous and restrained and with, in one corner, a lavatorium projecting into the cloister garth to be marked by a bold many-bladed shaft and minaret, with three shadowy basins inside rising in tiers. All this may be mere superimposition upon an English structure, and not exclusively Manoeline or Portuguese (for Gothic elsewhere can achieve similar effects) but it is enough to merit superlatives from the authorities: Sacheverell Sitwell describes the lavatorium as 'unique in beauty' while Mr Lees-Milne regards the doorway to the Unfinished Chapels as a marvel: 'It is just about the most extravagant piece of carving in western Europe', and goes even farther with regard to the cloister-bays: 'surely the most beautiful in

[1] *Baroque in Spain and Portugal*, (Batsford, 1960).

the world'. High praise, indeed, and sufficient, as we feel ourselves beginning to agree, to reconcile us for the loss of the Beckfordian monks, the lonely nightingale, the boys at their dusting accompanied by a stork and a flamingo (but the stork soon died), the liquors cooled in the snow, the fruit disposed about 'a rock of transparent ice, shining with a thousand prismatic colours'; colours, in fact, which had bathed them all at Mass in the Abbey church: 'We all partook of these gorgeous tints — the white monastic garments of my conductors seemed as it were embroidered with the brightest flowers of paradise.' No 'Woe to Portugal!' either but soldiers fiercely on guard at the patriotic tomb (which detracts if anything from the proportions of the Chapter House and its view into the cloister) and making the artistically minded visitor more of a lounging sybarite, a devotee of impressions and sensations, than he had intended to be.

Instead of nationalistic awe one grows lighthearted with Boytac's fantastic interpretations of nature. Quite clearly the sixteenth-century Portuguese were infatuated with their maritime discoveries. The Far East and India, Africa and Brazil contributed plant-forms and architectural motifs to the buildings with which they expressed their pride. The thrown fishing-net combined with memories of the grilles of the seraglio or the intricacies of the Chinese lacquered screen. The textures and tumescences of the jungle invaded the gardener's espalier and the herald's display of shields. Lotus flowers now crown the twisted columns which Boytac designed for Santa Cruz at Coimbra; its choir-stalls display the voyages of Vasco da Gama in gilt. At the Jeronimos beside the Tagus at Belem the cloister openings may have been abstracted from banana plants; the tracery in one of the arches portrays a galleon. At Tomar there are famous maritime buttresses and windows, weaving seaweed and coral with pulleys, cables and armillary spheres, or framing a round opening in a tied sail.

At one moment in our tour of the Abbey a cloud blew over and there was suddenly a violent storm of rain. The architecture went mad. Gargoyles sputtered and then full-throatedly spewed; the sky-ward stencils of deep and spiky balustrades, glorifying for hundreds of yards at three different heights the lily, the lotus, the uncurling fern (or whatever the objects might be) hissed from a dancing cloud of droplets; the many finials at the tops of their buttresses grew deformed as melting candles or jellifying plants; the box mazes inside the Royal Cloister pattered and drummed and the four tall cypresses in the much simpler cloister of Dom Alfonso V tossed and bent their shaggy sides;

indeed it only needed a little extra fancy to imagine Boytac's vegetable shapes on the point of burgeoning.

We returned again to those cloister-bays of his. Were the thin columns really tree-trunks? Alternate ones were certainly formed of a succession of pointed leaves like the leaves of an artichoke, and this is more or less the way a palm bole builds up as its sprays break off, leaving a kind of artichoke or pineapple armour, but the others were formed of triple twists of rope or cable between rows of balls, fruit or seeds which someone experienced in tropical vegetation might recognise as the interiors of pods. The alternating screens of tracery were also a matter for conjecture. Mr Lees-Milne says, apparently of both, that they call to mind 'neatly pleached hedges of lime or hornbeam'; Mr Sitwell quotes an authority as seeing in one pattern 'an elaborate network of briar-branches' and in the other a 'combination of the double Cross of the Order of Christ with the stems and blossoms of the lotus, evidently symbolising the enterprises of the Portuguese in the distant Orient' but then himself plumps for 'artichoke, cardoon and poppy' as influenced by the *moucharabiyes* of North Africa.

The sun came out again. We moved back through the Abbey church, which meant nothing new to me, being white and pure and as busily scraped as Alcobaça's, although the Chapel of the Fondador, an octagon in a square with windows of stained glass as gay as printed cotton and a ceiling of white lace doilies or snow-flakes in the form of a central fretted wheel and eight stars, was coolly delightful; we were looking for the entrance to the Unfinished Chapels, and we got there over rubble and mud. There is no denying that this is an extraordinary building: an octagon again, of seven chapels and the grand portal, to be covered by a dome which was never begun and to which buttresses of stacked columns — like bundles of reeds or asparagus tied together by horizontal courses — rise for only twenty feet above the usual tall balustrades, there to be sliced off flat and smooth: broad thrusts of truncated effect. The grand doorway is as intricate as anything in the Alhambra; successive fringes of lacy stone hang down in graceful ogival folds — how many are there? I lost count at about twenty-five; each moulded band of stone, running up those draped boudoir curves, is a honeycomb of cells or a fretwork in which each observer can make out for himself the plant-forms of his particular enlightenment...It was here of course, that Beckford spoke slightingly of 'scollops and twistifications'.

Afterwards we drank wine in the sunshine.

Temporarily deserting Mr Augusto Ova we drove south through Caldas da Rainha (which Beckford didn't like, partly because it was full of quince-coloured apothecaries) and past the walled almost medieval town of Obidos, to Ericeira on the coast. This was to be our base for the final Beckfordian jumble to Mafra, Cintra and Queluz.

Ericeira is perhaps even more dramatically situated than Nazaré. The town runs along cliffs above a relentlessly tormented sea; the fishing harbour seems no more than a ramp up which to escape from the waves: there is a café named after the Marialvas and a charming Rococo cinema with a china girl shaking a tambourine on its roof. To the left the cliffs crumble to a sweep of ground ending in a posh hotel and a huge thundering beach. Peacocks scream in the cactus of the hotel garden; its arbours and terraces are wet with spray; I had the greatest difficulty in imagining anyone bathing from its precincts. Everywhere the atmosphere was an invigorating but muddling combination of sun and salt mist.

At night it thundered.

At Mafra, the next morning, it was still windy and cold. The landscape hereabouts is much barer than I expected, a drift of sea-ward downs with several windmills but few trees of any size except in the gully bottoms, the pollarded planes scarcely more in leaf than at Vitoria or Breviesca; I should have remembered Beckford's account of its emptiness. 'The distant convent of Mafra, glowing with ruddy light, looked like the enchanted palace of a giant, and the surrounding country bleak and barren as if the monster had eaten it desolate' (July 19th, 1787). The platform before Mafra's church was all a-slime with a green moss or grass and the columns to the façade were deeply orange with lichen. Inside the atrium is very fine, the rest a soothing but rather empty classicism in mottled pink and slate-blue marble. Much of the palace is a museum through whose endless suites of rooms we pushed, half-angry with cold, bidding door upon door to be unlocked for us by a succession of guardians, refusing to look to left or right despite all their blandishments, for the pretty Rococo library at the end was all we wished to see: hideous paintings, Victorian furniture, a room decorated throughout in stags' heads and antlers could not distract us.

Out of this unpromising landscape the steamy wooded hills and crags of Cintra rise like an anomaly. The views of downs or plain may be 'languishing', (to quote Mr Sitwell) on a shimmering summer's day but I preferred the umbrageous lushness of the Serra. Having followed Byron to Patras, Preveza, and Missolonghi, I was glad to see a landscape celebrated in *Childe Harold*, and which gave rise to the well-known lines addressed to Beckford. Villas and quintas, not always in the best taste, peep from the woods; the Royal Palace, with its oast-house towers and Moorish decorations ('a confused pile' indeed but with windows 'all in a fantastic Oriental style, crinkled and crankled') is worth visiting at a slower pace than our sighing, coughing, finger-snapping guide allowed for the appreciation of ceilings decorated with magpies and swans (infinitely preferable to Ludwig of Bavaria's), glittering *azulejos*, a tank of water whose reflected ripples pulsed over a Persian carpet; and doubtless Beckford's villa of Ramalhão can be found, although I did not find it.[1]

Instead we went up through woods to the Capuchos, the Cork Convent, a tiny place hidden between great rocks and ferns in the filmy sunlight under the trees, with wicket-gate of cork and gnome-size cork-lined cells hewn from the rock, almost as great an object of romantic pilgrimage as the entirely different Grande Chartreuse. Higher still, the peaks of the Serra are crowned by a Moorish castle and by the Royal Castle of Pena, the Portuguese Balmoral, at whose gates we were con-tent to rest for some moments without trying to enter.

But the great, the overwhelming impression of the day was to be the Palace and in particular the Gardens of Queluz, discovered just to the left of the motor-way to Lisbon, near a rather ugly town and where the landscape of scrubbed wind-dried hills begins to be scarred by the radio aerials and blocks of workers' flats heralding the city. At first there is a kind of parade-ground of open space, vaguely reminiscent of Potsdam, around which various pink buildings are sprinkled; to one side a Town Hall, a clock-tower and some houses, to the other a low, rambling building whose main façade projects semi-circular wings. This is the Palace, whose ground-plan I should very much like to see, for it is clearly a superbly irregular shape, adapted to the nature of the ground on which it stands, or rather, to which it is so charmingly attentive: 'for it is,' as James Lees-Milne says, not so much a palace as 'a garden, in which have been raised a series of enchanting casinos in a style transitional from Rococo to Neo-classical.'

[1] I visited both Ramalhão and Monserrate in the summer of 1967. Ramalhão is now a convent school; the inland road to Lisbon passes under its grounds by means of an archway.

The interior of the Palace blazed with gilt decoration in the mid-eighteenth century when it was still in course of construction; the earthquake did not damage it; tastes, however, changed and Beckford found it smothered in patterned drapery, 'not a card or dining-table has escaped'. Now again, after the fire of 1934, the rooms glitter with the spirit of Chippendale, for here restoration has for once been successful, although much was lost, including a wallpaper depicting the Greek Wars of Independence and Byron himself amongst his Souliotes and white-kilted Evzones. To tell the truth, we merely peeped at these rooms, stealing up on them like children from the garden side, for we entered the Palace only to buy our tickets and then escape from the guides, running out through the nearest french-window into the gardens where 'the Rococo basked like a butterfly in the sun of fortune and content.'

Queluz is quite unlike Mafra. Its garden façades consist of three two-storeyed pavilions linked by one-storey wings and extending along two sides of a huge platform of box parterres, basins, urns and statues, below which the remainder of the big garden lies. The first impression is that it is all long windows and gently persuasive decoration, its immediate charm arising from the fact of its colour, which is a washed-out pink stucco emphasised by woodwork of faded and often blistered apple-green and given a stiffening of dignity by the grey-streaked stonework of its facings. It doesn't stare at its garden as so many Palladian buildings do, with their graceful aloofness; it smiles and participates. The central pavilion, beyond Neptune in his pool, has a narrow classical pediment with a decoration in pale blue and a balustrade along the roof supporting rather small white figures in the manner of the Chiericati Palace at Vicenza or Sansovino's Old Library in Venice. This classicism, however, is reduced to a feminine susceptibility by the soft curves at the top of the windows and the swagged pediments above them. The pavilion at right-angles to this main one — and which rises many yards off above its own topiary garden and pool — goes even farther. Its double roof has something of a pagoda curl at the ends while, instead of a pediment, it has a peculiarly swirling ogival gable enclosing a dormer. As for the third façade, the upper storey of this is on a line with the ground floor of the rest of the palace; it drops in fact below the platform to front a magnificent alley, of which one side is formed by the buttressed and peach-mantled wall of the platform and the other by a cypress hedge above a tiled kerb. Here, then, already is change of level and confirmation of rhythm and the unexpected. Nor is this façade without additional interest. Its centre is a deep round arch over which giant women recline, with bambini at their skirts; its corners are encrusted with chariots bursting into pennants, flying draperies or flame. As spiky, in fact, as a pineapple and with something of the same peculiar, slightly suspect richness.

We walked quickly and gaily into the Palace gardens as people who for once did not care a farthing for officials and their rules. No one could stop us. No bureaucratic cry would have the least effect. We belonged here; this was something we deserved. As we marched about, pointing and shouting to each other, we quickly suppressed our memories of less happy occasions when all this touristic excitement and sympathy (perhaps so childlike as to be ludicrous to others) had been blocked by a dreary crone jangling keys or an officious youth closing a door in our faces, by a Tourist Policeman with a whistle, or a Spanish caretaker with a hiss. In foreign countries one is frequently ignorant, wrong-headed, tongue-tied and absurd. The local inhabitants are entirely justified when they laugh at one's pretentiousness in claiming to know them and their culture sufficiently to set down one's findings, or illusions, in a book. But there are some things the tourist does know better than they. Crones and pimply-faced boys have no right to distract him from his passion for architecture and art; if payment has to be made (and why should one ever pay to enter a church?) then the transaction must be quickly and discreetly done.

Here, then, were languid but graceful statues, of which not a few had been turned bright orange by the lichen on their skins. The boys raised slim right arms, but the gesture signalled to nobody alive; self-insulating, it merely draped them in the attitude of salute. The girls hugged their breasts and, with heads faintly inclined, listened to a silence broken only by the drone of a fly or the unfolding of a bud. They rose amongst box topiary, the small shrubs cut into globes or pyramids, except that the pyramids bulged. Stone plinths bore urns, which looked fat and gently warm, or jugs, which were of a blue and white china and dispensed an opposing coolness. The parterres were intricately patterned, like a message in an unknown language. Emotion hovered there in the form of forget-me-nots, violas, polyanthus and other spring flowers.

Nearest to the main façade was the Neptune fountain, its stonework weathered brown, mauve and grey-blue. Above layers of maned and whiskered fish the god rose with his trident, accompanied by a boy with scaly legs who held the largest and most monstrous of the fish in his hand. From the rim watched women with scallop shells in their laps, and beside them jigged *putti* holding pots, and in between were globes encircled by snakes. Towards the end of the great garden platform, about which we moved in a maze of recognitions and reassurances, we came to the second basin. On a broad shell-like structure supported by figures blowing conches while, their under-parts turned green and furry in the water, there reposed an immense, bug-eyed fish. A woman rode this fish's back and at the same time flourished in the air what looked like the triple shelves of a cake-stand, only instead of cakes there were spouts for water and would have been splashing pools and tasselled fringes of over-flow if the fountain had been working. Nearby a mer-child thrust up a bigger tray while his younger brother thumbed a spout. In a kind of declivity of the un-dulating shell-structure a child in plump abandon sprawled beside a serpent. Not only did the shell's rim undulate, it provided convenient orifices or portholes through which peered a number of heavy-looking and rather flabby fish. The total effect was polymorphous and con-ceivably a trifle perverse. Indeed a lion on the basin's outer edge looked round at it, vaguely astonished.

Beyond this second fountain two sphinxes outstared each other, secure in the geometrical accuracy with which they were placed to each side of the central path. Where the balustrade broke to make an opening, two horses pranced and their riders blew trumpets in sil-houette. A gentle ramp led down to the darker, wilder garden.

But for the moment I was content to linger where I was, in the hope that I might understand some of the reasons for my delight. Like a chessboard, the platform had order and symmetricality although the sculptured objects placed there lent it the tension and significance of moves within a game which was perhaps still being played. The fountains of course had a Baroque or Rococo energy and fantasy; they flung themselves about, curving and swirling into the dramatic forms which should have borne the even greater restlessness of leaping and cascading water. The individual figures were, for all their turning and gesturing, simpler, smoother, until they approached the monolithic; even more than the fountains, their effect was associated with what I can only call 'depth' and 'silence'; for as I looked at them, I seemed to be aware of a stone falling into an enormously deep well, as though I listened for a hollow sound and then for the splash which never came. Thus were they rooted. But in their very stillness there was an aptitude for movement: not that they would necessarily move along the lines indicated by the position of their bodies, not that their motions would be naturalistic, but rather that the life which accumulated in them until it grew heavy would bear them through the air. In something of the same way that, when one looks up at a tower or a chimney outlined against racing clouds, one is rocked back on one's heels by the weight impending above one, and already floating free of the earth, so the absolute authority of these statues (who doubtless represented Apollo, Diana, Flora and so on, and were normally and conventionally executed) seemed to press through the flimsy nature of one's own presence. But this was a joyous, not a threatening thing. And possibly the fact that there was a number, a pattern of statues, and that there were parterres and pathways and basins and not the statues alone, diffused any particular, too personal tension.

For the main fact was the chequer-board under the soft April light (shortly afterwards, in fact, it began to rain for a little). The background was the charming and gentle palace itself. And one's pleasure derived, no doubt, as much from one's liking for the eighteenth century (and self-congratulation at having found such a transcendent example for oneself) as it did from the purely aesthetic qualities of sculpture or fountains. The chequer-board meant that anarchic nowhere was transformed into spatial somewhere, where points of focus were established and across which vistas of direction were laid. In such circumstances the overwhelming effect is that of an air of expectancy, of waiting. The garden is waiting for a series of events (a game to be played or, more likely, a ceremony) which does not belong to our order of time or our quality of existence. Statues and fountains in their mysterious association *exist more deeply than we do*. And our pleasure in them is caused by the fact that, despite our inadequate presence, we *can* to some extent collaborate with them as children or artists.

Once, on the 14th June, 1794, we know that this happened. William Beckford ran races here with the 'two Indian-looking girls of fourteen or fifteen'.

But, even without trying to probe into these various effects (and quite obviously I am no philosopher), I felt that I was face to face with a confirmation of some of my deepest longings. Here lay, in truth, my equivalent to T. S. Eliot's *Rose Garden*. Here was the enchanted place of whose presence I had been vaguely, troublingly aware in childhood and youth so that I could imagine myself having been at times within an inch of discovering its walls and gates, where they crossed perhaps some umbrageous, shadowy corner of my own muddled hinterland —

or even ran parallel, if only I had known it, with some rugged puritanical heath—so that a bird I observed with self-consciously nature-loving eyes had in fact just flown over from balustrade and urn, or a wind forlornly sounding notes of nostalgia and other-worldly yearning in a gorse-bush had a moment later strayed amongst camellias and roses, calmed in a shelter of cypress and laurel. There were, indeed, occasions when I seemed actually to have met inhabitants strayed from that parallel world, who filled me with so great a nervous excitement that I became shy and clumsy until I had made a self-destructive escape. On the physical plane there were certain gateways I had almost passed through, certain hedges, a façade glimmering beyond the turn of the road. At school, almost half-heartedly, I bought expensive art magazines which I presented to the reading-room of my house as a civilising gesture. When I had the De Quincey rooms at my Oxford college, I decorated them with ugly but gilded Victorian candelabra in which I lit candles. Imagining a political career to be glamorous, I enjoyed making speeches at the Union in white tie and tails. And afterwards, when those particular dreams faded or altered, I was still in love with something beyond the ordinary run of human experience; certainly I was always drawn to the oddity, the perhaps hidden richness and paradox of human character. Today I express this in my trinity of travelling companions, Boswell, Byron and Beckford. Indeed, in my teacher's way, I rationalise my personal predilections into a criticism of the ugliness and dullness of contemporary life. But, since I was not brought up as a candidate for aristocratic ease, let alone voluptuousness, it has taken me a long time to accept the more extravagant aspects of the eighteenth century; the Enchanted Garden, which can anyway mean so many different things, has often seemed a place restricted to dreams even if it has not also sparkled with guilt.

Even amongst gardens themselves I can think of possible rivals to Queluz. But Herrenhausen, as I remember it, is too formal and flat; the sweep between the Belevederes in Vienna too public, too mechanically connective of those palaces; the Mirabell Gardens are really part of a townscape; the terraces and vistas of La Granja outside Segovia are splendid but anomalous, pressed in upon by the mountains; and even Nymphenburg, which comes nearest, is misty and northern and too much a park. Only Queluz has the supreme patterning consequent upon its compactness and its relation to the pavilions embracing it, together with the varying elements of wildness and practical horticulture on the lower levels.

And now, from the bottom of the slope beyond the platform's end, we observed narrow pools running from left to right against the retaining wall, the water a velvety brown, sulky and secretive. Between the hedges in front of us the big alleys ran straight and clear, generally downhill, but there were also smaller passages, more slits in the foliage, which glimmered darkly. Was it here that Beckford raced the ladies-in-waiting at the command of the imperious Dona Carlota Joaquina? Surely he must have run on the level, and near enough to the Palace to justify the cautions about disturbing the melancholic queen.

We went down the central alley to a bearded grotto below a dribbling face, a grotesque monument presumably once alive with a cascade, and then turned right into a region of gardens either more decayed or more practical, a mixture of extravagant formality on a smaller scale than in the grand parterres and of the loamy scent, the gentle untidiness of kitchen gardens not much in use. Here children would certainly explore. There was a huge bedraggled dome, a beehive of cypress shaped like the Treasury of Atreus but full of aspidistras in earthenware pots; then a small hidden place framed in tiles of yellow scrolled with mauve and blue about pictured urns and flowers, and set with box-edged beds of candytuft, marigolds, nasturtiums, forget-me-nots, violas and daisies; another furry beehive nearby, smaller this time and with an open top; a pool with an asymmetrical swirl of rim, most Rococo of shapes, like the tendril-curl around a looking-glass; weeping willows; over there a wall hung with wistaria, morning-glory and passion-flower; a glimpse of practicality, vegetables, cucumber frames, against a line of prickly pears and pampas grass; and, stronger and stronger, the awareness of water.

The water rushed under trees, through banks of periwinkles. It pointed towards a gate faced by another semi-circle of the pedestal men. Beyond this gate lay the main road. But moving up against the current we found that the stream became a channel lined with tiles and thus revealed itself as the grandest and most imaginative of canals, where an English Envoy Extraordinary to Dom José once saw three galleys majestically afloat, subtly lit and bearing allegorical personages, while the royal fireworks died from the sky. As the stream approaches the Palace its banks gleam with *azulejos* depicting eighteenth-century figures indulging in villegiaturas and pastoral pursuits against prospects of palaces and temples which always include water and boats; it is balustraded with stepped plinths, also tiled in yellow, mauve and blue and holding urns; the biggest bridge is a noble affair, where a great pyramid of tiled decoration is combined with statuary. Opposite this, two stairways blend into one as they descend from a complex arrangement of angled loggias at the back of the palace. Although the water would probably have muffled their cries, it is here—on these level alleys, marked perhaps by a dark cypress above a pool—that I can best imagine Beckford running and dancing the *bolero* after he had been bewitched by the 'wandering lights' in the thickets and then discovered the odoriferous amphitheatre; he specifically mentions oranges and catalpas. It is tempting to imagine that he took much the same walk as we did: meeting the negro with the exuberant lips somewhere beyond the platform stairs, entering his 'pavilion' in the region of the cypress beehive and being discovered by Marialva near the bridge over the canal.

I paused for a long time by this bridge with the great staircase behind me. Alcobaça, Batalha and now Queluz; it was remarkable that in such stormy weather I had had generally fine days for all three expeditions: it was enough, in any case, that I had enjoyed them so much, lacy and flowery complements to wind-lashed Sitio and Ericeira. I was to see other gardens later—notably those of Mateus in distant Tras-os-Montes, together with the stairway gardens to the pilgrimage churches of Lamego and Braga; despite the shortness of my stay there was much more to do before I began to return home by way of almost the whole Atlantic coast of Spain; but the gardens in which I so happily stood, the work in fact of a Frenchman, J. B. Robillion, were the most beautiful I had ever been privileged to see. For years, too, I had been mildly intrigued by the figure of Beckford; recently, and rather to my surprise, I had spent much time reading and writing about him; and although he wasn't the pleasantest of men and too self-centredly lonely to be more than a day-dream candidate for the Orchards of Alcinous, he had come in my mind to possess a vivacity and fantasy which acquired a symbolic status altogether outweighing his shortcomings. Across the charm and serenity of these gardens he had flashed, in only temporary happiness, like some meteoric child. Up these stairs he had very likely returned to the Palace, a little out of breath with his exertions but full of an artist's satisfaction at the acquisition of a peculiarly romantic scene accompanied by a whole flight of images and potential anecdotes, to assist at the obsequies of a century if not of a monarchy, as the Queen shrieked 'Ai Jesous!' and the Regent mumbled darkly about rationalism and utilitarianism and the godless state of France, as we today might complain of the loss of tradition and the destruction of beauty.

But now I needed the presence of ordinary human beings and, as quickly as possible, a drink. I stopped at more than one café on the long drive back to Nazaré. And that evening, after dinner, I found myself again in the taberna of Mr Augusto Ova. Its barn-like darkness could have belonged to any of the last three centuries quite as much as it did to today. Enthusiastically I told Mr Ova about Queluz; he smiled but I don't think he had ever been there. After that I sat on my own, for my companion was determined on an early night. From the deepest recess came the sound of talk and occasional laughter. In just such a place James Boswell, that Ancient Scots Gentleman, had done his 'campaigning' and grown 'hearty' with friends. Was he now bargaining for a '*monstre*', whose hideousness was obscured by the fumes of drink, or had he drawn aside some lieutenant of artillery whose fondness for slumming he shared but whom he wished now to persuade of the truths of religion? Or was he (with a flash of that scarlet coat, a glimmer from the gold lace which had at least the air of being solid) — was he just showing off? 'Brilliant fancies were begotten and brilliant fancies were brought forth.' Meanwhile through the open door at my side I heard the thunder of the sea and caught, if I peered out, the distant, pale tumultuousness of the surf. One or two figures still moved beyond the sharp-prowed boats. It was not impossible to think of Julian and Maddalo riding along the shores of the Lido, with Beckford's toads perhaps still a-hop; it was not impossible to imagine a solitary figure whose 'beautiful, pale face' grew 'rapt' as he contemplated the splendid unrestraint of an element in which he had always felt free: 'Once more upon the waters! yet once more!'

I pulled out my note-book, thinking of the book that was almost completed, wondering whether personalities struck sparks off each other, atmospheres mingled, images cohered. Had I (a self-regarding thought) proved that I existed, that I had the right to exist? What (it sounded like one of the questions I have to set for examinations) was the relevance of all this to the problems of today?

For something, certainly, must be carried home.

Field House,
Gosfield Lake,
17. 12. '68

Index